African Feminist Fiction and Indigenous Values

Florida A&M University, Tallahassee
Florida Atlantic University, Boca Raton
Florida Gulf Coast University, Ft. Myers
Florida International University, Miami
Florida State University, Tallahassee
University of Central Florida, Orlando
University of Florida, Gainesville
University of North Florida, Jacksonville
University of South Florida, Tampa
University of West Florida, Pensacola

African Feminist Fiction
and Indigenous Values

Donald R. Wehrs

University Press of Florida
Gainesville · Tallahassee · Tampa · Boca Raton
Pensacola · Orlando · Miami · Jacksonville · Ft. Myers

Material quoted from *The Stillborn*, copyright 1985, 1989, 1995, by
Zaynab Alkali, is reprinted in this volume by permission of Pearson
Education Limited, Essex.

06 05 04 03 02 01 6 5 4 3 2 1

Library of Congress Cataloging-in-Publication Data
Wehrs, Donald R.
African feminist fiction and indigenous values / Donald R. Wehrs.
     p. cm
Includes bibliographical references and index.
ISBN 0-8130-1884-6 (alk. paper)
1. African fiction (English)—Women authors—History and criticism.
2. Feminism and literature—Africa—History—20th century. 3. African
fiction (French)—Women authors—History and criticism. 4. Women
and literature—Africa—History—20th century. 5. Feminist fiction—
History and criticism. 6. Indigenous peoples in literature. 7. Social
values in literature. 8. Sex role in literature. 9. Women in literature.
I. Title.
PR9344 .W44 2001
823.'91099287'0969—dc21   00-053664

The University Press of Florida is the scholarly publishing agency
for the State University System of Florida, comprising Florida A&M
University, Florida Atlantic University, Florida Gulf Coast University,
Florida International University, Florida State University, University of
Central Florida, University of Florida, University of North Florida,
University of South Florida, and University of West Florida.

University Press of Florida
15 Northwest 15th Street
Gainesville, FL 32611-2079
http://www.upf.com

To Lorna

Contents

Preface

This study traces how six representative African feminist novels contest the conceptual categories and evaluative assumptions that Western literary theory habitually brings to bear upon the reading of sub-Saharan novelistic discourse in general and women's writing in particular. Part 1 considers how "Africa" has been configured by a variety of seemingly mutually antagonistic Western discourses—anticolonial cultural nationalism, immanent critiques of the (Western) colonialist imagination, the feminist essentialism of Alice Walker, the antiessentialism of postcolonial theory and Western feminism.

Each of these ways of encountering Africa presents internal difficulties. If anticolonialism is understood as cultural nationalism or, more subtly, as the defense of difference against a totalizing colonialistic gaze, then difference taken as its own justification may underwrite an uncritical nativism. Immanent critiques of the Western colonialistic imagination, although useful as a branch of Western cultural studies, tend to view Africa, or any non-Western Other, exclusively as an effect, or a product, of a Western signifying economy; thus, the possibility of *any* noncolonizing cross-cultural knowledge seems to be discounted or occluded a priori. Alice Walker's feminist essentialism in *Possessing the Secret of Joy* (1992) universalizes contemporary Western ideas about identity and value in ways that preclude any rational critique of either those ideas or common inferences drawn from them. Postcolonial theories bound to postmodern premises, however philosophically antithetical to Walker's position, share with her a network of guiding assumptions, even similar tropes of language. For both postcolonial theorists and for Walker, the individual's relation to culture may be fruitfully divided between collaboration and resistance: acculturation is invariably linked to conditioning, to the generation of false consciousness; resistance is understood as undoing, or contesting, the violence internal to acculturation. Thus, freedom is taken to be at once an end in itself and an end so open-ended that it is definable only in terms of what it is against.

Postcolonial theory shaped by postmodernism is vulnerable to critique from new currents within philosophy and literary theory. In particular, the work of Emmanuel Levinas has thrown into relief how much postmodernism shares with the dominant strands of Western thought since the seventeenth century. Both in his critique of the egocentric violence at the heart of modern Western notions of liberation and in his derivation of speech, and thus the possibility of cross-cultural rationality, from the radical primordiality of ethics, Levinas's thought, surprisingly, dovetails with African indigenous structures of value and discursive traditions that inform diverse cultural practices. In particular, both colonialistic and masculinist patterns of appropriation and repression are understood, by ethnically and geographically diverse societies, to be forms of aggressively antisocial and self-aggrandizing individualism, a "mode of being" attributed to malevolent sorcerers who are characterized by the unrestrained pursuit of their interests and desires.

Part 2 considers in detail six African novels that are all in some sense feminist—Flora Nwapa's *Efuru* (1966), Zaynab Alkali's *The Stillborn* (1984), Mariama Bâ's *Une si longue lettre* (1979), Tsitsi Dangarembga's *Nervous Conditions* (1988), Ama Ata Aidoo's *Changes: A Love Story* (1991), and Buchi Emecheta's *Kehinde* (1994)—and argues that much of the textual surface of these novels, much of the plot, much of the implications of the sequence of events, simply cannot be accommodated within the interpretive frameworks that Western academic criticism frequently bring to bear upon them. Instead, the novels require a detailed knowledge of indigenous structures of value, history, and social practices. Each of these fictions is in part a reasoned argument about why notions of emancipation long dominant in the modern West are limited, impoverished, or self-defeating—not just for Africans but for people generally. A better account of the details of the texts and the coherence of the narratives may be achieved through exploring connections between what the novels are suggesting and, on the one hand, Levinas's account of how the ethical relation makes freedom, language, and reason answerable to something more than themselves and, on the other hand, Paul Ricoeur's account of how self-esteem and ethical solicitude are dialectically interrelated. There are, of course, tensions between Levinasian and Ricoeurian currents of thought, but the individual novels delineate forms of ethical reflection that, while intersecting with Levinas and Ricoeur at various points, are not reducible to one or the other, but comprehend in their own distinctive discourses elements of both. What is striking in the feminism of each of these novels is that it involves an unsparing critique of the sexism internal to both Western and indigenous social practices and conceptuality while nonetheless vindicating, though often in reformed modes, African traditions of ethical reflection that view Western "liberation" as self-impoverishment, and Western "ethics of resistance" as both unethical and, in terms of addressing what gives human life significance, clueless.

Connections between the critiques of modern Western thought that emerge from contemporary African writers drawing upon indigenous sources of moral discourse, and the critiques offered by Levinas and Ricoeur, are not merely coincidental. Levinas and Ricoeur are deeply influenced by scriptural hermeneutics, by Western traditions of ethical reflection anterior to, and disjunctive with, the egoistic orientation in Western thought from the Cartesian *cogito* and Hobbesian materialism on. Scriptural traditions, in both Islamic and Christian evangelical forms, have long been interwoven into African moral discourse. In some cases (especially for Islam but also for Christianity, as among the Yoruba, for example), this process has occurred independently of colonialism. Similarly, in evoking and reworking Aristotelianism, Ricoeur draws upon an ethical tradition that, through Islam, has long been part of African cultural life. Moreover, the striking parallels between Levinas's critique of the violence of imperialistic egoism and diverse African cultures' understanding of the antisociability of unrestrained appropriation (cognitive as well as material) may suggest how much the modern West's propensity to celebrate freedom understood as the self's open-ended expansion may be tied to a modern capitalist economy of surplus (made possible in part through Western colonialism) where freedom is implicitly likened to other commodities: more for me need not imply less for another. But, as Levinas argues, more for me is not of itself an ethical or humanizing goal.

This study seeks to combine intensive reading with extensive contextualization, providing sufficient historical, cultural, socioeconomic, and religious context for the implications of textual details to come into view. If we are to read novelistic discourse dialogically, in the sense of hearing the voices it evokes, then we must bring to our reading determinate knowledge about the cultures involved, a knowledge which in the case of Africa has been radically enlarged during the past thirty years. Because the relevance of such research for literature is best revealed through extended analysis of specific works, this study does not seek to represent the complete careers of authors or to survey all the major fiction of a country or region. Instead, it has endeavored to select works of sufficient variety to be representative and sufficient thematic and conceptual interconnections to suggest that challenges to the usual Western ways of reading African fiction come, not certainly from all writing in Africa, but from enough writing of acknowledged importance to be theoretically significant. Throughout, the study attempts to distinguish between "other" and "Other" in accord with the distinction between "autre" and "autrui" in French philosophical usage, where "other" refers to any other, to the singular of "others," and "Other" refers to the other as other, whose otherness is thematized or conceptually central. In its orthographic choices, the study seeks a middle ground between popular westernized transliteration and a degree of specialized orthography not standardized within the relevant field. The Islamic holy book is referred to as the Quran, not Koran or Qur'an, and when the Akan Twi language is cited, this study follows the practice of those scholars who deviate least from English orthography.

My debts to family, friends, teachers, colleagues, and students are, though deeply felt, too many to be acknowledged fully. Without Frank Ward, Tom Elmer, Bob Krieckhaus, and Don Gifford, this study could never have been written. The intellectual and personal debts I owe to Anthony Winner are reflected in every sentence. Laviece Ward, Alan Jacobs, Marc Silverstein, David P. Haney, and Harry M. Solomon graciously read and critiqued my evolving efforts. Melvyn New enhanced my understanding of Levinasian ethics and its relation to literary criticism. Robert Zabawa shared his expertise on Ghana and on the Twi language. Glenn Anderson and the Humanities staff of Auburn Library and the staff of the Emory University libraries have been unfailingly helpful. Susan Fernandez and Amy Gorelick at the University Press of Florida have been most kind and patient. My late father-in-law, Joseph Wood, assumed, in his early eighties, child-care tasks. My young children, Sylvia and William, impressed upon me the validity of Levinas's observation that sensibility precedes thematization. This study is incalculably indebted to my wife, Lorna Wood, whose critical insights and editorial skills have been invaluable

All errors of fact or interpretation are, of course, mine alone.

I want to thank the following publishers for permission to reprint passages from the following novels: for citations from *Changes: A Love Story* by Ama Ata Aidoo, Women's Press Ltd., 34 Great Sutton Street, London EC1V 0LQ, and Feminist Press at the City University of New York; for citations from *Nervous*

Conditions by Tsitsi Dangarembga, Seal Press, 3131 Western Ave., #410, Seattle, Washington; for citations from *Efuru* by Flora Nwapa and *Kehinde* by Buchi Emecheta, Heinemann Educational Publishers, a division of Reed Educational and Professional Publishing Ltd.; for citations from *Une si longue lettre* by Mariama Bâ, Les Nouvelles Éditions Africaines du Sénégal, 10 rue Amadou Assane Ndoye, B.P. 260, Dakar, Sénégal; for citations from *The Stillborn* by Zaynab Alkali, Pearson Education Limited, Essex, England; for citations from *Otherwise than Being* by Emmanuel Levinas, Kluwer Academic Publishers, Spuiboulevard 50, P.O. Box 17, 3300 AA Dordrecht, The Netherlands; for *The Politics of (M)Othering*, edited by Obioma Nnaemeka, Routledge, International Thomson Publishing Services, Cheriton House, North Way, Andover, Hampshire SP10 5BE, England.

I

African Fiction's Challenge to the Modern West

1

Encountering Africa in Contemporary Western Theory and Representation

Novel Theory and the Possibility of Cross-Cultural Discourse

Postcolonial theory has increasingly criticized its own colonizing tendencies, as in Chandra Talpade Mohanty's discussion of how "the production of the 'Third World Woman'" creates "a singular monolithic subject," or Obioma Nnaemeka's characterization of the double bind facing non-Western women writers: "[I]f they accord their traditional culture some modicum of respect, they are dismissed by feminists as apologists for oppressive and outdated customs; if they critique their culture, they are faced with put-downs and ridicule from the members of their own society for having sold out."[1]

Despite such concerns, criticism of African feminist fiction generally conforms to the assumptions governing Western literary theory. In recent years, criticism has moved from an introductory phase, where works were evaluated largely in terms of meeting Western genre expectations, through a secondary phase, where they were evaluated largely in terms of their social, political content, to a third phase, where they are viewed as contributing to "the African quest for freedom and identity."[2] All three phases understand African fiction as seeking liberation from the forms of thought that had made colonialism appear "natural" or "inevitable" for colonizer and colonized alike.[3]

Reading African fiction in terms of unmasking and liberation is certainly useful, but freedom is generally not in African writing the self-justifying good it often is for Western theory. Because pre-1960 critiques of colonialism involve more than a demand for national independence, novelistic rhetoric mobilized against British and French rule could be turned, after independence, against neocolonialistic African elites.[4] Kwame Anthony Appiah notes that postcolonial fiction often invokes "a *transnational* rather than a *national* solidarity," and so speaks "in the name of the ethical universal; in the name of *humanism*," making it "an agonist," not "an ally," of the postmodernisms that issue from the antihumanistic discourse of Derrida, Foucault, and others.[5] Many novelists who established international reputations during the 1950s and early 1960s turned with increasing insistence to the failure of the societies that replaced European rule to undo either the attitudes or the institutions sustaining political and economic subjugation.[6] The assault upon Negritude by Yambo Ouologuem, Wole Soyinka, P. J. Hountondji, and others prepared the way for the assault upon precolonial male chauvinism by Calixthe Beyala, Buchi Emecheta, and Mariama Bâ.[7] Within indigenous African cultures, the propensity of freedom to pass into unrestrained aggressivity is figured in the image of the witch or sorcerer, whose insatiable hunger leads to an "inhuman" indifference to the ethical claim of others upon us.[8] In African feminist fiction, as in African anticolonialist fiction generally, the entwinement of colonizing violence with the pursuit of freedom problematizes associations of liberation with the self's unencumbered pursuit of its desires and will to power.

"Novelistic discourse" here describes narrative techniques common to novels, short stories, and autobiographies, techniques easily traced to eighteenth-century Europe, where print culture, mass markets, and the scientific revolution generated both anxieties about the ease of fictive deceptions and standards of credibility through which fictions sought to hold suspicion at bay.[9] "Novelistic discourse" refers to the *kind* of discourse historically rooted in novels that now infiltrates other prose genres.[10] In Africa, novelistic discourse frequently opens up what Simon Gikandi, following Fredric Jameson, calls a "utopian" dimension, presenting itself as a way of imagining a community where the values invoked against colonialism would guide public and private life.[11]

While other non-Western fiction speaks to these concerns, orality would seem to make the novel more alien in Africa than, for example, in India, where print culture intersects with precolonial scribal traditions.[12] It has frequently been noted that the novel is tied not just to written discourse but also to print culture and hence to (European) modernity.[13] However, recent criticism, particularly by Africans, has insisted upon the role of oral storytelling traditions in shaping African fiction.[14] If the novel were an uncomplicated generic expression of European modernity, as novel theory from Dr. Johnson and Hegel on has tended to assume,[15] then African writers' appropriation of the form might suggest that the case against colonizing violence needs to be made, at least to the West or to those with Western educations, through cultural resources alien to precolonial African cultures.

This study argues, on the contrary, that the striking receptivity of the formal, aesthetic attributes of novelistic discourse to the political and ethical task of African anticolonialism and feminism demands that Western scholars revise their understanding of the novel. Mikhail Bakhtin points out that a culture comes to deeper self-understanding by hearing its words reaccented by voices from other cultures.[16] African writers and scholars have long brought Western forms of understanding to bear upon explorations of African cultures.[17] Alexis Kagame's consideration of Bantu animism in relation to Christian pneumatology, Kwame Gyekye's application of Aristotelian dialectics to African philosophy, and V. Y. Mudimbe's use of Foucault's power/knowledge matrix to examine the sexual politics of Luba praise-songs constitute diverse instances of placing one's own culture into appreciative dialogue with another culture.[18] Unhappily, the dialogue has been mostly one-way: Western scholars have seldom allowed African conceptions and values to enter into dialogue with Western modes of understanding.[19]

One purpose of this work is to redress that imbalance. African novelists may vindicate *some* traditional African forms of meaning and value without retreating into a nativism immune from rational critique.[20] As Kwasi Wiredu notes, precolonial African thought must be contrasted with *traditional* European thought lest the "basic non-scientific characteristics of African traditional thought . . . typifying traditional thought in general" be seen as "a peculiarly African way of thinking."[21] Non-Western voices may ask us to hear anew the Western discourses that precede modernity as well as those which constitute or contest its course. Only through such "hearing" can Western modernity cease to either assimilate Africa entirely to itself or treat it as an incommensurate, romanticized Other.[22]

African feminists, like other African novelists writing in French or English, tend to inhabit two or more cultural traditions much as Thomas Aquinas inhabits both Augustinian and Aristotelian traditions of moral enquiry.[23] Alasdair MacIntyre describes Aquinas as constructing a dialogical interweaving of the two, in which the deficiencies or impasses in each "call forth" the other, yielding an enlarged vision faithful to both.[24] African novelists often develop similar interweavings. Unlike Aquinas, however, African novelists tend to inhabit, in addition to two traditions, two modes of modernity as well, one suspicious of traditionalism, and one suspicious of modernity as embodied in the West. For

African writers, bilingualism passes into "biliteracy," being "literate" in the values and debates of two cultures.[25] Such biliteracy permits these novelists to apprehend what issues irresolvable within one tradition may be approached through other traditions,[26] but it also illuminates for them what issues belong to differences between cultural traditions and what issues belong to differences between traditional and modern ways of life.

Not all African novels resemble the works explored in this study. Some apply Western forms of thought to African circumstances; others provide uncritical affirmations of a romanticized traditionalism or revolutionary vanguardism.[27] This study attempts to characterize some central tendencies of a number of works of recognized quality. It seeks to delineate how African feminist fiction draws upon two networks of discourse (that of anticolonial fiction and that of indigenous structures of value), both of which allow novels to make the primacy of ethics the basis for dialogue between Africa and the West.

The Limits of Immanent Critiques of Colonialist Discourse

Western criticism has been reluctant to pursue African fiction's indebtedness to indigenous conceptualities. This reluctance derives, in part, from fear that treating Africa as an object of knowledge will reenact, cognitively, the West's colonizing of the Other. One way to avoid the problem is to analyze only Western writing about the non-West, to engage in immanent critiques of colonialist discourse. The trouble with this genre, however, is that its lack of curiosity about the "truth" is inconsistent with its insistence that Western discourse misrepresents what is really the case. Noting Marianna Torgovnik's argument that the West constructs "the primitive" in ways that have "little to do with the reality it is supposed to depict," Eugene Goodheart remarks, "I doubt that Torgovnik means to suggest that all the wishes that she ascribes to the Western psyche (the desire for beginnings and endings, for integrating the spiritual and the physical) are not shared by the native people," but the effect of insisting that "the West's understanding of the primitive is no more than a projection" is to "almost willful[ly] . . . defamiliarize a world that may be more familiar than the . . . critic would like."[28] As Goodheart observes, an "insistence on the sui generis character of cultures . . . easily turns into obscurantism."[29]

In his criticism of V. S. Naipaul's writings on Africa, Selwyn R. Cudjoe declares, "The imperialist intent of Naipaul's work seems to make itself more manifest in his willingness to argue that 'certain countries and certain peoples have allowed themselves to be exploited and abused' not because of the cruelty of others but because of internal flaws and 'the limitations of their civilization or their culture.' The blame of colonialism and imperialism is removed from its external, exploitative source and made into an internal and inherent flaw of the colonized."[30] Without defending Naipaul's oft-criticized portrait of Africa, we may note that internal conditions often give shape and opportunity to external forces, and external activities may be rebuffed or redirected through responses shaped by internal circumstances.[31] One way the West justified colonialism in Africa was to conceive it as passive, without history.[32] Investigations, such as those by Patrick Manning and John Ralph Willis, of the ideological, political, and economic roots of the African side of the slave trade must be ruled out in principle if we follow Cudjoe in believing that calling attention to sources of exploitation within the culture of the exploited is of necessity "imperialistic."[33]

In another critique of Naipaul, Rob Nixon takes to task "The Crocodiles of Yamoussoukro," Naipaul's account of his visit to the Ivory Coast, for establishing "the icon of the crocodile pit as the embodiment of an African essence." At the presidential residence, an artificial lake contains crocodiles to whom live chickens are sacrificed daily. Nixon argues that Naipaul makes the crocodiles "do a great deal of figurative work; they become emblematic of the ineluctable ills of the Ivory Coast and, beyond that, of all Africa. For it is Naipaul's thesis that Africa can achieve only a veneer of modernity because magic and make-believe are the real rulers of the continent. He therefore interprets the existence of the croc-pit as testament to the futility of African quests for social development." Nixon complains that Naipaul spends too much time with European, American, and Caribbean expatriates who, like him, are guilty of "cultural essentialism," but omits all mention of Naipaul's own use of African sources.[34] At the time of his visit, a major newspaper story concerned strange fires, attributed to the magic of the Evil Spirit, at a schoolteacher's house. Naipaul visited the house and heard from a number of African informants that the Evil Spirit caused the fire by possessing a member of the schoolteacher's family and so had to be battled by exorcism.[35] Naipaul links this episode with the forms of solidarity and identity that slaves in the Caribbean were able to maintain: "There was the world of the day; that was the white world. There was the world of the night; that was the African world, of spirits and magic and the true gods."[36] Naipaul associates this dual sense of reality with the crocodiles: "The metropolis, the ruler's benefaction to his people, belonged to the world of the day, the world of doing and development. The crocodile ritual—speaking of a power issuing to the president from the earth itself—was part of the night, ceaselessly undoing the reality of the day." To support his claims, Naipaul cites an African professor, Mr. Niangoran-Bouah, who goes unmentioned by Nixon.[37]

Nixon argues that since belief in spirits and magic functions immanently in colonialist discourse as a sign of primitive superstition, Naipaul reveals his colonialist imaginary by placing interpretative stress upon belief in spirits and magic. Such readings leave unclear how *any* discussion of beliefs in spirits and magic would not be vulnerable to similar critiques, as Goodheart points out.[38] In listing the characteristics of Ghana's cultures, Wiredu cites "reverence for ancestors and other departed relatives who are believed to be able to affect the living; elaborate rituals of mourning; the belief in the existence and influence of lesser gods as agents of the one Supreme God, and in witchcraft and a variety of spirits, fetishes and powers, both good and bad."[39] Appiah observes, "Most Africans, now, whether converted to Islam or Christianity or not, still share the belief of their ancestors in an ontology of invisible beings."[40] Appiah, Wiredu, and Hountondji even suggest that widespread acceptance of an invisible spiritual world does indeed impede scientific and technological activity; Abiola Irele argues that "the inability of our traditional world concept to break free from the prison of the mythopoetic imagination" works against the development of formal deductive logic, which is required for "the scientific spirit itself, which governs the whole functioning of the scientific and technological civilization we now wish to appropriate."[41]

Connections between belief in spirit worlds and African accounts of power, of which there are quite a few,[42] have no place in Nixon's argument for reasons of academic genre. Here, as opposed to elsewhere,[43] the discussion is not about Africa but an immanent critique of Naipaul's representation of Africa. However, we would learn more about Naipaul's representations and more about Africa if we did not separate an analysis of the one from a study of the other. Appiah notes, "Concentrating on the noncognitive features of traditional religions not only misrepresents them but also leads to an underestimation of the role of reason in the life of traditional cultures."[44]

To cite one among many African discourses that bear upon Naipaul's argument, the Kaguru people of Tanzania tell a folktale that reveals the cognitive side of African spirituality. In the tale, a man plants maize in his gardens, but his wife discovers that wild pigs have entered the gardens and broken stalks.

Angered, the man goes to a blacksmith, who transforms his hoe blades into spears. The man hides at night, sees the pigs, and stabs one with a spear. The next morning, he follows a trail of blood up to a cave in the mountains. When he enters the cave, he discovers that it opens into "a country with mountains, villages, and gardens"; arriving at a village, he hears moaning and discovers "his spear at the head of the bed of the sufferer. That one was that man's dead mother's brother and the person nursing him was that man's dead mother who had borne him." His mother remonstrates, "We are ghosts of the dead. If we stop eating in your garden, where shall we eat?" When the man insists that he did not know the wild pigs were ghosts of the dead, his mother's brother tells him that when his own efforts to protect his gardens fail, he should consult a diviner, who might determine if they are ghosts; if they are, he should make beer to offer libations and sweep their graves. The mother's brother then declares, "Here in the land of the spirits there is tobacco seed which you yourself don't know about." When the man returns to the world of the living, his relatives are uncertain whether to believe him. But when tobacco grows, they believe him. The man introduces a crop that stimulates trade and increases prosperity.[45]

Without entering into details peculiar to Kaguru society,[46] it ought to be apparent that the story insists, like Naipaul, upon constitutive distinctions between the worlds of daylight and darkness, of the living and the dead, while arguing, again like Naipaul, that the two worlds interpenetrate and counterbalance each other. Even Naipaul's argument that the pursuit of development and modernity is complicated by the interplay between the world of daylight and night finds support in the story. When the wild pigs threaten his gardens, the man seeks out the blacksmith, the communal agent of instrumental mastery. But this is futile. However, the story also challenges Naipaul's association of spirits and magic with a passivity that always "undoes" development and modernity. In the spirit world, the man is told that he needs to tend to spiritual as well as material "realities." But he is also told how to grow tobacco, how to combine piety and prosperity.

The story yields rich implications. The man learns to "hear" the voices of the dead only after his act of violence makes visible, through a line of blood, his path to them. That the line of blood should lead to a cave and an alternate world suggests initiation and rebirth. This moral education precedes his practical empowerment. Growing tobacco brings innovation into the world of the living, connecting personal prosperity to communal prosperity. Tobacco was indeed, at one time, an innovation—introduced by the Portuguese from America—that became an important commodity.[47] In the early nineteenth century, as Omani Arabs established clove plantations and a trade center on Zanzibar, demand for slaves and ivory increased, leading to an intensification of trade between the coast and interior.[48] "[T]rade in tobacco was continued parallel with the 'new' export trade," and as markets expanded currency and its equivalents came into use, so that exchange became an increasingly important source of a community's material well-being as the nineteenth century progressed. This expansion of trade occurred against a background of considerable famine and disease: the folktale's portrait of the difficulty of making a living and the closeness of the world of death has a context.[49]

One might argue that the story reinforces the diviner's authority and legitimates innovation (growing tobacco) by revising the past (the ancestors started the practice). While this is valid, the cost of reducing the folktale's interpretative-evaluative content to power politics or ideological mystification would be high: it would then only confirm links between discourse and power already inscribed in the modern West. The folktale claims, on the contrary, that spiritual and material goods are implicated in one another: it is not that doing good is a cover for doing well, but rather that doing well (increasing material well-being for oneself and one's community) can only come about through moral *and* cognitive enlightenment. The challenge that the folktale's rationality poses for the modern West is similar to the challenge that, according to J. M. Bernstein, modern art poses: "to think through what truth, morality, and beauty (or its primary instance: art) are when what is denied is their categorical separation from one another—a separation . . . constitutive of modernity. It is the entwinement of art and of truth, the experience of art as somehow cognitive and of truth as sensuous and particular . . . that constitutes the challenge."[50] Bernstein associates such "entwinement" with both the promise of art and the link between practical knowing, *phronêsis*, and political action, *praxis*, that lies at the heart of Aristotle's account of the *bios politikos*—the life that realizes fully the goods intrinsic to human being. The folktale's concern with articulating such goods need not suggest a complete convergence between African oral literature and Aristotle's project, but it does suggest that contemporary forms of assimilating non-Western discourse to Western terms and value are intensely implicated, as Wiredu suggests, in the assumptions that estrange Western modernity from its past.

Placing an Ethics of Resistance in Africa:
Walker's *Possessing the Secret of Joy*

To say that Africa has been exploited by a West that constructs an Other against which to measure its own "advanced" civilization does nothing to address what Pearl Cleage describes as the feminist ethical challenge of Alice Walker's *Possessing the Secret of Joy* (1992): "When Tashi [the heroine] can finally admit that the legendary wisdom of the male elders of her tribe and the fervor of the present-day African revolutionaries have in common a tolerance for, and glorification of, female circumcision, she almost cannot bear it." Similarly, Laura Shapiro's *Newsweek* review declares, "There is no dogma in this narrative and little typecasting. Instead, we have a true rarity: a novel that's strengthened, not strangled, by its political mission." Cleage argues that reading the novel "requires courage and a willingness to admit to a terrifying reality."[51] Similarly, Kimberley Joyce Pollock claims, "Because of *Possessing the Secret of Joy*, women are able to speak the unspeakable. This becomes true not only for the women in the novel, but for the women who read the novel as well."[52] By contrast, the Kenyan scholar Nwikali Kieti argues that "Walker's portrayal of Africans sometimes reveals latent Eurocentricism." Kieti subjects Walker to an immanent critique similar to Nixon's critique of Naipaul: Walker is, like Naipaul, influenced by Conrad; she essentializes and universalizes, "changes the 'oppressed woman' into the 'oppressed third world woman' category Mohanty critiques."[53] Such a critique, however, cannot address the central issue: Walker insists that certain cultural practices are ethically indefensible in ways that no amount of contextualizing or sensitivity can diminish.

Possessing the Secret of Joy describes how the heroine, Tashi, raised as a Christian in the fictional African country of Olinka, joins anticolonial guerrillas and seeks out excision as an act of cultural-political solidarity. When Olivia, her best friend and an African American missionary's daughter, pleads with her to reconsider, Tashi turns on Olivia with rage: "You want to change us, I said, so that we are like you. And who are *you* like? Do you even know? . . . And the nerve of you, to bring us a God someone else chose for you! He is the same as those two stupid braids you wear, and that long hot dress with its stupid high collar!"[54] When Adam, Tashi's future husband, traces her to a guerrilla camp, he finds a woman whose spirit has been mutilated along with her sexuality (40, 43–44). Adam takes Tashi back to America and marries her, but she has been so psychically violated that she spends some thirty years in therapy in Europe and America. Treated by Carl Jung, among others, Tashi comes to recognize that she has been suppressing her own knowledge of the misogynistic violence inherent in the initiation, a violence that assumes overwhelming immediacy in her recovered childhood memory of having seen her own sister's severed clitoris thrown disdainfully to a cock to devour (80).

Walker uses the techniques of psychoanalysis to construct a narrative that is in part, like *Oedipus Rex*, a murder mystery. But in line with much contemporary popular psychology and Western theory, the guilt is traced not to the natural desires of individuals but to the cultural practices of society; therefore, healing involves not acknowledging desires that one must repress and redirect, but learning how not to cooperate with one's victimization by society. Whereas Freud would argue, for the most part, that psychic health involves moving from crushing, self-destructive violence against oneself to moderate, civilized self-limitation, much Western popular psychology would locate psychic health in directing violence away from the self (the victim) by turning it against society (the victimizer).[55] In Walker's psychological murder mystery, we come to learn with Tashi that the murderer is African traditional culture. Her rage turns upon the woman who performed her circumcision, the aged M'Lissa, who is celebrated by the independent government as a guardian of tradition.

Tashi is aided in her progress toward liberating recognitions by Adam's illegitimate son, Pierre, an American-trained anthropologist. Pierre reads to her the Dogon account of the origins of excision, in the God Amma's intercourse with the earth, as described by Marcel Griaule in the classic anthropological text *Conversations with Ogotommêli*: because the clitoris is a locus of masculinity, it must be excised lest an ambiguous sexuality block intercourse; similarly, male circumcision removes the "female" prepuce (169–73). Pierre suggests that anxiety about feminine sexual ambiguity is particularly intense because women can experience pleasure without men (178). Behind male jealousy of female pleasure lies a desire for conquest, manifest in the political history of Olinka (193). Both political and patriarchal repression depend upon effacing an earlier fertility cult (196). Tashi learns that M'Lissa herself has been brutally victimized and is capable of declaring that "the God of woman is autonomy" (216).

Convicted of murdering M'Lissa, Tashi is sentenced to be executed. But, despite an official campaign to demonize her, she becomes a source of inspiration to Olinka women, who now grasp that they might rebel. In a final revelation of the truth of African history, Tashi learns from Pierre that the great curse in some African countries is "son of an uncircumcised mother," because uncircumcised women were captured slaves: "But what is less noted about these people, these women, is that in their own ancient societies they owned their bodies, including their vulvas, and touched them as much as they liked. . . . In short, . . . early African woman, the mother of womankind, was notoriously free!" (276). Armed with this knowledge, Tashi faces her executioners as relatives and friends unfurl a banner with a message that her entire life, and the entire novel, has worked to construct: "RESISTANCE IS THE SECRET OF JOY!" (279).

Walker's indictment cannot be brushed aside. Female circumcision can be persuasively linked to notions that feminine sexuality needs to be curbed, submitted to a larger order, in order to become human rather than bestial. Jean Comaroff describes female initiation (*bojale*) in precolonial Tswana society as involving dramatic and sustained habituation to subordination: the right thigh of a girl was cut, into which the "glowing end of an ignited stick was twisted," to which the girl was expected to respond "with fortitude"; this was followed by the piercing of the hymen by a tuber and sexual instruction "punctuated by severe flogging carried out by older women or widows."[56] Kieti's observation that "[w]hereas circumcision traumatizes many women, separating it from the production and reproduction relations where it occurs is inadequate as a means to address the problem"[57] may be useful if "the problem" is cognitive, a matter of understanding the origins and place of such practices, but for Walker "the problem" is ethical, the traumatizing of women.

Nonetheless, while Walker, like Gayatri Chakravorty Spivak, suggests that African cultures surgically literalize forms of sexual oppression enforced largely through psychic manipulation in the West,[58] her novel's structure and values are as reflective of the contemporary West as Olivia's braids. The pursuit of psychic health becomes a matter of recovering the self anterior to social inscription, and ethical life centers around separating that recovered self from cultural impositions.[59] Walker argues that an acultural selfhood, found through affirming "ownership" of our bodies, grounds the ethical life of any conceivable just community.[60] On the one hand, sources of identity and value are imagined as standing outside culture and history; on the other hand, Walker suggests an original, matriarchal, sexually liberated society. Of course, there is an actual culture with a history of affirming acultural selfhood, and that is the modern West. Even the notion of a primordial matriarchy circulates within contemporary Western feminism.[61] By drawing upon Jung, Walker emphasizes the transcultural, ahistorical nature of the identity repressed by diverse societies.[62] Jungian psychology, modified by contemporary Western feminism, replaces or modernizes the Enlightenment categories of rationality and fellow feeling as the sources of a universalistic ethic capable of judging the superstitions and prejudices of various cultures. Pollock summarizes, "Without resistance, there is a life without joy. Without resistance, self-love is impossible."[63]

Walker's critique of African modes of cultural formation, although derived from essentialist sources, accords with the association of acculturation and ideological mystification one finds in antiessentialist contemporary literary theory, the conviction, derived largely from Gramsci, Lacan, Althusser, Derrida, and Foucault, that to accept shaping into a "civilized" form is *of necessity* to become an accomplice in society's crimes against the self.[64] The oddity that essentialist and antiessentialist positions should yield a shared view becomes less strange upon reflection: for an essentialist, to accept cultural "shaping" violates one's "real" self; for an antiessentialist, to accept cultural "shaping" submits desire and will to the false, essentializing claims of cultural authority and so binds us, arbitrarily, to power structures that rest upon insupportable foundationalist claims.

The great difference, of course, is that the antiessentialist believes any notion of "essential self" to be the product of repressive "shaping."[65] However, even this difference may be less great than at first appears, for both the essentialist and the antiessentialist locate freedom and value in what resists shaping. Peter Dews notes that by seeking difference "through an immersion in fragments and perspectives," poststructuralism neglects Adorno's insight that "this splintering is itself the effect of an overbearing totality [modern capitalism], rather than a means of escape from it."[66] Indeed, the subsumption of any notion of sustained, developed individuation to the violence of cultural shaping tends to work against any ethics not reducible to classical liberalism's negative liberty.[67] The tension of adhering to an antiessentialist position that replicates liberalism's critique of how cultural shaping "violates" an essential self is evident, for example, as Richard Bernstein notes, in how Foucault's "talk of ethics and freedom" is undermined by "genealogical analyses" that make unaccountable "any talk of agency which is not a precipitate of power/knowledge regimes," and in how Derrida, despite evident "moral passion," "seems to call into question the very possibility of 'warranting' ethical-political positions."[68] J. M. Bernstein argues that Derrida can only keep deconstruction's political mission of "combating the totalitarian risk" from collapsing into "liberalism's (illusory) agnostic stance towards the question of the good life" by valorizing "unconditional affirmation" in a manner that leaves unclear how "this unconditionality . . . has come to be revealed as prescriptive for us now (at the closure of metaphysics?)" and that makes the moral "prior to knowledge and truth" in a way that reduces politics to "a question of strategies and rhetorics."[69] In postulating "strategic essentialism," using essentialism in the service of antiessentialist disruption, Spivak most explicitly illustrates the parallels between essentialist and antiessentialist critiques of cultural "shaping," as well as the difficulties of using concepts derived from one culture to combat the formation demanded by another culture without a theory that allows for cross-cultural rationality.[70] Absent such a theory, on issues that matter, like excision, there will be no way to avoid wavering between relativism and antirelativism.[71]

Both essentialism and antiessentialism imply overly simple oppositions between resistance and incorporation. Anthony Giddens observes that Talcott Parsons's functionalism and Louis Althusser's version of Marxism both reach "a position in which subject is controlled by object. Parsons's actors are cultural dopes, but Althusser's agents are structural dopes of even more stunning mediocrity."[72] Parsons argues that society molds many of our desires, so we come to want the attributes necessary to fulfill specific social roles; Althusser's state ideological apparatus thoroughly and insidiously works to ensure that we will know ourselves in ways that "naturalize" whatever makes us into "supports" of the system.[73]

Such assumptions lead to seeing narrative primarily as a vehicle for producing cultural or structural dopes. Distinguishing between narrative's performative and pedagogical dimensions, Homi K. Bhabha ascribes positive value only to the performative dimension's "disruption" of the pedagogical dimension, which implies that narrative desire to teach is (always?) regressive and totalizing.[74] Edward Said argues that "narrative fiction and history . . . are premised on the recording, observing powers of the central authorizing subject, or ego," which creates an imperialism internal to narrative.[75] By contrast, Paul Ricoeur argues that a capacity for ethical-political agency is tied to gaining a narrative sense of identity, that narrative has a positive value in the individuation of identity.[76]

If narrative as such is implicated in the "violence" of cultural formation, then good criticism must work against narrative designs by valorizing resistance *as such* (thus affirming our "real" nature).[77] Walker's treatment of "resis-

tance" as the substance of ethical self-realization is axiomatic in much contemporary Western theory.[78] It is not surprising that Laura Shapiro finds "no
dogma" in Walker's novel, for it teaches what the West has long naturalized.

V. Y. Mudimbe points out that in postwar intellectual discourse the "nineteenth-century *a priori* assumption about primitive images as contemporary . .
. symbols of Western prehistorical experience" is challenged, and Abiola Irele
notes that "the position of cultural pluralism and cultural relativity which began to mark anthropology in the inter-war years and finally came to dominate
it after the Second World War" ushered in both "avowed anti-imperialism"
and "a new and positive evaluation of non-Western cultures."[79] If reading African works only confirms the West's *own* rejection of ideological justifications
of colonialism a half century ago, such reading becomes an incredibly safe
activity. By contrast, readers open to encountering a "difference" that has not
been colonized in advance to Western conceptuality must be, like Nietzsche's
ideal readers, willing to be "profoundly wounded" as the precondition for being "profoundly delighted."[80]

2

Postmodernism, Cultural Otherness,
and the Ethical Stake in Close Reading

Postmodernism and Postcolonial Theory

Postcolonial theory offers little resistance to privileging modern Western terms of analysis and value, for what is peculiar to the non-West tends to be swallowed by what is general to Western postmodernism.[1] Indexes of prominent anthologies on postcolonial theory reveal numerous entries for terms derived from postmodern thought—hybridity, deconstruction, essentialism, hegemony, orientalism, etc.—but no entries for terms that speak to indigenous African thought and experience, such as ancestors, witchcraft, spirits, and patron-client relations, nor is there any entry for parastatals, the public-financed large-scale industrial and agricultural organizations central to the economic history of postcolonial regimes. Leela Gandhi notes that "the intellectual history of postcolonial theory is marked by a dialectic between Marxism . . . and poststructuralism/postmodernism," for "in its current mood postcolonial theory principally addresses the needs of the Western academy."[2] Rosemary Marangoly George cites Ama Ata Aidoo, among others, to the effect that "when it comes to publication in today's global market, 'Someone can declare that your manuscript doesn't read like a manuscript from a third world person.'"[3]

Postcolonial theory has not lessened its dependence upon Western frameworks, despite a history of appeals to do so. In *The Empire Writes Back* (1989), Bill Ashcroft, Gareth Griffiths, and Helen Tiffin argue that postcolonial literature is characterized conceptually by syncreticity (whereby previously separate linguistic and cultural formations merge) and formally by hybridity (a blending of culturally historically distinct generic norms).[4] The terms have gained wide currency (as the index entries indicate), in part because, as Vijay Mishra and Bob Hodge note, *The Empire Writes Back* provides the Western academy with "a good, teachable text," in part because the terms do allow one to point to the heterogeneity of cultural, linguistic, generic models embedded in many postcolonial works.[5] However, the postcolonial world's openness to syncretic vision is attributed almost entirely to the West's effect upon the non-West, and syncretic values replicate postmodern norms.[6]

Mishra and Hodge argue that this theory "ends up" homogenizing particularities "into a more or less unproblematic theory of the Other." They point out that Ashcroft et al. are aware of these dangers, for the latter cite Benita Parry to the effect that syncretism assimilates "native 'difference' into a new hegemonic totality," but they nonetheless insist, "Syncretism is the condition within which post-colonial societies operate."[7] Mishra and Hodge suggest the corrective of considering precolonial texts as sources for the syncretic and hybridized, since "an indigenous precursor tradition" may have "some of the features of postmodernism."[8]

The terms that postcolonial theory deploys matter greatly. Hybridity, Robert J. C. Young points out, originated in nineteenth-century Western racial discourse and connoted "forcing incompatible entities to grow together (or not)."[9] In our time, hybridity has become a term of celebration because cultural mixture is taken to imply a gain in postmodern decentering and destabilization. Homi K. Bhabha argues that hybridity "reverses the effects of the colonialist disavowal, so that other 'denied' knowledges enter upon the dominant discourse and estrange the basis of its authority"; by making possible "the *production* of hybridization," colonial power "enables a form of subversion."[10] Alongside hybridity, a conception of creolization emerges in which "creoles, patois and Black English decentre, destabilise and carnivalise the linguistic domination of 'English.'"[11] The biological, linguistic overtones of these terms occlude the rational element in cross-cultural discourse. Through a metaphorics of forced breeding, these terms reinforce the postmodern "rage against reason"[12] that reduces discourse to a stark interplay of domination and self-assertion.

Young points out that Bakhtin distinguishes between "organic [linguistic] hybridity" and "intentional hybridity," in which a specific instance of "double-voiced hybridized discourse serves a [conscious] purpose."[13] In organic hybridity one may well find linguistic effects of material domination that may be mobilized for subversive purposes. Bakhtin's intentional hybridity, however, opens a space for dialogue and rationality because it rests upon a conception of language that emphasizes a relation of "active responsive understanding" on the part of both speaker and listener: "[W]hen the listener perceives and understands the meaning . . . of speech, he simultaneously takes an active, responsive attitude toward it. He either agrees or disagrees with it (completely or partially), augments it, applies it, prepares for its execution, and so on. . . . And the speaker himself is oriented precisely toward such an actively responsive understanding. . . . [H]e expects response, agreement, sympathy, objection, execution, and so forth."[14] The "active role of the *other* [Bakhtin's emphasis] in the process of speech communication" opens us to friendship (agreement, sympathy) and invites rational dialogue (agreement, disagreement, augmentation): "There can be no dialogic relationship with an object. . . . Understanding is always dialogic to some degree."[15] For Bakhtin, as for Levinas, the Other does not expose the complicity of language and rationality in totalizing violence, but rather discloses the ethical dimension of language that makes reason possible. Levinas argues, "[T]he relation with the Other . . . introduces into me what was not in me. But this 'action' upon my freedom precisely puts an end to violence and contingency, and, in this sense also, founds Reason. . . . The other is not for reason a scandal . . . , but a first teaching."[16]

By contrast, most postcolonial theory attends more to how language undermines its own claims than to how genuine dialogue may yield cross-cultural understanding.[17] In "DissemiNation," Bhabha claims that the narrating drive toward presence is undermined by temporal fissures *within* narration that disrupt the "fullness of narrative time": "In the production of the nation as narration there is a split between the continuist, accumulative temporality of the pedagogical, and the repetitious, recursive strategy of the performative."[18] Postmodern claims about language as such—presence conceals absence, rhetorical figuration undermines grammatical denotation—are transposed into claims about national identity as such.[19] A national minority "does not simply confront the pedagogical, or powerful master-discourse with a contradictory or negating referent," but "[i]nsinuat[es] itself into the terms of reference of the dominant discourse" as a "supplementary antagoniz[ing] the implicit power to generalize, to produce the sociological solidity." Bhabha focuses upon how minority voices reiterate abstract claims already inscribed within Western postmodernity: "The aim of cultural difference is to re-articulate the sum of knowledge from the perspective of the signifying *singularity* of the 'other' that resists totalization. . . . [A]ll forms of cultural meaning are open to translation because their enunciation resists totalization."[20] While resisting totalization is an

important good, if singularity's significance resides exclusively in resisting totalization, then its value becomes co-extensive with its general negative effect.
Such a way of valuing difference opens itself to Hegel's comment upon Schelling's dissolution of all oppositions into underlying identity: it's a matter of all
cows being black in the night.[21]

The specificity of non-Western culture and thought is lost in blanket affirmations of difference. Kenneth Harrow points out that African literature in
French and English constitutes its own tradition and suggests that one can
distinguish three types—literatures of *témoignage*, revolt, and postrevolt—
each of which establishes paradigms that the others contest. While Harrow
considers how African content may complicate Western schemas, the readings
that emerge tend to confirm postmodernism's self-portrait. Harrow draws upon
Dennis Duerden's argument that traditional African cultures managed conflict by assigning different social roles to different age-grades and by rejecting
writing lest it create a static, totalizing system. Through Duerdon's work, Harrow finds an indigenous precursor tradition that refuses "to accord a fixed symbolic meaning to objects, to masks or statues, or to social roles" and that resists
"the totalizing pressures of a permanent authority."[22] The literature of *témoignage* is assimilated to classical realism. This literature is subverted when the
unified subject is recognized to be a fiction. Because movement toward the
postmodern is associated with both a gain in truth and a return to an indigenous difference, Harrow can use extensive citations from Western theorists as
commentary upon African fiction, absorbing the postcolonial into the postmodern.[23]

The ethical value that Ashcroft et al., Bhabha, and Harrow implicitly place
upon destabilization rests upon what Seyla Benhabib calls "the specifically
modern achievement of being able to criticize, challenge, and question the
content of . . . [socially, culturally] constitutive identities and the 'prima facie'
duties and obligations they impose upon us." There can be compelling autobiographical reasons for appreciating that achievement. Spivak argues that
"the postcolonial teacher can help to develop this vigilance" about the culturally constructed processes of value-formation in part because "[s]he says 'no' to
the 'moral luck' of the culture of imperialism while recognizing that she must
inhabit it, indeed invest it, to criticize it."[24]

If postcolonial theory relies upon a postmodern ethics, however, it must
either engage contemporary criticism of that ethics or risk intellectual provin-
ciality. Although postmodern features may be found in both indigenous tradi-

tions and postcolonial texts, there is no theoretical reason why one might not also find some features of communitarianism or the second-generation Frankfurt School, for example. Such "alternative" precursor traditions are not sought, because Western criticism takes as axiomatic a conflation of ethics with affirmations of difference that underwrites, paradoxically, a totalizing hermeneutics. As Geoffrey Galt Harpham notes, deconstruction becomes a neo-Kantian "ethical necessity," a "law" to be applied to "all discourse."[25] Postmodernism's tendency to equate the ethical with epistemological skepticism, with the procedures of negative theology,[26] raises both theoretical and practical concerns. By arguing that *différance* is primary and, as in Derrida's notion of "iterability,"[27] *alone* generative of resistance to totalization, postmodernism portrays norms and values as invariably guilty of violence to the extent that they promote *any* stabilizations, regularities, consistencies. Determinate contexts have only the strategic value of promoting "'unconditional' affirmation" of difference.[28]

Such a view severs ethical concern from rational discussion. Even if we accept that instability or *différance* are emancipatory, and that we each individually desire unconditional affirmation, it is unclear why we should concern ourselves about anyone else's unconditional affirmation.[29] In terms of praxis, moreover, the undermining of unified subjectivity and rationality threatens to make theoretically impossible any account of agency. Moreover, the circumscription of ethical activity to negativity (working *against* totalizing claims) tends to replicate and reinforce classical liberalism's marginalization of discourse about the good in favor of demarcations of (negative) rights (here, the "right" to "unconditional affirmation").[30]

To the extent that postmodernism challenges any ethical universalism, it poses serious obstacles to any discussion of human rights. Thus postmodernism, while allied with feminism, is blocked from embracing the ethical universalism that feminism's relation to the politics of human rights would seem to demand. Spivak observes that "the political claims that are most urgent in decolonized space are tacitly recognized as coded within the legacy of imperialism: nationhood, constitutionality, citizenship, democracy, even culturalism." If these are to be seen, as she sees them, as "regulative political concepts" tied to "the social formations of Western Europe," for which "no historically adequate referent may be advanced from postcolonial space," then they become concept-metaphors without adequate referents, "catachreses."[31] Spivak argues that her own position as a displaced non-Western female intellectual in

the American academy is emblematic of postcoloniality: "Claiming catachreses from a space that one cannot not want to inhabit and yet must criticize is,
then, the deconstructive predicament of the postcolonial."[32] When asked
about discussing "'universal' oppression of women . . . in terms of the effacement of the clitoris, . . . whereby clitoridectomy can be considered a meton-
omy of women's social and legal status," Spivak declares, "I chose a universal
discourse . . . because I felt that rather than define myself as repudiating universality—because universalisation, finalisation, is an irreducible moment in any
discourse— . . . I should see what in the universalising discourse could be
useful. . . . I think we have to choose again strategically, not universal discourse, but essentialist discourse." When pressed about how one can "*use* universalism, essentialism, etc., strategically" without an "overall commitment"
to these concepts, Spivak replies, "[Y]ou *are* committed to these concepts,
whether you acknowledge it or not. . . . I think it's absolutely on target to take
a stand against the discourses of essentialism, universalism as it comes in terms
of the universal—of classical German philosophy or the universal as the white
upper-class male . . . etc. But *strategically* we cannot. . . . You pick up the
universal that will give you the power to fight against the other side, and what
you are throwing away by doing that is your theoretical purity."[33]

But to use a concept strategically that one repudiates philosophically suggests sophistry. Indeed, Spivak's military language raises the question of
whether despair of reason does not occasion a metaphorics of violence. The
moral passion of postcolonial theory's political concerns drives it toward exploring the conditions necessary for cross-cultural ethical discourse, but its
intellectual dependence upon postmodernism blocks that exploration.

In the work of Edward Said, that blockage takes on a particular poignancy.
Said's *Orientalism* has generated many useful accounts of Western constructions of non-Western others.[34] However, such work contributes primarily to
scholarship *about* the West. Its own terms of analysis do not provide a space for
cross-cultural ethical discourse. As James Clifford argues, *Orientalism* wavers
between maintaining "that all cultural definitions must be restrictive, that all
knowledge is both powerful and fictional, that all language distorts" and making "frequent appeals to an old-fashioned existential realism."[35] The epistemological question is whether critical understanding can be a rational aspiration,
or should we see ourselves as locked within culture-specific fictions, as Lyotard
suggests.[36] The ethical question is whether there are determinate values that
can be rationally, cross-culturally defended. Clifford argues that Said waffles.[37]

Similarly, John McGowan claims that Said's "tendency to appeal to transcendent values like freedom and justice conflicts with his adherence to the doctrine that 'there is no point of view, no vantage, no perspective available like an Archimedean principle outside history' . . . that allows for disinterested knowledge," which leads Said to pay "too little attention to how parasitic the whole concept of an other [to champion and accord recognition to] is on liberal traditions of individualism."[38]

One might expect Said to address such concerns in *Culture and Imperialism* (1993). Early in the text, Said scorns the idea that "the outlying regions of the world have no life, history, or culture to speak of, no independence or integrity worth representing without the West."[39] Yet, in over three hundred pages, only twice does Said briefly mention non-Western cultural sources of value and intellectual historical momentum: he notes that Abn al-Rahman al-Jabarti attributes the French conquest of Egypt to God's punishment of his people; he lauds the poet Adonis, or Ali Ahmed Said, for challenging "what he regards as the ossified, tradition-bound Arab-Islamic heritage" by seeking to legitimate "the dissolving powers of critical modernity" by arguing that "at the heart of the [Islamic] classical tradition—including the Koran—a subversive and dissenting strain counters the apparent orthodoxy proclaimed by the temporal authorities."[40] Said sympathizes with Jabarti's experiences, but does not take his reading of history seriously, and Said values Adonis's work because it allows him to find an "indigenous precursor tradition" with "some of the features" of critical modernity ("a subversive and dissenting strain").[41] Said praises other non-Western figures but in the context of their commitment to modes of valuing and interpreting derived from engagement with the modern West.[42]

Said locates an ethics of anticolonialism in a rehabilitation of humanism, appealing to his readers "as intellectuals and humanists" to stand against both Western imperialism and "resurgent nationalisms, despotisms, and ungenerous ideologies."[43] Arguing that Frantz Fanon's final work looks beyond both the limitations of "imperialist culture and its nationalist antagonist" toward "liberation," Said "conjectures" that Fanon read Lukács's *History and Class Consciousness* as he wrote, deriving from Lukács the notion that fragmentation and reification "could be overcome by an act of mental will, by which one lonely mind could join another by imagining the common bond between them," thereby effecting "reconciliation and synthesis between subject and object." Thus, in Said's reading, "Fanon's violence, by which the native overcomes the division between whites and natives, corresponds very closely to

Lukács's thesis about overcoming fragmentation by an act of will. . . . In Fanon's world change can come about only when the native, like Lukács's alienated worker, decides that colonization must end—in other words, there must be an epistemological revolution."[44] Said argues that liberation is distinguished from nationalism by its commitment to humanism: "National consciousness, [Fanon] says, 'must now be enriched and deepened by a very rapid transformation into a consciousness of social and political needs, in other words, into [real] humanism.'"[45] Said insists that while Fanon "could not make the complexity and anti-identitarian force of [his] counter-narrative explicit . . . , there are enough poetic and visionary suggestions to make the case for liberation as a *process* and not as a goal contained automatically by the newly independent nations."[46] Since Lukács was decisively influenced by Schiller and Hegel, who were much concerned with fragmentation and alienation, there is a certain plausibility in Said's account.[47] Spivak, however, has noted the oddity of coming at the non-Western world by beginning with Frantz Fanon, "a Christian psychiatrist from Martinique."[48] Even if we take Fanon as an unproblematic spokesman, there are problematic parallels between Said's reading of Fanon and a standard account of Romantic poetry's response to the replication of absolutist consciousness in the French revolution. Whereas Romantic poets want their revolution to heal the subject-object breach through poetry, Fanon, on Said's account, hopes to heal the breach through "violence," but in both cases healing involves "imagining the common bond" between lonely minds.[49]

Since Said adopts the position he attributes to Fanon, its implications demand consideration. First, the association of liberationist humanism with an "anti-identitarian . . . counter-narrative" connects this position with Adorno's, where the subject-object dialectic produces reification because conceptualization emerges from the need to know the world in such a way that one may control it: "The system is the belly turned mind."[50] Adorno argues that conceptualization drives toward the absorption of the nonidentical into the identical. To "change this direction of conceptuality, to give it a turn toward nonidentity" is the "hinge of negative dialectics." The goal is to move toward "reconciliation," which Adorno argues would "release the nonidentical, would rid it of coercion, including spiritualized coercion," by allowing "the thought of the many as no longer inimical."[51] Adorno's valorization of anti-identitarian thought accords with postcolonial theory's valorization of singularity's contestation of totalization. Such valorization can also come from Derrida, but Said, like Terry Eagleton, is wary that in Derrida singularity's value is exhausted by its abstract difference, leaving "deconstruction . . . either silent or negative about the notion of solidarity—a value without which no significant social change is even conceivable."[52] Adorno can be seen as offering *both* appreciation of singularity's detotalizing work *and* ethical-political solidarity.

But Adorno refuses to give concrete content to the reconciliation that negativity serves. Praising Marx for not picturing utopia, Adorno argues that since "the spirit's liberation from the primacy of material needs in their state of fulfillment" is beyond our current conceptual capacity, any delineation would be both abstract and idolatrous.[53] However, Eagleton observes that by confining itself to vague notions such as "emancipation of human powers," the Marxist "sublime" does not adequately confront the material reality that "human powers are far from spontaneously positive" and thus there will remain "the need to discriminate among human powers" even if one grants as absolute "the unquestionable virtue of a rich all-around expansion of capacities for each individual." Eagleton argues that Marx's position is "in entire agreement" with the earl of Shaftesbury's: "To live well is to live in the free, many-sided realization of one's capacities, in reciprocal interaction with the similar self-expression of others."[54] Because acceptance of this abstract ideal does not exhaust ethical reflection, there is something dangerous about substituting for the work of ethical thought Shaftesbury's aesthetic cultivation of moral feeling or, in our language, heightened sensitivity.[55] In a similar vein, Albrecht Wellmer questions whether Adorno does not unnecessarily, and regrettably, exclude communicative rationality from his conception of reconciliation. By contrast, J. M. Bernstein argues that Adorno views art as gesturing, alone in Western modernity, toward the lost connection between *phronêsis* and *praxis* upon which reconciliation depends.[56] On both accounts, however, Adorno's concept of reconciliation resists the theorization of how reconciliation may be achieved and maintained. Adorno assumes an end to history in which the release of the nonidentical, like Marx's release of "a rich all-around expansion of capacities for each individual," entails freedom somehow becoming an uncomplicated, self-regulating good. Simply imagining the future as radically discontinuous with the present, however, does not address what Levinas describes as the violence inherent in freedom's spontaneity: "[R]educed to itself [freedom] is accomplished not in sovereignty but in arbitrariness. . . . To approach the Other is to put into question my freedom, my spontaneity as a living being, my emprise over the things, this freedom of a 'moving force.'"[57]

The limitations of Adorno's negative dialectics are evident in Said's use of them. When Said speaks of "consciousness of social and political needs" yielding "real humanism," he implicitly acknowledges a bond between what *is* and what *ought to be*. Harpham notes, "Ethics entails a necessary and principled confusion: the ethical *is* is an *is* that *ought* to be; the ethical *ought* is an *ought* that *is*." Such "principled confusion" underlies novelistic discourse as well as ethics: Harpham argues that "if narrative is powerless to render either *is* or *ought*, it can, and ceaselessly does, figure a process of turning from a disjunction of the two, through resistance, towards their union."[58]

Neither abstract affirmation nor resistance to the identitarian can address how *is* and *ought* are implicated in one another. J. M. Bernstein notes that for Adorno, "Affirmation, . . . in the Nietzschean mode, is violence and guilt."[59] It is telling that Eagleton's questioning of the Marxist sublime, which can critique Adorno's as well as Marx's version of utopia, can equally challenge Derrida's unconditional affirmation: "human powers are far from spontaneously positive"; there will always remain "the need to discriminate among human powers," and so simply affirming "a rich all-around expansion of capacities for each individual" will not exhaust ethical discussion.

Said's reliance upon Adorno impedes concrete discussions of the good, for Adorno's Marxism shares with Derrida's Nietzscheanism a heritage of Romantic individual expressivity, which, paradoxically, can fit comfortably with classical liberalism's marginalization of rational discourse about the good. Linking Marx's narrative of the movement from "the realm of Necessity" to "the realm of Freedom" with Freud's narrative of therapeutic movement toward the patient's freedom, Harpham argues that "Marx and Freud imagine an ideal narrative leading to an unconditioned freedom in which the very determinism on which they had insisted all along simply vanishes."[60] Such a realm of unconditioned freedom derives from a modern Western conceptuality incapable, as Brian Schroeder notes, of putting in "question the capricious spontaneity of personal freedom," an incapacity that is itself the legacy of Western cultural history.[61] By contrast, ethical reflection in African cultures takes the violence internal to freedom quite seriously. Chinua Achebe draws upon such discourse when he declares that "fulfillment is not . . . uncluttered space or an absence of controls, obligation, painstaking exertion. No! It is actually a presence—a powerful demanding presence limiting the space in which the self can roam uninhibited."[62]

To the extent that modern Western thought takes aesthetic cultivation to be a substitute for, rather than an ally of, moral deliberation, the mere recognition of difference will be taken as ethically adequate, as all the other can ask of us. Harrow notes that one purpose of African autobiographical works of *témoignage* was to give "voice to a new cogito, 'me voici,' with the community voice simultaneously echoing 'nous voici.'"[63] While granting recognition is crucial to opening an ethical relationship, it is too frequently treated as exhaustive of that relationship. Peter Dews notes that whereas for Habermas, "linguistic intersubjectivity is the medium within which claims to truth, in the cognitive sense, as well as claims to rightness and authenticity, can be raised and arbitrated," for Lacan, "'Speech is *essentially* the means of being recognized.' . . . It is this conception which lies behind Lacan's celebrated formula: 'Moi, la vérité, je parle.'"[64] A similar view attends Derrida's essay, "En ce moment même dans cet ouvrage me voici,"[65] and even Adorno's vague description of reconciliation as "the thought of the many as no longer inimical."

Paradoxically, such uncritical hearing replicates the kind of scholarly detachment from the other that Hans-Georg Gadamer criticizes in traditional "disinterested" historical positivism (the effort simply to put texts in their "own" contexts): "The text that is understood historically is forced to abandon its claim to be saying something true. We think we understand when we see the past from a historical standpoint—i.e., transpose ourselves into the historical situation and try to reconstruct the historical horizon. In fact, however, we have given up the claim to find in the past any truth that is valid and intelligible to ourselves. Acknowledging the otherness of the other in this way . . . involves the fundamental suspension of his claim to truth."[66]

The Resurgence of the Ethical
and the Rehabitation of Narrative in Literary Theory

The tendency of postmodern thought to reduce the ethical to abstract negativity has helped provoke a resurgence of moral philosophy,[67] just as the privileging of disruption has stimulated interest in connections between ethics and narrative.[68] Levinas's work allows the end of metaphysics to be considered in ways that yield neither relativism nor a "rage against reason."[69] Zygmunt Bauman's *Postmodern Ethics* (1993) is representative: After restating the now-familiar story of how a "grounding" of ethics and reason in "truth" became untenable, Bauman embraces Levinas's claim that ethics, rather than metaphysics, is "first philosophy," that is, the branch of philosophy anterior to all other branches, as well as Levinas's depiction of ethics as an unconditional obligation or responsibility that flows from experiencing the face of the Other as something that "cannot be comprehended, that is, encompassed," which allows the Other to remain forever irreducible to an object of cognition.[70] Because ethics grounds philosophy, it is unconditional and so anarchic, before the beginning (archê). Bauman argues, "The moral self is also a self with no foundation," and "Morality is a *transcendence* of being," for "Confronting the Other not as a person (*persona:* the mask worn to signify the role played, that role having been first described and prescribed in the scenario), but as the *face,* is already the act of transcendence." Bauman thus conserves postmodernism's understanding of Western thought's journey toward antifoundationalism while relying upon the primordiality of ethics to keep the epistemological skepticism of postmodernism from liquidating all value and meaning.[71]

If ethical responsibility does not vanish after deconstruction has done its work, the question arises of what keeps the relation between unconditioned ethical responsibility and specific moral understanding and practice from being an exercise in arbitrary will. Levinas attempts to mediate the relation between the absoluteness of the call to responsibility and the "difficult freedom" of daily practices and choices by distinguishing between ethics and morality.[72] Harpham notes that for Levinas, "morality performs the worldly work of ethics," for morality constitutes, Levinas argues, "a series of rules relating to social behavior and civic duty. But while morality thus operates in the socio-political order of organizing and improving our human survival, it is ultimately founded in an ethical responsibility toward the other. As *prima philosophia,* ethics cannot itself legislate for society or produce rules of conduct whereby society might be revolutionized or transformed."[73] For Harpham, Levinas's distinction dovetails with similar distinctions by Bernard Williams and Stanley Cavell to suggest that "[e]thics leads into conflicts only morality can settle."[74] For Bauman, "the obsessive, almost compulsive urgency with which [Levinas] returns in his late writings and interviews to the 'problem of the Third'" raises the question of whether "ethics, born and grown in the greenhouse of the twosome [face-to-face] encounter [can] withstand the assault by the Third party [entry into society, the realm of morality]." Indeed, Bauman claims that Levinas's writings "do not confront the possibility that . . . the work of the institutions which Levinas wishes to be dedicated to the promotion of justice may have consequences detrimental to the moral values."[75]

While Levinas's work is almost obsessively focused upon the radical unconditional anteriority of the ethical, Levinas does provide a sketch—through his defense of reason, meaning, and language—for how linking ethics and morality, answerability to the Other and a politics of justice, might be pursued. In *Totality and Infinity* (1961) Levinas claims, "The order of responsibility . . . is also the order where freedom is ineluctably invoked. . . . This bond between expression and responsibility, this ethical condition or essence of language, . . . permits us to extract language from subjection to a preexistent thought, where it would have but the servile function of translating that preexistent thought on the outside, or of universalizing its interior movements. . . . The face opens the primordial discourse whose first word is obligation. . . . It is that discourse that obliges the entering into discourse, the commencement of discourse rationalism prays for." Because language "comes to me from the Other and reverberates in consciousness by putting it in question," because the "action" of the Other upon me "puts an end to violence and contingency, and, in this sense also, founds Reason," "language does not only serve reason, but is reason," for the "introduction of the new into a thought, the idea of infinity, is the very work of reason. . . . The rational is not opposed to the experienced; absolute experience, the experience of what is in no way a priori, is reason itself."[76]

In *Otherwise than Being* (1974), Levinas distinguishes between "the saying" and "the said," the former, "[a]ntecedent to the verbal signs it conjugates, to the linguistic systems and semantic glimmerings, a foreword preceding languages, . . . is the proximity of one to the other, the commitment of an approach, the one for the other, the very signifyingness of signification," which "weaves an intrigue of responsibility," while the latter is the determinate, fixed, thematized, historically, culturally conditioned meaning that in one sense always "betrays" the "pre-original saying" and that in another sense is always ethically answerable to it: "The correlation of the saying and the said, that is, the subordination of the saying to the said, to the linguistic system and to ontology, is the price that manifestation demands. . . . [But] thematization . . . and theory and thought, its contemporaries, do not attest to some fall of the saying. They are motivated by the pre-original vocation of the saying, by responsibility itself."[77] The relationship between saying and said parallels that between ethics and morality; indeed, language as said is bound to the realm of morality as language as saying arises from the realm of ethics. But what binds the saying and the said, ethics and morality, to each other, and both pairs to one another, is reason: "Reason consists in ensuring the coexistence of these terms, the co-herence of the one and the other despite their difference, in the unity of a theme. . . . Reason, in which the different terms are present, that is, are con-temporaneous in a system, is also the fact that they are present to consciousness inasmuch as consciousness is representation, beginning, freedom."[78]

Levinas's crucial difference from postmodernism lies in his not taking the otherness of the Other as a refutation of reason—a refutation that, Christopher Norris notes, "necessarily leads to some version of the postmodern incommen-surability thesis."[79] Rather, answerability for an Other whose otherness infin-itely outstrips our conceptualizing, "colonizing" gestures grounds reason, even as the abiding tension between ethics and morality, the saying and the said, gives reason its vocation. The concrete work of making determinate mo-rality answerable to ethics constitutes the labor of ethical rationality—an inter-play of *phronêsis* and *praxis* no longer mortgaged to metaphysics. By freeing reason from subservience to metaphysics and subjectivism, Levinas opens a space for rethinking what Paul Ricoeur argues is undeveloped in his (Lev-inas's) own thought: a postmetaphysical, neo-Aristotelian consideration of the shaping of moral identity through deliberative agency over time, a process linking identity to a narrative unity of aiming for the good.[80]

If reason articulates relationships of "contemporaneousness" between eth-ics and morality, it is a false dilemma to argue that one must choose between, on the one hand, a Levinasian emphasis upon the ethical as disruptive of an egocentric, totalizing psychic economy and, on the other hand, a Ricoeurian emphasis upon the ethical as solicitude, as bringing to encounters with others an identity shaped by aiming, over time, for the good.[81] Levinasian reason may be inaugurated by the face of the Other putting the self-justification of my freedom into question, but reason's commitment to "the coherence of the one and the other despite their difference" works to moderate the extremism, what Ricoeur calls the hyperbole,[82] of the ethical and the saying taken in theoretical isolation. Reason "ensur[es] the coexistence" of what might seem mutually antagonistic: reason thinks through the implications of the face to face where "[i]n proximity the other obsesses me according to the absolute asymmetry of signification," while acknowledging that "[t]he relationship with the third party [the socio-political order, morality] is an incessant correction of the asymmetry of proximity in which the face is looked at. . . . In the comparison of the incomparable there would be the latent birth of representation, logos, consciousness, work, the neutral notion *being*. . . . Out of representation is produced the order of justice. . . . Justice requires contemporaneousness of representation. It is thus that the neighbor becomes visible, and, looked at, presents himself, and there is also justice for me. The saying is fixed in a said, is written, becomes a book, law and science."[83] Despite Levinas's own attack on artistic representation in "Reality and Its Shadow" (1948), his major work opens a path to linking ethics and aesthetics through reason, and it provides a basis for justifying representational narrative as, at least potentially, moral labor, a position anticipated by his own readings of Proust and Dostoyevsky.[84]

If cultures resemble languages, they do so by bearing a relation to ethical transcendence, to what Levinas calls the "otherwise than being," similar to the relation of the said to "the pre-original Saying." Precisely because cultures, like any "said," speak to something beyond themselves, they are not incommensurate formal systems—for in speaking *to* something outside the *being* their conceptuality constructs, cultures can speak *to* each other, and so cross-cultural rationality becomes possible.

Levinas might seem an odd ally of feminism, for his theorizing either assumes a male viewpoint or it de-emphasizes gender. Indeed, Levinas's association of the feminine with hospitality, discretion, tenderness, and silence has provoked critiques from Simone de Beauvoir and Luce Irigaray.[85] Moreover, the status of ethics as first philosophy might seem, as Derrida argues, to privilege one form of difference (ethical) over another (sexual).[86] However, Tina Chanter points out that Levinas contests "any theory that presupposes the sameness or similarity of individuals, and which does so by taking for granted the priority of the whole," and so challenges such effacements of otherness as, for example, letting sexual difference be subsumed into a generalized "human" essence: "For Levinas, ethics is prior to logic, the Other comes before the I. Once it is understood that the main attempt of Levinas's thinking is to depart from the model of the Other as determined by the I, it is also necessary to recognize that to think the feminine as other takes on a new meaning in

Levinas. . . . Levinas is upsetting, not accepting, the traditional values which identify the egoism of male dominance as superior to female sufferance."[87] Indeed, the saying is exemplified in, prefigured in, maternal tenderness. Ethics and rationality begin in the arrest, through encountering the Other, of freedom's spontaneous unfolding and enjoyment of goods. But enjoyment presupposes habitation, hospitality, and thus the "welcoming" of the feminine. Chanter notes, "It is the I of enjoyment who gives to the Other when called upon in the face-to-face relation. But until the I has learnt to identify itself as an I and as distinct from that which it enjoys, there can be no bread to give to the Other. The feminine being is the one who encourages the I to break from its life of pure enjoyment and conserve its goods. It is in this sense that the feminine is presupposed by the face-to-face."[88]

To the extent that feminism is understood as simply a variant of liberal individualism or Romantic expressivism, Levinas's thought may be seen as uncongenial to it. However, if feminism is understood not as an expression but as a critique of the egocentricism of modern Western conceptuality, and of the abstraction of reason from values, experience, the nontotalizable, the body, then feminism and Levinas may be understood as sharing common insights and concerns. The derivation of the rational from the ethical, and the concern of reason to hold in "contemporaneousness" the ethical and the moral allows the articulation of concrete feminist political demands (ending domestic violence, gaining property rights, etc.) and promotes the attainment of feminist "spiritual" goods (self-respect, inner integrity, intellectual and moral freedom) without predicating such demands and goods upon a network of modern Western assumptions that may easily be seen, within African contexts, as inherently dubious, intrinsically "colonizing," and vulnerable to patriarchal counterattacks.

To follow the ethical rationality of African feminist novels requires a "close reading" not to be confused with New Criticism. Whereas narrative theories inspired by Foucault or Derrida see the "violence of representation" manifest in the constraints of plot and textual pretensions to discursive coherence, narrative theories influenced by Levinasian ethics stress the "colonizing" *of* the text by critics who ignore the claim of the Other, the narrative, upon them. In *Getting It Right* (1992), Harpham argues, "[I]n narrative plot . . . we see the law in productive resistance to the freedom of the reader. . . . Indeed, the effect of narrative is to produce the clear idea of freedom only within and through the clear idea of obligation. The image of plot as the law is useful, too, as a response to those who see the 'ethics of literature' as being based on the priority of the 'special or unique features' of the particular instance over and against the reductive indifference to the particular."[89]

Once such a resistance to readerly freedom is taken as analogous to the suspension of arbitrary freedom before an ethical Other, then the "image of plot as the law" implies that attending to the text sufficiently to subordinate oneself, for the time of the reading, to its coherence involves a responsibility at least analogous to ethical responsibility—so that what is seen by Nancy Armstrong and D. A. Miller as narrative's disciplinary practices may be recast as narrative's calling of the reader to responsibility.[90] Adam Newton's *Narrative Ethics* (1995) attempts to "braid together" Levinas, Bakhtin, and Cavell to articulate a "triadic structure of narrative ethics," first, "a narrational ethics," which he associates with Levinas's "'Saying'—the dialogic system of exchanges at work among tellers, listeners, and witnesses, and the intersubjective responsibilities and claims which follow from acts of storytelling," second, "a representational ethics," which involves "the small but still momentous distance that lies between person and character, or character and caricature, the gains, losses, and risks taken up when selves represent or are represented by others," and third, a "hermeneutic ethics," for "textual interpretation comprises both private responsibilities incurred in each singular act of reading and public responsibilities that follow from discussing and teaching works of fiction."[91]

While correcting facile equations of narrative with imperialism, Newton associates morality (in Levinas's sense) with prescription and old-fashioned moralistic criticism in ways that lead him to minimize "the mediatory role of reason," going against Levinas's own stress upon the "contemporaneousness" of the ethical and the moral, the saying and the said.[92] An ethical encounter does not consume itself in mere recognition of alterity. Instead, reason returns the ethically constituted subject to the question of how one can be, in the realm of concrete daily life, answerable to the Other. Because the ethical both "grounds" and leads back to the moral, to the realm of *phronêsis*, *praxis*, and thus politics, the ethical rationality of feminist fiction involves assessing cultural values, patterns, systems in ways that may lead to repudiation, modification, valorization.

By exploring how African feminist writers are able to employ the techniques and themes of the novel in anticolonialist, antipatriarchal work, we may see that the novel generically, like aesthetics theoretically,[93] anticipates the end of metaphysics, the death of traditionalism. Anthony Giddens notes, "A post-traditional order is not one in which tradition disappears—far from it. It is one in which tradition changes its status. Traditions have to explain themselves, to become open to interrogation or discourse."[94] Traditions become part of the morality assessed by ethics, part of the conceptuality put in question by the ethical encounter, which is itself analogous to the aesthetic encounter ("arresting" or "overflowing" a potentially totalizing conceptuality).[95] The ethical relation gives rationality its vocation and thus cross-cultural discourse its possibility.

II

Reading African Feminist Fiction

3

Culture's Relation to Identity and Value
in *Efuru* and *The Stillborn*

The Ethics of Empowerment in Flora Nwapa's *Efuru*

Efuru (1966) describes a young woman's coming to terms, in the Igbo village world of the late 1940s, with two failed marriages and the early death of the one child she had been able to conceive. Although a successful trader, Efuru faces the communal judgment that she has failed as a woman. As the novel progresses, she begins worshiping Uhamiri, the goddess of the lake, who cares for the community and brings wealth but who has no children. As Lloyd W. Brown notes, "Uhamiri's symbolic presence . . . is an assurance that in developing into a more self-sufficient and independent woman, Efuru is not growing into the kind of self-contained individualism which would break away from the cultural and religious heritage represented by Uhamiri herself. Efuru['s] . . . . individualism is sanctioned by one set of the community's traditions," although it departs from another set.[1] On the one hand, Brown notes how Nwapa portrays a culture that is far from monolithic. In doing so, Nwapa accords with recent theorizing by Derrida, Jameson, Trinh T. Minh-ha, and others.[2] On the other hand, Brown's reading leaves somewhat obscure how cultural formation sustains individual integrity and how self-assertion is entwined with communally mediated notions of right.

Brown argues that "the traditional marriage structure is incompatible with [Efuru's] sense of self" and that she is characterized by an "independent spirit," a "general capacity for self-fulfillment," and "individualism." Perhaps this language leads Brown to describe Efuru as choosing to "dedicate herself as special worshiper of Uhamiri, . . . reject[ing] marriage and motherhood . . . deci[ding] to be a single, childless woman . . . elect[ing]" independence. Thus, he sees the novel as emphasizing "not . . . specific roles, but . . . the woman's need for a free choice of roles."[3] In fact, Efuru does not quite choose any of this: she becomes a worshipper of Uhamiri as a result of recurrent dreams, her father's interpretation, and a dibia's [diviner's] advice. She loses her one child to infant illness; her marriages fail because her husbands fail her; and she is childless not out of choice but because she cannot conceive.

Later studies tend to reinscribe Brown's vocabulary. Naana Banyiwa-Horne argues that Efuru "demonstrates a marked sense of independence and a determination to lead a fulfilling life," "searches for options for self-actualization," seeks a "new definition of a sense of self," and so becomes "an actor in her own, in woman's right." Similarly, Theodora Akachi Ezeigbo argues that "the most important attributes of [Nwapa's] female protagonists are strength, self-determination, and physical beauty. And . . . she deconstructs 'motherhood' by giving it a secondary position to woman's empowerment and economic independence."[4] Elleke Boehmer argues that the female dialogue which saturates Nwapa's text functions as "a mode of self-making" that works toward "fullness" and "autonomy," a "spirit of pride and self-reliance," while Ada Uzoamaka Azodo argues that, according to Nwapa, "Women should feel free to engage in motherhood when it pleases them or withdraw from it anytime, through will or awareness. This implies that the self should be at the center and that personality and behavior should aim at satisfying the needs of the total self."[5] Carole Boyce Davies wonders whether Efuru's achievement of a "free and independent state" is not diminished by the hint that she regards the collapse of her second marriage as a "misfortune."[6]

Employing a postmodern vocabulary alters very little. Introducing a recent collection, Obioma Nnaemeka criticizes those who translate the concerns of African women writers into the terms of First World feminism, but her own conceptual framework does exactly that: "In their studies of female victims who act in resistance against their victimization, . . . [three of the contributors] recast the victim status that is fundamental to feminist scholarship by foregrounding agents of insurrection and change operating within an oppressive situation. What is important is not whether these agents survive their insurrection or are crushed by it; what is crucial is the fact that they *choose* to act."[7]

As in Brown, choice is not just a good but *the* good, for self-empowerment is understood as "insurrection," as "resistance," as seizing upon a capacity for negative liberty. Describing how "the explosive language of pain erupts tragically," Nnaemeka characterizes "these eruptions as women's desire for freedom," a desire that often assumes the form of counterviolence, but also "other channels, such as writing and solidarity/sisterhood through which women survive and gain freedom."[8] The description of pain—physical, psychological, moral, spiritual—is indeed central to African feminist fiction, but its implications cannot be contained within a formula like "desire for freedom" without collapsing back into a critical discourse where a "general capacity for self-fulfillment" and a "marked sense of independence and a determination to lead a fulfilling life" make African feminist heroines indistinguishable from Ibsen's Nora or Hollywood's Thelma and Louise.

While it is partially true, as Nnaemeka asserts, that "female characters are victims of multiple oppressions that are internally generated by oppressive customs and practices and externally induced by an equally oppressive, in-egalitarian world order," such formulations exclude any consideration of how female characters' relations with either internal or external cultural forces may assume forms that cannot be described in terms of "multiple oppressions"— that is, how culture may have a positive, constructive role in shaping character, and how one might distinguish between a cultural influence that constrains the violent spontaneity of freedom in a way that is oppressive and a cultural influence that constrains such freedom in a way that is not. In the absence of thinking through such questions, one is left with vague axioms such as "women should [not] accept the status quo without question but rather . . . equip themselves for *effective* resistance and participation in societal transformation."[9] Such an axiom is unobjectionable because it is vacuous. On the other hand, specific claims, such as Azodo's characterization of Nwapa's view of motherhood as something one can "withdraw from . . . anytime, through will or awareness," either implies that Nwapa endorses family planning, which is true but underscores a point on which she concurs with First World feminism, or it implies that motherhood is a relation that one can terminate at any time, depending (only?) upon one's "will or awareness"—a position that a careful reading of *Efuru* cannot support.

While *Efuru* certainly argues that a woman's worth should not be limited to her role as mother, and while Efuru becomes increasingly assertive and self-reliant, criticism reliant upon the vocabulary of Western liberal individualism or postmodernism tends to occlude aspects of the work that question the vocabulary's assumptions. The vocabulary itself raises the question of whether Igbo culture somehow generates values and expectations that receive full ar-

ticulation in liberal individualism or postmodernism, or whether human beings "naturally" seek autonomous self-actualization. Following in Heidegger's
(or Sartre's) footsteps,[10] one might locate the essence of the human in lack of
essence, so that a core of nonidentity, negativity, *différance* would ground resistance in ways that effectively obviate the essentialist/antiessentialist distinction. Such strategies, however, reinforce what is implicit in the vocabulary of
liberal individualism — autonomy, self-actualization, self-fulfillment, a free
and independent life, etc. All of these terms turn attention away from intersubjectivity and from ethical connection with others; all derive from a peculiar
(modern Western) intellectual history that theorizes an inherently adversarial
relation between self and others (taking capitalistic exchange as the model for
human relations).[11] By contrast, Efuru's acquisition of her own identity is tied
to her ethical solicitude for others: her care for her daughter, her devastation at
her loss, her attentiveness to her child maid, Ogea, and to other children, her
charity to Ogea's impoverished parents (Nwosu and Nwabata) and to the old
woman Nnona, her affection and respect for her father, her considerate treatment of her co-wife, Nkoyeni, and her two mothers-in-law. All this goes largely
unmentioned in the commentaries cited above.[12]

The assumption that Nwapa's novel can be confined to the message that
female self-worth may be found outside motherhood or that her novel is a
female "nous voici" supplement to Achebe's male-centered delineation of
Igbo life neglects the way that *Efuru* is carefully structured to engage in rational dialogue Western expectations of self-fulfillment as well as Igbo assumptions of female subordination.[13] The novel's very evocation of Igbo life in
English prose implies an "outsideness" and thus a position from which to
"raise new questions."[14] As Harrow notes, African fiction constitutes its own
tradition but is "heir to multiple traditions," including those "inherent in the
European languages."[15] Rather than locating African discourse in the margins
of the West, which produces needless anxiety and unwarranted romanticiza-
tion,[16] we should explore how African discourse engages the Western voices
inscribed into its own margins.

Efuru begins with an act of self-assertion that disturbs the village's expectations of female subordination.[17] Efuru, daughter of a great man of the village,
marries Adizua, a man of low status and insufficient funds for a dowry, without
her father's knowledge or consent. The first paragraph emphasizes the speed
and autonomy of Efuru's decision: "They saw each other fairly often and after
a fortnight's courting she agreed to marry him. . . . When the woman saw that

[the man] was unable to pay anything, she told him not to bother about the dowry. They were going to proclaim themselves married and that was that." The subversive nature of this activity is immediately noted through a male cousin's remark, "I don't know what is wrong with young women of these days" (2).

When Efuru's mother-in-law presses upon her the need for excision, Efuru is reincorporated into the community in ways that enforce passivity and immobility: first through the pain of the operation and the healing process, then through the inactivity of a ritual feasting against which Efuru finally rebels: "Her mother-in-law wanted her to continue feasting for two months, but she refused saying that the life was a dull one. She wanted to be up and doing" (15). Efuru is then ritualistically exposed in the market. That evening many people congratulate her and her mother-in-law: "'Your daughter's face is good,' they told her, meaning that she was popular with people. 'Your daughter has the face of people,' others told her, meaning the same thing" (17). The chapter ends, however, with the narrator observing that "underneath, something weighed Efuru down" (17).

The structure of the first chapter, moving from Efuru's assertion of autonomy to her "violent" reincorporation into patriarchal community to her vague unease about this assimilation, invites placing her story within the familiar scripts of liberal individualism or postmodern resistance to essentialist acculturation. Within African literature, this opening appeals to the theme of young love confronted with traditional impediments articulated in Achebe's "Marriage Is a Private Affair" (1952), Obi Okonkwo's relationship with Clara in *No Longer at Ease* (1960), and Ngũgĩ's *The River Between* (1965).[18] However, Nwapa complicates the application of these interpretative matrices. Farmers on the land Adizua works wonder why a woman of "very good family" and "daughter of Nwashike Ogene" would marry "that imbecile" (7). Indeed, the novel introduces the communal commentary that, as Brown and others note, functions as both chorus and disciplinary mechanism,[19] with the remark, "People wondered why she married him" (1), and the end of the chapter reiterates a collective negative judgment: "He is not known. And nobody knows why she ever married him" (16). One farmer speculates, "If it were in his youthful days, Nwashike would have taught that fool a lesson. Things are changing fast these days. These white people have imposed so much strain on our people. The least thing you do nowadays you are put into prison" (7).

Nwapa implies that Efuru's freedom is a product of colonialism's restrictions on patriarchal power. More important, though, she vindicates the collective judgment upon Adizua by the narrative that follows: he is lazy and improvident, lives off his wife's industry, then abandons her and his child for a "low" woman. This complicates any reading of the novel that simply celebrates autonomy and self-assertion by requiring a rereading of the opening, in which the break with deference to others ("They were going to proclaim themselves married and that was that") contains overtones of gratuitous willfulness. If one follows the community in asking why Efuru would marry someone like Adizua after "a fortnight's courting," one finds only this answer: "One moonlit night, they went out. . . . Efuru told him that she would drown herself in the lake if he did not marry her. Adizua told her he loved her very much and that even the dust she trod on meant something to him" (1).

Read in light of what follows, these declarations acquire a "double-voiced" quality: on his part, we hear the fatuous clichés of a young man who can offer only the ardor of the moment; on her part, we hear the triumph of passion over judgment. Far from presenting self-assertion or resistance as an uncomplicated ideal, Nwapa suggests that unalloyed self-assertion ("that was that") tends to isolate us from others and from our own rationality. At the same time, the repressiveness of Igbo culture is emphasized by the extended description of the painfulness of the excision, euphemistically called a "bath"—"Efuru screamed and screamed. It was so painful" (10)—and by Efuru's desire to be "up and doing," to be an active agent rather than a passive representative of her husband's family's status.

If both incorporation into a rigid conventional identity and willful self-creation are flawed alternatives, the question turns to how one may find a form of life that answers the just claims of what we "owe" ourselves and what is due to others. Ricoeur argues that selfhood involves "two major meanings of 'identity' . . . depending on whether one understands by 'identical' the equivalent of the Latin *ipse* or *idem*. . . . Identity in the sense of *idem* unfolds an entire hierarchy of significations, . . . [in which] permanence in time constitutes the highest order, to which will be opposed that which differs, in the sense of changing and variable. . . . [S]ameness as synonymous with *idem*-identity . . . [is opposed to] selfhood (*ipseity*). . . . [I]*pse*-identity involves a dialectic complementary to that of selfhood and sameness, namely the dialectic of *self* and *other than self*."[20] That which is continuous and determinate in the self, *idem*-identity, interacts with, shapes, and is shaped by that which makes the self inseparable from a putting in question of the self's sameness, an *ipseity* that calls upon the self to justify itself. Similarly, *ipse*-identity is shaped by the interaction of the self and the other than self. Thus, the self that is formed culturally in determinate and continuous ways, and the self that is capable of self-creation, resistance, self-assertion, may be bound to one another intimately (which makes possible an assessment of the constructive as well as the oppressive aspects of cultural formation), and the very capacity for change, for putting the determinate and normative in question, may disclose how the self's irreducible particularity, its *ipseity*, is co-extensive with its intersubjective constitution, its ethical answerability to what is other than itself. Such interconnections lead, Ricoeur argues, to the question of "what dialectic of the Same and the Other replies to the demand for a phenomenology of the self *affected* by the other than self."[21]

On the one hand, Nwapa portrays the social reproduction of patriarchy within Igbo culture through Efuru's ritual kneeling when she drinks at the reconciliation ceremony (23), Efuru's pride at meeting the social expectation of becoming pregnant (29), Ajanupu's (Efuru's mother-in-law's sister's) admonishment to Ogea, Efuru's child maid, when sweeping, "Bend down properly, you are a girl, and will one day marry," and when eating, "Put your legs together and sit like a woman" (50), the expectation that all housework and cooking, as well as trading or farming, will fall to the woman (58), and the separate advice of Ajanupu, her father, and her mother-in-law that she should be "patient" about Adizua's neglect and adultery (76). When Adizua begins to ignore her, Efuru contemplates urging him to marry a second wife, thinking to herself, "It is only a bad woman who wants her husband all to herself" (62). When she consults her father, he repeats the same words (75), which allows us to realize that Efuru has internalized a patriarchal maxim. This thread in the novel accords with Pierre Bourdieu's argument that dispositions necessary for "voluntary" cultural reproduction are "unconsciously" reproduced through daily habits.[22] Nwapa has elsewhere observed, "A woman who says she is oppressed and then . . . treats [her son] like a king, . . . is perpetuating the problems."[23] The novel traces a clearly oppressive strand of what Ricoeur calls *idem*-identity.

On the other hand, Nwapa portrays Efuru's resistance both to Adizua's neglect and to the advice to be passive as also deriving from culturally sanctioned forms of identity and value: "I am a human being. I am not a piece of wood. . . . I don't object to his marrying a second wife, but . . . I want to keep my position as the first wife, for it is my right" (62–63); "God in heaven knows that

. . . I have been faithful to him. . . . But [he] has treated me the way that only slaves are treated" (68); "Our ancestors forbid that I should wait for a man to drive me out of his house. This is done to women who cannot stand by themselves, women who have no good homes, and not to me the daughter of Nwashike Ogene" (76). Efuru's sense of self, her *ipseity*, is linked to a notion of right that involves hierarchy (first wife, not a slave, daughter of Nwashike Ogene), determinate values (female fidelity in marriage), and appeal to an absolute context of judgment (God, our ancestors), and thus an *idem*-identity, one shaped by narrative unity and specific hierarchies of value. Indeed, Nwapa suggests that Efuru's success as a trader—her brains (39), self-discipline, resourcefulness—has something to do with her being the daughter of a man whose yams "were the fattest" and whose own father fought "single-handed . . . . against the Aros" (7). By contrast, we learn that Adizua is following his own father's example of irresponsibility, abandonment, and philandering (69–73). Family standing and material well-being seem to be connected with moral and intellectual qualities, thus disclosing the metaphorical insight of Igbo beliefs that our ancestors influence our lives and that we inherit their spirits. Efuru's success in trade links material and spiritual goods, for—as Ifi Amadiume notes—female trading activity combines self-assertion and solicitude for one's family and it constitutes an avenue for the recognition of excellence and thus political influence.[24]

Nwapa also underscores, however, the human cost behind opportunities to cultivate a strong sense of self. When Efuru's father dies, a cannon announces his death because distinguished families, which "took part actively in slave dealing," received cannons as payment (255). When Efuru thinks of what is due her as a wife, she contrasts her right with that of a slave, reminding the reader that until well into colonial times the slave was part of Igbo daily life and so is part of Efuru's social imagination. Similarly, while Ajanupu is, as Maja-Pearce notes, "a marvelous creation, a strong, forceful woman" (in contrast to her submissive sister), she treats Ogea quite roughly, succeeds in trade because she is relentless in demanding payment of debts (51–56), and has a strong sense of self in part because she has raised herself from poverty to wealth.[25]

Nwapa seems to suggest, in accord with Adorno and Benjamin, that the conditions necessary for cultivating our highest qualities depend in part upon benefiting from a history of violence or competitive struggle.[26] The aspects of *idem*-identity that structure or reproduce oppression and the aspects of *idem*-identity that give rise to, or provide reasons for, resistance, for an *ipse*-identity that refuses to be absorbed into a violent, objectifying totality, are entwined in ways that complicate an identification of resistance with the moral purity of victimhood.

It might appear that Nwapa places us in the uncomfortable position of seeing resistance to Igbo patriarchy issuing from a sense of self embedded in Igbo networks of inequality: family status, material success, free-born condition, etc. However, Efuru's development only begins with tensions between gender and class categories. Efuru's difficulty conceiving, loss of her child, and subsequent infertility press upon her and the reader the realization that projects of self-creation and willed identities are checked by more than cultural impediments, that limitation and dependence are inscribed materially, bodily, into the human condition. When Efuru does not become pregnant right away, her mother-in-law assures her that "a child would come when God willed it" (23). Her father takes her to a dibia who tells her to sacrifice regularly to the ancestors; after she does so and delivers a girl, at the naming ceremony, the same dibia breaks a kola nut in response to a prayer for more children and exclaims, "Our fathers forbid. God forbid. God won't agree to this" (37). When the child dies, Efuru's devastation takes the form of "ask[ing] the gods and her ancestors where and when she offended them" (84). "Oh, my chi, why have you dealt with me in this way?" (89). After Ajanupu scolds one woman for "comforting" Efuru by recounting her misfortunes (88), another woman relates how she lost eight children in infancy, declaring, "Nobody owns this world. . . . So have heart. We cannot explain the mysteries of life, because we are mere human beings. Only God knows" (90–91), after which Ajanupu adds, "That's how to sympathize with a woman who has lost her only child." (91).

Solidarity here is not a matter of victims finding in a shared struggle against oppression a collective self-interest. Rather, it is a concern for the suffering, wounded Other that tears one away from self-interest—as when the woman recounts, and so relives, the loss of her eight children because she cannot be indifferent to Efuru's loss of her one. In Ajanupu's rebuke to the one woman and praise of the other, there is an implicit assumption that another's suffering compels our concern, that, in Levinasian terms, "[t]o hear [the Other's] destitution which cries out for justice is not to represent an image to oneself, but is to posit oneself as responsible. . . . More, for my position as *I* consists in being able to respond to this essential destitution of the Other, finding resources for myself."[27]

Ethical action, genuine comforting of Efuru, making language a "saying" addressed to her, is commanded by the absolute reality of her bereavement. The point is not a sociological one (that Igbo women comfort one another over the loss of children); it is that Igbo women's proximity to immediate, visceral human suffering—as in the frequent loss of young children—places them face to face with the nonarbitrary absoluteness of ethical obligation. Jealousy of Efuru's wealth, resentment of her social status, a self-love that consoles itself with viewing others as "less lucky" than oneself—these no longer have a place. "Responsibility, the signification which is non-indifference, goes one way, from me to the other. In the saying of responsibility, which is an exposure to an obligation for which no one could replace me, I am unique."[28]

Nwapa portrays a mother's loss of her only child as the site where the radical anteriority of ethical obligation discloses itself with utmost intensity, for the meaning of the loss of a child cannot be contained by Igbo patriarchal ideology's construction of it—a woman loses prestige, children are associated with wealth, children are evidence of divine favor, etc. Efuru's unspeakable pain transcends all that, for the maternal relation to a small child incarnates saying. "Saying is communication, to be sure, but as a condition for all communication, as exposure. . . . The plot of proximity and communication is not a modality of cognition. The unblocking of communication . . . is not due to the contents that are inscribed in the said and transmitted to the interpretation and decoding done by the other. It is in the risky uncovering of oneself, in sincerity, the breaking up of inwardness and the abandon of all shelter, exposure to traumas, vulnerability."[29]

Because maternal love incarnates saying, it discloses how exposure to another, being-for-another, anchors identity, in both its *idem* and *ipse* dimensions. Bereavement such as Efuru's, where being-for-another is torn from the soul like flesh from bone, reveals how much the interplay between *idem*- and *ipse*-identity is inseparable from an ipseity constituted by a love in which ethical answerability uproots egoism. Similarly, in understanding the obligation that Efuru's suffering imposes upon them, Ajanupu and the other woman respond to a maternal imperative, at once realizing the Igbo cultural ideal of older women treating younger ones as daughters and transcending it (leaving behind, momentarily, the patronizing aspects of gerontocratic "care") by acting toward Efuru as she can no longer act toward her own child.

While Nwapa suggests that the institution of dibia is open to abuse and that modern medicine can limit the extent of our powerlessness, she also implies that the competitiveness, sexism, and class-consciousness of Igbo society can, at times, be transcended by culturally mediated recognitions that the vulnerabilities and limitations intrinsic to our humanity call us to concern for one another. When Adizua does not return for his daughter's burial, Efuru searches for him and then declares the marriage over by returning to her father's compound; she takes over her dead mother's room, cleaning it and putting "in very beautiful designs typical of her people," then rubs "her father's room and his obi and scrub[s] the Ofo, the Chi and many other things" (109). Her decision is communally sanctioned (110) because she has proved a good wife to a bad husband. This return to her father's compound, after her own project of "self-making" has failed partly through calamities she could not prevent, recalls Okonkwo's exile to his mother's village after he inadvertently kills a clansman in *Things Fall Apart*, but unlike Okonkwo, who never learns to temper his investment in willful self-creation by attending to his maternal uncle's lecture on the inherent fragility of all human blessings,[30] Efuru begins to use her intelligence and influence to help other people.

Whereas Okonkwo's insistence upon his "masculine" self-sufficiency leads to isolation, rigidity, and self-destruction, Efuru's growing assertiveness in deciding when her first marriage is over, in pursuing her trading career—for which she gains communal recognition: "She is a good woman. . . . Her hands make money. Anything she touches is money" (154)—and in contracting a second marriage with a man who "loved and respected her" (170), is combined with a growing ethical solicitude for others. Ricoeur argues that solicitude and self-esteem are intimately connected: "To self-esteem, understood as a reflexive moment of the wish for the 'good life,' solicitude adds essentially . . . the fact that we *need* friends. . . . Solicitude adds the dimension of value, whereby each person is *irreplaceable* in our affection and our esteem. In this respect, it is in experiencing the irreparable loss of the loved other that we learn, through the transfer of the other onto ourselves, the irreplaceable character of our own life. It is first for the other that I am irreplaceable."[31]

In a manner that accords with Ricoeur's "dialogic structure" of self-esteem and ethical solicitude,[32] Efuru comes to stand up for herself and achieve material independence without isolating herself within a narrow individualism. She seeks out information about the illness of Ogea's father, Nwosu, arranges for his hospitalization, and pays the bills (113–29), doing the same for a lame old woman (160–66). Only after these actions does she have dreams about diving into the lake and seeing an elegant woman. Her father interprets these dreams as signifying that "Uhamiri . . . has chosen you to be one of her worshippers" (183). We learn that Efuru's mother had similar dreams and that she was equally successful in trade and upright in conduct (187–88). When Efuru marries a seemingly better man, Gilbert, and again cannot conceive, she realizes that Uhamiri has no children and so cannot bring her any (207–8). Efuru generously lends Nwabata and Nwosu ten pounds while sharply reminding them that they did not repay the last loan (209–16). She makes up what Nnona loses to thieves (216–17), offers to find Gilbert a second wife so he can have heirs (219–20), takes the new wife under her wing (247–50), and is willing to marry Ogea to an increasingly distant and despondent Gilbert (273), an act that would discharge Ogea's parents' debt to Efuru, for which Ogea is a pawn.[33]

While Efuru's identity becomes increasingly defined by ethical engagement with others, she does not become spineless. In her second marriage, she finds a degree of equality and intimacy that surprises the village: "Gilbert was very happy with his wife. He was proud of her and respected her. They were so much together that people admired them. They went to the stream together, there they swam together, they came back together, and ate together" (171). Even though Efuru loans Nwabata and Nwosu more money, she does so while insisting upon her rights: "You don't know the value of goodness. . . . Poverty does not affect the reasoning power or the innate goodness in human beings. Poor people do not behave foolishly. . . . Am I not a human being? Am I not free to be angry when I am provoked?" (215). When she learns that Gilbert did not attend her father's funeral because he was jailed in another town, where he had fathered a child before their marriage, she "felt very sorry at first, then suddenly, she was filled with fury. She was angry because her husband, with whom she had lived for nearly six years, could, at that stage of their married life, hide something from her" (265). When she becomes mysteriously ill and an unscrupulous dibia attributes her condition to adultery, a charge Gilbert is willing to entertain, she first goes to a medical doctor and receives a cure, then undergoes ritual vindication, and finally renounces Gilbert (273–80): she insists upon freeing herself from false cultural inscriptions, and she breaks decisively with Gilbert when he slanders her, having the power to do so because of her success in trade.

Nwapa clearly notes that a life of ethical involvement with others, however "dialogically" interwoven with increasing self-esteem and self-assertion, makes one vulnerable to being taken advantage of in ways that the Igbo expectation that women will exhibit maternal care exacerbates. Moreover, the novel ends with Efuru wondering why women worship a goddess who cannot give them the joys of motherhood (281). Igbo culture's ability to valorize the full humanity of women remains impaired by patriarchal assumptions and practices. Despite the respect Efuru receives for her industry and rectitude, Nwapa strongly suggests that Efuru will not receive her just due until Igbo culture internalizes the ways of seeing women that her novel makes available. Until then, the resources for *idem*-identity will not be adequate to the demands of *ipse*-identity in both its self-creative and ethically responsive dimensions.

Nwapa's novelistic presentation of Efuru's story discloses colonizing aspects of Igbo culture, reveals the injustice of those aspects, and suggests that the implicit sources of feminism within Igbo culture can be empowered by making novelistic explorations of identity and value part of Igbo culture. Through what Newton calls "a narrational ethics" and "a representational ethics,"[34] novelistic discourse may provide, in Levinas's terms, an ethical assessment of the morality it represents.

While emphasizing that Efuru fails to receive full justice from either her culture or other people, Nwapa places a folktale at the beginning of Efuru's new career of active self-assertion and ethical responsiveness that suggests the sustaining of life depends upon a willingness not to demand perfect justice. When a spirit becomes enamored of a beautiful girl and threatens to take her to the spirit world as his bride, she appeals to her four sisters, who are named after days of the week. The first three refuse to help her because she had refused to lend them household items. They do their sister justice, which means consigning her to death. The fourth sister, named for the market day, Nkwo, agrees for no reason at all to help her sister trick and defeat the spirit (131–37). Notably, the story is told by a male, Eneke, to children, apparently of both sexes, after Efuru has sent for him, because he is known for telling stories beautifully (130) and for his way with children. Sharing the story creates a moment of solidarity between male and female, adults and children; the circumstances of the story's telling involve a companionable collaboration between the sexes.

Susan Arndt, writing against the tendency to equate the presence of strong women in folktales with a protofeminist message, notes that this folktale, *Ifo*, follows a common generic pattern of portraying feminine transgression leading to punishment: here, the girl disobeys her mother by not staying indoors, which leads the spirit to see and desire her. Arndt argues that "the unpleasant husband embodies divine justice—a punishment for wanting autonomy."[35] While the tale certainly admonishes the young to listen to their elders, there are good reasons why Igbo culture might teach deference to the judgment of mothers and elders, why it might warn against arbitrary self-will, other than to impose the lesson that "[d]aughters (or any women) who violate social norms by ignoring social prohibitions and by showing self-determination are punished with a life full of problems and suffering."[36] Most obviously, the mother's prohibition speaks to a sociohistorical world where unattended children—especially girls—were vulnerable to being seized by slave raiders; such a threat was a constant feature of Igbo village life throughout the eighteenth and nineteenth centuries and into the twentieth.[37] Neglecting this context, Arndt is led to contrast what she takes to be a completely patriarchal discourse with Nwapa's feminist subversion of that discourse, arguing that by having Nkwo help her sister in distress, Nwapa emphasizes Nkwo's "sense of solidarity. . . . By outlining the benefits of mutual help, Nwapa clearly affirms women's solidarity and sisterhood as a means of reforming patriarchal societies," whereas the other sisters' unwillingness to help shows "the importance Nwapa attaches to women's solidarity."[38]

Although female solidarity is a value Nwapa affirms, the folktale demonstrates that solidarity is *not* self-grounding. Common vulnerability does not motivate collective resistance; otherwise, all the sisters would behave as Nkwo does. Instead, the other sisters claim that their captured sister has done nothing to deserve their aid, that her own selfish conduct has absolved them of obligation. What is suggested by the folktale, in contrast to Igbo preoccupations with right, hierarchy, and competitive advantage, and in contrast to Arndt's notion that feminist ethics rest upon seeing the other as another me, is that only suspension of justice, in the sense of reciprocity, quid pro quo, only a return of good for ill, makes life in time and genuine ethical association with others possible. The ethical relation binding Nkwo to her sister is "asymmetrical" in Levinas's sense. It is not a return for what the other has done or can do for oneself, nor is it a consequence of group identity or group interest. Instead, it is a "responsibility for another" that "the strict book-keeping . . . does not measure," for "in responsibility for the other for life and death, the adjectives unconditional, undeclinable, absolute take on meaning" by grounding a freedom that transcends "being" or "ontology," a freedom that cannot be resolved into the play of interest or egocentric psychology.[39]

Just as Nkwo preserves humanly significant time and community (indicated by the days of the week) through unmotivated ethical action, and thus, like a mother, ensures the continuance of human life, so Efuru acquires a type of fertility and thus her own identity, one whose freedom is not an illusory effect of self-interest, self-aggrandizement, revenge, or will-to-power, when, like the fourth sister, Nkwo, she treats others better than they deserve. Since Nkwo is the market day, and Efuru's wealth (the material source of her freedom of action) is made in the market, the implication is that doing well for ourselves is ultimately consistent with, if not predicated upon, reaching out to others. Ethical solicitude and self-esteem imply one another in ways analogous to how the production and circulation of wealth in the marketplace enriches the trader; material and spiritual goods are entwined, for the paradox of the market, antithetical to the zero-sum logic of warrior cultures where wealth is generated from plunder at another's expense (exemplified by slave raiding), lies in a practice where what is socially beneficial is also self-enriching. However, the "dialogic structure" of solicitude and self-esteem, illustrated by the market's production of wealth from nonviolent, sociable exchange, ultimately rests upon the asymmetry of the ethical relation (Nkwo conserves a world where trade is possible by refusing to make herself a commodity, by giving herself in exchange for nothing at all). If the exposure of the other calls us to ethical action, makes it "undeclinable," and if "nobody owns this world" and so our blessings and misfortunes are not entirely our own work, we can, like Nkwo, enter into a solidarity that sustains life only when we do without complete justice—which is not to say *no* justice—from the culture and the gods.

Feminism in an Islamic Context: Zaynab Alkali's *The Stillborn*

Alkali's *The Stillborn* (1984) begins with thirteen-year-old Li's return from school to her native village; her physical confinement in the back of an overcrowded lorry anticipates the psychic-political confinement she faces: "After a few weeks at home, Li began to find the atmosphere in her father's compound suffocating. . . . 'It's worse than a prison,' Li complained" (3). When her older sister, Awa, remonstrates by asking if Li would rather be in one of the "heathen homes," Li responds, "Those people you call heathens may not have embraced anybody's religion but they have their own ancestral gods" (3). This exchange suggests that Li's "free and gay" (3) experience at boarding school has helped destabilize traditional certitudes. Anthony Giddens notes that "globalization" has given rise to "a post-traditional social order," one in which "[t]raditions have to explain themselves, to become open to interrogation or discourse."[40] By contesting the word *heathens*, Li denaturalizes the worldview it entails. Thus, Li, at thirteen in rural northern Nigeria, assumes the role that Roberto Mangabeira Unger argues is characteristic of modernity; she disputes taking "a particular form of social life as the context of all contexts—the true and undistorted form of social existence."[41]

Li questions a political-moral division of the world between the realm of Islam (*dar al-Islam*) and the realm of warfare (*dar al-harb*).[42] Awa's disdain for heathens draws upon centuries of piety intensified by the Fulani *jihad* of 1804–12, when the armies of Usman dan Fodio conquered Hausaland (northern Nigeria), after which, in order to prevent "impious" mixing of the sexes, the seclusion of women (*kulle*) to their husbands' compounds became normative and largely remains so.[43] Li is teased repeatedly about having been born in the outhouse (4–7) to check her "stubborn streak" (7), which exemplifies patterns of acculturating girls into expectations of subordination.[44]

Li finds sources of subversion within the compound as well as without, however. While her father, Baba, is a cowardly authoritarian, her father's stepmother, Grandma, is "[s]hrewd and dominating," having driven "three other wives from the household" (8). But while she demonstrates that a woman need not be crushed by patriarchal culture, her selfishness makes her a moral monster. In Grandma, Alkali associates moral deformity with heathenism and an absence of restraint, especially sexual restraint: "I was married fourteen times in the eastern part of this land. I left for this part because I could find no lion among them. . . . This village is full of lizards, snakes, worms and by the gods of my ancestors, cold slippery fish" (53). Li likes her "funny stories but dislike[s] her dirty habits and foul language" (8). Li has a much more positive relation with Baba's father, Kaka, who is "warmhearted" and "fond" of Li (13) and who dislikes his son's excessive discipline (25); his moderation and concern for others seem connected to his religious ecumenicalism: he sacrifices to "the gods of his ancestors" and attends Christian and Muslim festivals (25). By contrast, Baba views his family as a *jihad* leader views the *dar al-harb*: "A heathen woman [Li's mother] can only have heathen children. . . . And even after I have civilised you, you still behave like heathens" (13).

Li's rebelliousness is linked to destabilizing modernity (the school), a heathen heritage (polytheistic but also nature-affirming), and the ethnically heterogeneous environment of the village. Unger notes that the "less the individual sees himself as occupying a natural position within a society that itself has a natural order," the more he "experiences himself as the center of his own world" and feels "a will to self-assertion and to the satisfaction of a desire that knows no fixed boundaries."[45]

In part, Li's rebelliousness follows this pattern. When she escapes her father's compound to attend a dance, she encounters a young man, Habu, to whom she attaches her longings for freedom. Alkali emphasizes the sexual dimension of her attraction: "Li noticed his muscular thighs under a pair of brown shorts" (17). When her friend, Faku, asks if Habu is handsome, Li replies, "Like a god," upon which both "burst out laughing" (34). Sexual pleasure and freedom are connected with spatial distance: in a cave away from the village, Li, Awa, and Faku meet Habu, Awa's male friend, the local headmaster Fiama, and Habu's dissolute friend from the city, Garba. Although Garba describes the city good life in terms of keeping a number of wives who "slave" for the man, Faku finds his "city wisdom" (45) attractive: "What was this love the rest were cracking their heads about? . . . [O]nce she married, living with her mother was over. They would no longer have to work their fingers sore . . . because someone else would be responsible" (46).[46] By contrast, Awa wants to marry because Fiama has promised to put her in charge of education for older women: in Awa, self-definition, self-empowerment, and ethical activity are bound together: "I have always wanted to do something big in the village" (56–57). Li, however, connects marriage primarily with escape to freedom: "She was dreaming of a paradise called 'the city.' A place where she would have an easy life. . . . She was going to be a successful Grade I teacher and Habu a famous medical doctor, like the whitemen in the village mission hospital. The image of a big European house full of houseboys and maids rose before her" (55).

As in *Efuru*, a bid for self-creation comes to grief. Habu marries Li, but immediately leaves her for the city, sending for her only after four years. When he does, Li discovers a distant, cold man who has a second wife in another part of town; when she returns to the village to help her dying father, Habu does not seek to reclaim her. Faku and Awa suffer related misfortunes: Garba leaves Faku secluded in city poverty, under the thumb of a senior wife; Fiama is replaced by a more educated "brown man" and takes to drink, while Awa resigns rather than suffer a reduction in position and status (87). Li's dream is obviously "colonized" by Western images of freedom and success: along with "the big European house" there is "the smooth body, the long silky hair" (57). Li's dream images, like Madame Bovary's, are contaminated by tawdry, vulgar notions of self-fulfillment. Indeed, the very conception of self-fulfillment comes under scrutiny in the two descriptions of Li's dream (55, 57), where public service (being a teacher or physician) functions as an instrument for getting things and status.

The first description of Li's dream (55) comes at the end of a chapter dominated by Li's Grandma's ferocious public humiliation of the village hunchback (52–55). While Grandma's uninhibited assault on the patriarchy may be relished,[47] Alkali portrays her as no role model; when she learns that Li is seeing Habu secretly, she uses that knowledge to extort money and service (35–36). By moving from Grandma's shameless speech to Li's dream, Alkali implies a connection that is reinforced by Li's association of Habu with both sexuality and freedom, Li's describing Habu's appearance as godlike, and her associating city life with paradise. All this places Li's rebellion within the register of the Islamic term *fitna*, which connotes rebellion, disorder, and chaos and is particularly understood as resistance to the hierarchy among goods that Islam would enforce: the spiritual over the material, the rational over the natural.[48] Li conflates the divine and the human, heaven and earth, expecting to find in the material, temporal world ultimate value and significance. Fatima Mernissi notes that *fitna* also means "a beautiful woman — the connotation of a *femme fatale* who makes men lose their self-control."[49] Thus *fitna* is an intellectual and moral disorder to which female desire is especially prone.

On the one hand, Alkali's novel presents a scathing critique of northern Nigerian patriarchy; on the other hand, it questions Li's forms of rebellion in ways consistent with Islamic suspicions of impious, Western-influenced conflations of identity with self-will and happiness with self-fulfillment.[50] After Li tells off Habu in language similar to her Grandma's for not proclaiming himself divorced,[51] she returns to the village, receives a "flow of suitors," and is "oblivious to everything" (83), until the village women attack her at the well. She then leaves the village to make "an independent life for herself" (85), giving her daughter to Awa's care. Five years later, she returns with an advanced teaching certificate and then becomes the "man of the house" at the compound of her now dead father (85). As a successful teacher, she can modernize the compound (101); when a seemingly repentant Habu tries to make up, she rebuffs him coldly (91–92).

Within frameworks of liberal individualism or postmodern resistance, all this can only be read as triumphs of self-assertion, but such readings make the novel's conclusion incomprehensible, which is how Maja-Pearce sees it: "Habu has been involved in an accident which leaves him paralysed, and . . . his other wife has left him. . . . [Li] has a vision of herself as an old woman full of regret at a wasted life," and so resolves to return to him: "So much for the feminist point of view that a beautiful, elegant, intelligent woman in the prime of life should so willingly sacrifice herself to a man who can offer her nothing."[52]

For the conclusion not to appear as a betrayal of the novel's feminism, it is important to see that Li's "vision" is the last in a series of prophetic night dreams, which contrast with her "colonized" daydreams. The tension between Li and her father is introduced by a description of how she "stared at him fearlessly" and how Baba "hated to admit even to himself . . . those piercing eyes . . . stripped him naked and saw through his soul; assessing, judging and condemning him" (9). This passage evokes Hegel's celebrated description of how the lord's objectification of his bondsman is contested by his need to be recognized as lord by the bondsman, a description that from Sartre to Fanon to Albert Memmi to Edward Said has shaped the theorizing of how "colonizing" cognitive violence works and how it is subverted.[53]

Hegel and Sartre associate reification with a violence internal to cognition. Hegel associates realized freedom with determinate (as opposed to abstract) identity, whereas Sartre opposes freedom to being, like Levinas, but presents as the opposite of being not the ethical call but nothingness—a capacity for decision and action irreducible to circumstances, interests, forces, or drives.[54] For Sartre the gaze induces shame by making one see oneself as objectified by the Other: "[S]hame supposes a me-as-object for the Other but also a selfness which is ashamed."[55] Alkali's passage presents the father as a lord disconcerted by a "bondsman" who turns upon him a Sartrean objectifying look. Even the metaphorics of sexual aggression in Alkali's text ("piercing eyes . . . stripp[ing] him naked") recall Sartre's description of the effects of the gaze. However, we learn that Baba's "unease" has a specific source: when Li was eleven she had a dream of disaster and attempted to warn her father not to go to a Friday prayer meeting because of the "feeling" the dream provoked. Baba attributed the dream to "the work of the devil" and went to the meeting. The prayer house collapsed, causing much death and injury (10–12). Similarly, when she is in the city with Habu, Li dreams that her father's hut has collapsed; two weeks later she learns he is gravely ill (73–76). When she visits Faku, neglected by Garba and dominated by a senior wife, she dreams that Faku is tilling dry, barren land, and therefore advises her to leave (80). Later Faku does leave Garba, apparently works as a prostitute, and ends up a "social welfare worker" (93–94, 102). Since prostitution is one of the few means of independence open to women, it is not an entirely disreputable expedient.[56]

Each of these dreams articulates feelings that carry intuitive knowledge. Alkali links the cultural devaluation of women to masculine dismissals of knowledge that comes through feelings. Trinh T. Minh-ha notes that dismissal of "mother's talk," of women's speech, is shared by many sub-Saharan cultures: "Commonly enough, . . . Mother's dignified speeches failed to command (men's) respect. . . . 'A woman will find ninety-nine lies, but she will betray herself with the hundredth,' says a Hausa proverb; while a multitude of Fulani sayings warn: 'If your mother has prepared food, eat; if she has concocted [a plan for you], refuse'; because 'He who follows a woman's plan, is bound to drown.' . . . The wisdom attributed to men is one that generally works at conserving the social group, while the wisdom attributed to women is consistently equated with a supernatural malefic power."[57] It can be argued, however, that such dismissals violate antimisogynistic currents within Islamic piety and tradition, for—unlike in intensely ascetic variants of Christianity—the material and natural *are* goods, albeit subordinate ones, and women have scripturally mandated rights to consideration, though not to equality.[58]

While Minh-ha draws a sharp distinction between women's speech that is "discreet," conforming to the patriarchal status quo, and "indiscreet," being subversive, indirect discourse, Connie Stephens points out that Hausa oral folktales (*tatsuniyoyi*) told by women "repeatedly offer a counterpoint to . . . [patriarchal aspects of] Islamic ideology," showing "heroines consistently challeng[ing] and best[ing] husbands," because the heroines are associated with "natural and supernatural" powers that are in turn linked to "supernatural abilities to nurture and produce life."[59] In one story, the King of the East refuses to pay his debt to the King of the West until the latter's son comes to collect the debt, but as the King of the West only has a daughter, he sends her accompanied by a magical stallion, who helps the daughter fulfill tasks only a boy is supposed to be able to perform. As Stephens notes, the tale celebrates the girl's pluck and capacity, linking both to her ability to derive knowledge from the interconnectedness of the natural and the supernatural (the stallion).[60] On the other hand, self-assertion is positive only if it fits into an appropriate hierarchy of goods (the daughter is helping her father).

Crucially, the generic structure of *tatsuniyoyi* contests postmodern divisions of discourse, such as Minh-ha's, into speech allied with culturally constructed inequitable power relations and speech that undermines or subverts those power relations. *Tatsuniyoyi* celebrate the empowerment of women at the same time that they acknowledge an imperialistic violence internal to will to power; only through making one's freedom answerable to values and purposes beyond itself can one reconcile self-empowerment with sociability. In *tatsuniyoyi*, self-realization, maternal nurturing of particular others, and the conserving, or building, of just social orders are generically and conceptually linked.

It is important to see that Li's third dream, which authorizes active resistance to patriarchal violence, draws upon sources of identity and value embedded in the first two dreams, despite their seemingly conventional or collaborationist function of guiding the daughter to serve her father. It is equally important to see that Alkali makes the moral knowledge and call to ethical action conveyed through the dreams' sensuous particularity the model and ultimate source of similar knowledge and similar calls conveyed through novelistic discourse. When Li describes the first dream, she notes how human faces impressed themselves upon her: "There were many people sitting in the dust with their backs to the wall. . . . Their faces were long and sad and nobody spoke to me. Nobody moved or smiled at me. I noticed some had dust on their hair and on their faces" (10). When Li runs to the site of the disaster that her dream has predicted, she finds among the dead and injured "a middle-aged woman . . . , covered in red earth . . . . She was stripped to the waist. Both hands were clasped to her breasts. Her eyes were wild and slime ran from the corners of her mouth. She had lost two sons in the disaster and was demented with grief" (11). Just as the dream calls Li's attention to the suffering and vulnerability manifest in the faces of others, so the novelistic description impresses upon the reader the middle-aged woman's exposure—physical nudity suggesting corporeal fragility. As in *Efuru*, the destitution wrought upon a mother by the loss of her children exposes us—Li and the reader—to an ethical call anterior to culturally specific discursivity and determinate morality. In exposure to such a call, we acquire an identity that "transcends" what an oppressive society would construct us to be.

Li's dream, and the novelistic discourse that insists upon its truth, communicates the primacy of saying in constituting identity. What matters is not so much that Li's dream predicts the future but that the dream's predictive "power" testifies to the primordial reality of an ethical relation that the father's male pride, his embrace of a narrow rationalism, can neither understand nor respect. Levinas argues, "Saying approaches the other by breaking through the noema involved in intentionality. . . . The exposure to another is disinterested-ness, proximity, obsession by the neighbor, an obsession despite oneself, that is, a pain. . . . [Thus, the] for-another characteristic of sensibility . . . does not enact the play of essence, does not play any game, [for it] is the very seriousness that interrupts the pleasure and complacency of games."[61]

Just as Li's dream moves from self-preoccupation (concern that no one is noticing her) to concern for others (noticing the dust on hair and faces), so her encounter with the mother demented by bereavement momentarily "breaks through" an intentionality organized around desire, justified resentment, and wounded pride. The father's anxiety before Li's "piercing eyes" derives not simply from his inability to objectify her; it is rather that he associates those "piercing eyes" with a prophetic dream that has already revealed Li's access to a power and a truth that exceed his grasp, a power and truth whose very ethical constitution (as opposed to a female insubordinate egoism his ideology could easily "contain"), *even* when expressed in maternal and daughterly care, can-not but undermine the equation of truth with male-regulated discursivity upon which Islamic patriarchal authority grounds itself.

Alkali makes clear that patriarchy needs to discount the moral knowledge that comes from attentiveness to the sensual particularity of other people and the material world. When Baba dismisses Li's dream as "the work of the devil" or "simply what you think during the day," Li feels "cheapened in his eyes," and she instinctively resists: "Li had always hung on to her father's words as the ultimate truth but, somehow, what he had said about dreams being reflections of earlier thoughts did not sound right to her. She knew there wasn't a streak of evil in her and she never thought of bad things during the day" (10). Li recog-nizes as intrinsically wrong Baba's refusal to "see" her because she knows her-self to be more than either a culturally arbitrary construct or a locus of self-regarding, self-pleasuring desire. Baba's words wound her self-esteem, and Li internally recognizes and protests their injustice, their misrepresentation, but her self-esteem here, as opposed to the narcissism implicit in her daydreams of living in a big house with many servants, derives from a knowledge of herself as motivated by ethical solicitude.

Since Alkali places this moment of patriarchal colonization and feminist estrangement between the description of the dream and the description of the bereaved woman, she calls her reader's attention to what is shared by the dream of the disaster and its novelistic description. In both, sensuous particularity communicates its "own" ethical rationality, irreducible to abstract conceptuality and mere subjective sentiment. An internal, "aesthetic" coherence gives voice to a truth that contests patriarchal monopolizations of truth. Because the "natural" or "nonarbitrary" emergence of ethical rationality from sensuous particularity challenges the equation of "father's word" and "ultimate truth" in a way that mere female desire never can, patriarchal power needs to treat any claim of preconceptual or extraconceptual meaning and value as deluded or willful. Thus, when Li dreams that her father's hut has collapsed, it is "as vivid as if it were real" (73). Her husband, occupying the patriarchal position and so acting like Baba did when Li was eleven, dismisses the dream as a "nightmare" (74), as one of the subjective delusions to which women especially are prone.

The bond between ethical knowledge conveyed through novelistic realism and ethical knowledge conveyed through dreams is reinforced when Li, having left Habu, visits Faku at Kano, the capital of Hausaland. At first, she can hardly recognize Faku in "the gaunt-looking woman before her," and she is shocked to find her "[f]amished in body and no doubt famished in soul" (77). When Faku lamely insists that she is happy, Li notes, "Our people believe happiness shows itself in the flesh and the face of a person tells the story of their soul" (79), a remark that ascribes to their "people" an intuitive and perhaps pre-Islamic understanding of the interpenetration of flesh and soul that her own dreams bear out. After Li learns that a senior wife is "master of the house," that Garba is constantly away "on business," she realizes that while she had "felt cold and lonely, . . . here was someone . . . she sensed felt much colder and lonelier" (79).

The implications of what Li learns through seeing Faku, and what the reader learns through the novelistic description of their encounter, are elaborated in the dreams that Li has that night. She first dreams that she is looking into Faku's room, where she sees "Faku, naked, standing in the middle of the room" (80). The room is also bare, and as Li is about to speak to Faku, she notices Garba leaving the room: "He walked straight without turning back and Li was surprised to see the door of a new building open in front of him" (80). After this, Li dreams of Faku tilling land that remains barren. The second dream delineates the consequences of the state of affairs revealed in the first. By seeing Faku naked, Li sees the destitution of body and soul to which Garba has reduced her, but her nudity, like the nudity of the demented middle-aged woman, suggests the corporeal vulnerability that calls for a "clothing" in ethical solicitude. Instead of offering some equivalent of the maternal care in which the ethical relation is most clearly figured and prefigured, Garba leaves, refusing to see Faku's nakedness. Because her nakedness means nothing to him, for her to remain in the marriage would be to till barren soil (it would be to inflict upon herself a spiritual sterility that does violence to marriage's justification in terms of literal and metaphoric fecundities).

To the extent that Garba's indifference has been culturally encouraged, the culture is indicted. The nakedness of the other demands acknowledgment in Cavell's sense (it is not an object of "knowing" that can be dissolved by epistemological skepticism but a subject whose acknowledgment constrains the free movement of skepticism). The Levinasian ethical call incarnate in nakedness arrests the freedom that would turn away from or "move beyond" an object that impedes one's course.

Li is impressed through the dream with a vivid, sensuously particular image of a young woman utterly naked. Alkali's novelistic discourse impresses the reader with that same image—an image which in an Islamic context epitomizes everything the practice of *kulle* is intended to prevent, and which, brought to the reader's imagination through a feminist novel, might be taken as confirmation of Islamic suspicions of Western cultural influence's "immoral" consequences. The Islamic feminist scholar Fatima Mernissi points out that the "ban on producing images of human beings forever links in the Muslim unconscious two things that have emerged as supreme in the modern information age: the image and individualism. Creation, imagination, individuality—so many facets of a fabulous, dangerous energy—are like mirrors and dreams. . . . The words that mean 'to create,' like *khalaqa* and *bid'a*, are dangerous and stamped with bans."[62]

Mernissi argues that Islam crucially defines itself as offering peace, love, and community in exchange for renouncing "*shirk*, the freedom to think and choose [one's own] religion, which was incarnated by the 360 gods enthroned in the Ka'ba," a renunciation exemplified by the Prophet's destruction, in 630 A.D., of the 360 idols displayed in Mecca, an event that crystallized Islam's investment in two major assumptions: "The first is fear of personal freedom, from which comes the ban on the artistic reproduction of the human face.

The second is the exclusion of women from politics, which is tied to the triumph of the monotheistic One. Among the 360 gods of the Ka'ba, the most powerful were goddesses. These goddesses did not have the face of *rahma*, the tenderness associated with the nurturing mother, for they wallowed in the bloodbaths of the sacrifices they demanded. . . . The feminine would be doubly stamped with the sign of invisibility. Women would be veiled, first because they were identified with the violence of the goddesses, and then in order to homogenize the *umma* (community) and cleanse the city of everything that smacked of the pre-Islamic disorder."[63]

Mernissi notes that "Arabic has a special word for women's rebellion — *nushuz*" and that it "is linked to one of the most individualistic concepts of Islam, the concept of *bid'a*, that is, innovation," so that a "woman who rebels against her husband" is understood to be "also rebelling against the *umma*, against reason, order, and, indeed, God. The rebellion of a woman is linked to individualism, not community (*umma*); passion, not reason; disorder, not order; lawlessness (*fitna*), not law."[64] Such rebellion is figured in terms of an imperialistic self-will that invests meaning and power in its "own" images and imagination, and so refuses to submit to a preexistent, pretextualized reality (*haqq* — the truth co-extensive with God's will).

Clifford Geertz points out that the Quran comprises God's "direct speech, the syllables, words, and sentences of Allah. Like Allah, it is eternal and uncreated, one of His attributes. . . . The metaphysics are abstruse and not very consistently worked out, having to do with Allah's translation into Arabic rhymed prose of excerpts from an eternal text, the Well-Guarded Tablet, and the dictation of these . . . by Gabriel to Muhammad, Muhammad in turn dictating them to followers, the so-called Qur'an-reciters, who memorized them and transmitted them to the community at large."[65] Within this context, the "said" of the Well-Guarded Tablet and its earthly recitation would appear to be more primordial than any "saying"; indeed, the "saying" manifest in sensibility, like the "aesthetic" coherence and nonconceptual communicative power of images or novelistic discourse, would seem to be so much *shirk* associated with a reversion to pre-Islamic chaos and violence.

Thus, the daring of Alkali's use of Li's dream image of a naked woman, and her novelistic depiction of that image, to communicate *rahma*, Li's "maternal tenderness" for Faku, and to evoke the reader's "maternal tenderness" for them both, is remarkable. Here, rebellion against patriarchal "veilings" of various sorts is carried out not in the name of *fitna* but in the name of *rahma*, and *rahma* itself is linked to the "natural" power of images and of sensuous particularity to call us to ethical answerability *through* what David Haney would call their aesthetic autonomy,[66] and thus both images and sensuous particularity are able to call the cultural "said," determinate moralities, to justify themselves ethically. Alkali seems to associate the ethical power of novelistic discourse with its ability to represent, to disclose, women's access to natural and supernatural sources of meaning and value that, as in *tatsuniyoyi*, empower women by disentangling an agency predicated upon *rahma* from one expressive of *fitna*. In an interview, Alkali notes that part of what motivated her to write was being "irked" at how "most women have been trained to see themselves as 'weak' and 'incapable' of attaining the highest peak of intellectual development."[67]

However, to link a defense of women's capacity for ethical rationality to the aesthetic integrity, the autonomous "power," shared by dream images, concrete sensuous experience, and artistic representation is to confront distinctive problems within an Islamic context. If, as Newton argues, the ethics of narrative is tied not just to an aesthetic work's ability to communicate in a way irreducible to conceptuality, but to a Levinasian primacy of the saying over the said, then an aesthetic, nonconceptual communication, like a dream's communication, is especially well suited to impress upon us ethical significance that cannot be circumscribed into any said.[68]

But if the novel insists upon, or makes manifest, the primacy of saying to said, then it would seem to be generically committed to making ethics the ground and thus the judge not just of morality but of the revealed word itself. Indeed, the novel's origins in eighteenth-century England are tied up with the emergence of ethics as the judge, as the hermeneutic guide, for the reading of Scripture. In *Tom Jones*, Henry Fielding has Mr. Allworthy counter Captain Blifil's citations of Scripture to justify the abandonment of illegitimate infants with the argument that it "was indecent, if not blasphemous, . . . to represent [God] acting against *the first Principles* of Natural Justice, and against the original Notions of Right and Wrong, which he himself had implanted in our Minds; by which we were *to judge* not only in all Matters which were not revealed, but *even of the Truth of Revelation itself*" [my emphasis].[69] Martin Battestin points out that Allworthy's position echoes that of Anglican Latitudinarian divines over the previous half century.[70] Despite Fielding's metaphysical language, a legacy of his classical and Renaissance humanist education, his claim that ethics constitute "first Principles" by which everything else, even the "Truth of Revelation," is judged, anticipates Levinas's postmetaphysical insistence that ethics is the source of reason, language, signification.

In an Islamic context, however, the metaphysical priority of the revealed word would seem to deny "saying," and thus ethics, such radical primordiality. For Levinas, "Ethics is the breakup of the originary unity of transcendental apperception. . . . Witnessed, and not thematized, in the sign given to the other, the Infinite signifies out of responsibility for the other, out of the-one-for-the-other. . . . The metaphor of the inscription of the law in consciousness expresses . . . in a remarkable way [the reconciling of] autonomy and heteronomy. . . . The inscription of the order in the for-the-other of obedience is an anarchic being affected, which slips into me 'like a thief' through the outstretched net of consciousness."[71]

For Islam, by contrast, while there is certainly a direct relation between obedience to God and responsibility for the other, "the Infinite" would seem not to signify "*out of* responsibility for the other," or "an anarchic being affected," but to signify through the Divine Word that commands responsibility. God's direct word, rather than the face of the Other, would appear to be the trace that inaugurates meaning, language, reason, as many Quranic verses attest: "Surely, the (true) religion with Allah is Islam. And those who were given the Book differed only after knowledge had come to them, out of envy among themselves. And whoever disbelieves in the messages of Allah—Allah indeed is Quick at reckoning" (3:18–19). Knowledge—*ilm*, at once cognitive, ethical, and religious understanding—comes only *after* the Book is *given*, and once knowledge is available through the Book, dissension is explicable only in terms of moral failing (envy) or willful disbelief, both instances of *fitna*.

The subtle violence of Alkali's use of the image of a naked woman against Islamic patriarchy, which implies not only that sexist oppression is unethical but that the ethical can impress itself as a divine command "naturally," makes the final dream even more puzzling. In that dream, Li's great-granddaughter awakens her to receive a blessing for her marriage, and Li replies, "Don't be like me. I spent my entire life dreaming. I forgot to live." When the great-granddaughter protests that Li was "a success" and contributed to "the welfare of the people," Li replies that some dreams are "aborted," others "stillborn" (104). Upon actually awakening, Li realizes "that the bond that had tied her to the father of her child was not ruptured. And in spite of everything, in the soft cradle of her heart, there was another baby forming. This time Li was determined the baby would not be stillborn" (104–5). Here, Li situates herself within biological bonds and within her capacity to "nurture and produce life" in ways that repudiate the notion that Western-style individualism is sufficient to be successful.

As Callaway notes of her experience discussing feminism with educated northern Nigerian women, "[A] woman thinks of herself in terms of her family—her father's family and her husband's family. Women think of themselves as 'actualized' through bearing children and living in a large family group; the notion of living alone is incomprehensible to them."[72] Li is motivated again by *rahma*, but whereas the "nurturing maternal tenderness" she felt for Faku crystallized her consciousness of the brutality of patriarchal exploitation, and whereas the *rahma* that had shaped her ethical solicitude for her father allowed her to know herself in a way that could repudiate his misogynistic constructions of her, the *rahma* that seems to animate Li's dream this time turns her away from being satisfied with success as an independent, educated woman.

Alkali here seems to separate herself from Western feminism by aligning Li's discontent with a suspicion of the egotism implicit in self-assertion. Mernissi points out that desire, *hawa*, is a generally negative term in the Islamic tradition: "*Rahma*, peace in the community, can exist only if the individual renounces his *ahwa* (plural of *hawa*), which are considered the source of dissension and war. The *jahiliyya* [pre-Islamic era] saw the unbridled reign of *hawa*, desire and individual egotism. . . . *Hawa* means both 'desire' and 'passion,' but it can also signify 'personal opinion.' It is the unbridled individual interest of a person who forgets the existence of others in thinking only of his own advantage."[73]

Through her dream, Li appears to accept that a dehumanizing antisociability undermines or accompanies her life of self-sufficient success. The challenge Alkali's novel poses for Western readers is to do justice to the coherence of a work that seems, from Western perspectives, to juxtapose feminist and nonfeminist elements. While Alkali argues that she was prompted to write to counter the training of women to see themselves as weak, she responds to a question about the impact of the women's movement upon African women writers by suggesting that "the movement interferes with women's writing" because people tend to see women's writing only as "feminist literature."[74]

The Stillborn's conclusion involves a complex set of negotiations. The intuitive knowledge, carried by feeling and drawn, as in *tatsuniyoyi*, from natural and supernatural sources, that the "bond to the father of her child" is not broken, takes possession of Li in a way that recalls the *bori* spirit possession cult, which thrives alongside Islam in northern Nigeria. Nicole Echard notes, "In *bori*, a spirit, seized by violent love-desire, 'attacks' a person," thereby allowing a space for "amorous passion" that is largely denied women in Islam.[75] In the *bori* cult, one may see female resistance to the circumscription of value and meaning to the knowledge given by the Book; as in Li's dreams, the *bori* cult valorizes the insight and empowerment that comes from being affected. But unlike in the *bori* cult, being affected does not imply a loss of self for Li. Instead, this final dream, like the previous ones, leaves Li knowing herself to be the one called to specific ethical obligations.

Indeed, Habu is no longer much of an object of love-desire. Awa reminds Li that Habu is now lame (105). His lameness may be seen, like Rochester's blindness in *Jane Eyre*, as a way of suggesting that a truly humane love requires the radical subordination of sexual desire. But when Li replies, "We are all lame," she suggests that true ethical activity depends upon a recognition of shared and intrinsic vulnerability, which alone can motivate a willingness not to exact a "sterile" perfect justice. When Awa asks whether she wants to walk before or behind Habu, Li replies that "side by side we will learn to walk," which implies a degree of equality and companionableness. When Awa says, "May the gods of your ancestors guide you," Li replies, "May the good God guide us all" (105). The juxtaposition of gods and God suggests a space for ecumenicalism, but it also suggests the priority of God over gods, thus reinscribing Li within Islam. A woman's walking "side by side" with her husband is fused with being "guided" by "the good God," which suggests not only that the redressing of women's just claims against patriarchal violence and a pious deference to God are reconcilable but that the latter is the necessary context for the former.

Both sisters take as axiomatic that the divine should guide human actions, that human freedom is answerable to something more than individual desire. This situates Alkali's text within the context of northern Nigerian educational and political reform for women associated with Aminu Kano's career and picked up after his 1983 death by the Federation of Muslim Women's Associations in Nigeria (FOMWAN), whose efforts to improve the lot of women, the Hausa journalist Bilkisu Yusuf notes, involve opposing lesbianism, the abstraction of the individual from "all concrete and collective bonds," and "negative Western influences." FOMWAN "hopes to develop the full personality of Muslim women as a model for other women, based on the belief that true Islam makes adequate provision for women," and seeks to "put an end to a situation where Qu'ranic verses are misinterpreted by ignorant scholars to legitimize the oppression and humiliation of women."[76]

Understood within this context, the conclusion of Alkali's novel need not be seen as either gratuitous or a retreat. Li's decision to go to Habu does not imply that a woman must have a man to complete her, but that—just as any patriarchy that refuses to "see" the ethical claims implicit in women's humanity is without legitimacy—a life oriented only toward individual achievement will not do justice to our own internal, intrinsic needs for ethical solidarity, and so will fall short not only in duty to others but in offering us genuine self-fulfillment. Immediately before Li's final dream, Faku arrives and her beloved grandfather, Kaka, dies. Faku is "on the way to becoming a social welfare worker herself" (102). Her life with Garba is irrevocably over because that life can only be one of "oppression and humiliation." The novel valorizes Faku's independence, but becoming a social worker, not achieving negative liberty or pursuing *hawa*, constitutes fulfillment. "Li felt happy for her friend who had found fulfillment at last" (102). Li then thinks of her sister, Awa, who is also in effect an independent woman (because her husband has retreated to drunken isolation) and who spends her days supervising a large extended family. "[Awa] was everywhere at the same time. This was another person who had given her life for the happiness of others. Could she, Li, make some sort of an impact in her society?" (102). Li links Faku's public activity (her nontraditional, professional role) with Awa's private activity (a traditional enactment of *rahma*) in a way that contests standard Western separations of career and home; similarly, the parallelism between giving one's life for the happiness of others and having an impact in one's society contests standard Western oppositions of self-sacrifice and self-realization. Immediately after this passage, we learn that Kaka has just died. His death recalls to Li and the reader the constancy of his kindness to a "marginalized" granddaughter. Surely it is significant that Li contemplates the examples of Faku, Awa, and Kaka just before the final dream. That the examples include a man as well as women, and that the two women embody ethical activity in both modern and traditional forms, suggest that Alkali is not ascribing a separate ethics for women, ascribing a masochistic "self-sacrifice" as the duty of women, nor is she suggesting that female fulfillment must come through connection with a husband.

Rather, Li's dream reveals that what is wrong with Li's success is not that it involves the modern career of teaching but that (unlike Faku's externally similar fulfillment) it has been oriented toward self-assertion, *hawa*, and *fitna*. Alkali draws upon metaphors of biological interconnectedness ("the bond that had tied her to the father of her child," "in the soft cradle of her heart, there was another baby forming") to suggest the spiritual impoverishment inherent within a denial of the claims of connectedness internal to our human materiality.

Nonetheless, Li's willingness to return to Habu remains disturbing. While he does not display Garba's indifference during courtship and while he is last seen begging for her to return (92), the novel does not provide enough information to reassure the reader that Li is not being too good to a bad husband. Perhaps Alkali withholds sufficient information to underscore the need for faith, but it is arguable that Alkali, following FOMWAN and much northern Nigerian thought, is too ready to associate Western influence with negative egotistic individualism, and so leaves Li vulnerable to patriarchal insinuations. On the other hand, the novel makes a strong case for the insufficiency of egotistic individualism.

While the content, the said, of Alkali's text accords with a reformist Islamic piety, the novelistic form of her discourse articulates the priority of ethics and saying in ways that are potentially irreconcilable with Islamic doctrine. There is a radical difference in arguing, as Yusuf and FOMWAN do,[77] that, if interpreted correctly, the knowledge given in the Quran and other early Islamic texts and traditions do not authorize the oppression of women and what Alkali, through her use of prophetic dreams and through the aesthetic "autonomy" of novelistic discourse, seems to suggest—that the Infinite is "witnessed," not "thematized," that the Infinite signifies "out of responsibility for the other."

If *rahma* is communicated by, and manifest within, a "saying" anterior to conceptuality, then *rahma*, a term that would seem to be a support for patriarchal order, may suggest on the contrary that tenderness signifies the Infinite with a directness that at least rivals the directness of the sacred word. Judaism and Christianity, understanding Scripture to be words about God written by many hands over many centuries, can and have accommodated ethical critiques of the sacred texts in ways that Islam, conceiving Scripture as God's own speech, has not. Mernissi notes, "Opposition to the One would forever have a negative color," as do "words like *hizb* (party) and *shi'a* (group with a different opinion). . . . The concept of *shi'a*, which means 'those who see things differently,' is condemned in the Koran as 'those who split their religion and become sects.' . . . The Prophet Muhammad, the last Messenger of God, came to correct the division and bring everyone back to the right path—that of Islam."[78]

Whereas the primacy of the ethical in the West is tied to notions of continuous revelation (so that ethical critique of religious doctrine can justify itself through assuming the mantle of prophecy, as in Blake), in Islam prophecy is emphatically consummated with Muhammad. Thus, the very cross-cultural ethical rationality that emerges from the aesthetic integrity and coherence of novelistic discourse would seem to risk, from the perspective of Islamic piety, the disturbing overtones of *hawa, fitna, bid'a,* and *shirk.*

4

Tenderness, Piety, and Cosmopolitan Humanism
in *Une si longue lettre*

Memory, Language, and the Other

While published earlier than *The Stillborn*, Mariama Bâ's *Une si longue letter* (1979) seeks to negotiate many of the tensions that Alkali's novel brings to light. Bâ's narrative presents itself as a long letter written by a fifty-year-old Islamic Senegalese woman, Ramatoulaye, to her best friend, Aïssatou, upon the occasion of her husband's sudden death. The husband, Modou Fall, had been living with his much younger second wife. Aïssatou's similarly prominent husband, the doctor Mawdo Bâ, had also wed a second, much younger woman. In response, Aïssatou had ended the marriage and established herself as an independent professional woman.

Une si longue lettre is frequently read as a record of the heroine's movement toward or away from Aïssatou's feminist independence.[1] Keith L. Walker characterizes the letter as "a groping toward significance, self-determination, self-definition, and subjectivity."[2] Glenn W. Fetzer argues that letter writing allows the heroine to acquire "the therapeutic tools needed for self-realization," for "finding a voice" affirming the self.[3] Bâ herself, however, stresses how one's own word responds to another's. The novel begins, "Dear Aïssatou, I have received your letter [*mot*]. By way of reply, I am beginning this diary, my prop in my distress [*point d'appui dans mon désarroi*]."[4] Aïssatou's "*mot*" functions as the verbal equivalent of a caress or a squeezed hand. Significantly, in the early days of her widowhood, Ramatoulaye also hears Quranic verses, described vaguely, never quoted, as signifying the impossibility of indifference of the speaker, who is God. By placing verses from the Quran and "noble words of consolation" (2) in apposition, by characterizing the reading of the Quran as comforting, "réconfortante" (*USLL* 13), Bâ indicates that both Aïssatou's and the Quran's words communicate as saying to a distraught Ramatoulaye. This is not to suggest that the discourses are identical. The hortatory tenor of Quranic discourse has a strongly paternal flavor. There is even the suggestion that Ramatoulaye hears in Quranic discourse external commands that she, in her "désarroi," experiences as overwhelming (5). The text affirms, nonetheless, that the Quran's words are at once "nobles" and "consolatrices" (USLL 9).

The reassuring, maternal "mot" from a feminist friend and the intensely masculine Quran both comfort Ramatoulaye because, in their dimension as saying, maternal and paternal discourse intersect. Annemarie Schimmel notes that Sufi Islam turns "to the maternal realm for some of their symbols. . . . It was soon realized that the word *rahma*, 'mercy,' the root of the constantly re-peated divine names *ar-rahman*, 'The Compassionate,' and *ar-rahim*, 'The Merciful,' derives from the same root as does *rahim*, 'mother's womb.' Rumi [the thirteenth-century poet] tells us . . . that, just as God is always a refuge for humanity, so is the mother for her child."[5]

God's compassion and mercy are expressed in two gifts that parallel gifts of maternal tenderness: creation and language. Levinas notes, "Language is not enacted within a consciousness; it comes to me from the Other."[6] Language consoles and commands simultaneously. It inaugurates a "paternal" symbolic order that confers identity in relation to an Other that would be Lacanian, except that the "maternal" comfort signified in divine speech anchors signifi-cation and reason not, as in Lacan, in "arbitrary" metaphorization, but in the ethical relation.

Although the Quran's positive enjoining of responsibility—to widows, or-phans, strangers, as in Sura 4:10, "Those who swallow the property of the or-phans unjustly, they swallow only fire into their bellies"—may be consonant with viewing the Quranic said as arising from divine *rahma*, it is difficult to see how divine *rahma* could be isomorphic with a Levinasian responsibility that tears one away from the "oneself proper to consciousness," grounding the self—as opposed to the ego—in "the complete being 'for the other'" character-istic of maternity.[7] According to Levinas, "for the other" is experienced as a duty that "strips the ego of its pride and the dominating imperialism character-istic of it," placing in question the "oneself proper to consciousness" and thus all our thematizing.[8] God understood in the light of such maternal exposure "is neither an object nor an interlocutor." Rather, "[h]is absolute remoteness, his transcendence, turns into my responsibility . . . for the other." The absolute-ness of divine transcendence means that God supersedes any said, language's bond with what Derrida calls a metaphysics of presence: "The sentence in which God gets mixed in with words is not 'I believe in God,'" but "the 'here I am' . . . by which I announce . . . my responsibility for the other."[9]

By contrast, Islam insists that God's *rahma* is consummated in His gift of determinate words. The eleventh-century ethical theorist Ghazali (or Al-Ghazali) begins his book on Quranic recitation and interpretation by declaring, "Praise be to God Who has bestowed favour upon mankind by sending His Prophet . . . and by revealing His Book. . . . The Qur'an is an illumination and a light; by it is obtained deliverance from error and deception; and in it lies the healing of those [diseases] which exist in men's souls."[10]

Ramatoulaye describes her letter in terms that could equally describe how Islamic piety experiences the Quran, as the "point d'appui dans mon désarroi" (*USLL* 7). Walker notes that, at times, "the letter assumes the cadences of Koranic discourse."[11] Her text's evocation of the sacred word suggests that Ramatoulaye has at hand a refuge of words against "désarroi"—not the simple "distress" of the translation but "disorder, disarray, confusion," as in "the disorder and confusion predating the year 630."[12]

The letter's words, like God's, move the soul away from "désarroi" to a peace that rests upon an order of language which should structure a just community. Such a community must include justice for women. In this way, divine discourse and feminist discourse mutually reinforce one another. However, Levinas suggests, "Revelation, described in terms of the ethical relation or the relation with the Other, . . . discredits both the figure of the Same and knowledge in their claim to be the only site of meaning," thus forcing reason to "awaken," in "obedience" to God's word, to "this disruption which can never be absorbed, of the Same by the Other, in his difference": "Surely we should think of the Revelation, not in terms of received wisdom, but as this awakening?" Levinas notes, "We may ask questions about the manifestation of these things within what is said [*dit*]. But can we convert transcendence as such into answers without losing it in the process?"[13] Levinas's understanding of Revelation leads to the kind of sacred hermeneutics that Fielding advocates, a hermeneutics crucial to the cultural authority of novelistic discourse: ethics guides even theology because Revelation as "awakening to unfulfillable obligation" has precedence over Revelation as "received wisdom."

Whether Islam can accept such hermeneutics is ambiguous. Barbara Freyer Stowasser notes that Mernissi's feminist rereading of Quranic texts "leaves most [even modernist interpreters] behind. . . . In pitting the Prophet's early vision of gender egalitarianism against demands later imposed upon him by Medinan *realpolitik,* this author stipulates that the Qurʿanic dicta on . . . women . . . are of unequal 'value.'"[14] Such an application of feminist ethics to sacred hermeneutics would seem to place in question the Quran's status as Revelation in its entirety, as well as challenge the doctrine that the Quranic word as literal inscription is both primary and eternal. On the other hand, Ghazali argues that since "all forms of knowledge are included in the works of God," and these forms "have no end, but in the Qurʿan there is an indication . . . of their confluence," the "understanding of the Qurʿan" is not identical with "mere outward exegesis." Ghazali speaks of "the essence of the Qurʿan," which resists every effort to be contained within what human cognition can grasp. Thus, Ghazali argues that the Quran's "essence," while not opposed to "outward exegesis," cannot be delimited by such exegesis.[15] Thus, the very divinity of the Quranic word works against the idolatry implicit in any metaphysics of presence.

Bâ's evocation of Quranic cadences in a secular, literary text raises the question, however, of whether the human word can echo the "essence" of the Quranic word rather than set itself against "outward exegesis." While the first clause of Ramatoulaye's description of her letter likens it to the Quran, the second underscores how human ethical experience, especially female companionship, gives her the heart to speak: "Our long association has taught me that confiding in others allays pain" (1). Such lessons come from the radical singularity of our own sensations and their rootedness in an intersubjectively constituted being-in-time. Ramatoulaye tells Aïssatou, "Your presence in my life is by no means fortuitous. Our grandmothers in their compounds were separated by a fence and would exchange messages daily. Our mothers used to argue over who would look after our uncles and aunts. As for us, we wore out wrappers and sandals on the same stony road to the koranic school" (1). The identity Ramatoulaye finds in memory to support her against "désarroi" is indissociable from—indeed, springs from—memories of immediate sensuous experience: the "same stony road" is equally constitutive of each woman's individuality because its distinctive pressure was repeatedly experienced on a shared journey that was both communal and spiritual—the path led to the Quranic school.

Through holding memory "intact," Ramatoulaye is able to reach Aïssatou imaginatively: "I conjure you up. The past is born, along with its procession of emotions. I close my eyes. Ebb and tide of feeling: heat and dazzlement, the woodfires, the sharp green mango, bitten into in turns, a delicacy in our greedy mouths. Ebb and tide of images" (1). Invoking, calling in, the Other through memory's melding of emotions, sensations, and images, Bâ "conjures up" precisely the "truth" that novelistic discourse makes the support, the rational ground, of its own determinate evaluative claims. However, to do so "conjures up" goods distinctive to the modern West—goods that Charles Taylor has summarized as "inwardness," "the affirmation of ordinary life," the "voice of nature," and "subtler languages."[16] Describing what is retrieved as a "cortège d'émotions," "flux et reflux de sensations," "flux et reflux d'images" (*USLL* 7), Bâ evokes Proust's characterization of involuntary memory. As Kristeva notes, Proustian memory reveals nonarbitrary bonds between sensation and image.[17]

Locating identity in immediate sensation, however, as Proust repeatedly observes, gives rise to confusion and disorder (as when the narrator awakens and is led by the position of his body to imagine that he is in another bedroom belonging to his past), a confusion and disorder that in turn give rise to delusory desires, as when we imagine that a sensation is produced by what is contingent to it (a woman, a name, a place).[18] Taylor notes that for Proust, "the original experience . . . dominates our attention and obstructs the vision behind it, as it were. Only when we recall it in memory can we see behind it to what was revealed through it."[19] Escaping conceptual and moral "désarroi" demands recapturing connections. Kristeva remarks, "The chronicle-like construction of *In Search of Lost Time* is innately ethical. To the disarray of the world and the self [*au désarroi du monde et de soi*], Proust adds a never-ending search for the lost, invisible temple of *the sensory time of our subjective memories*."[20]

For Bâ as well, the past must be retrieved in memory—that is, in language—because immediate sensation, as Islamic piety also argues, disorders the self. Because "désarroi" cannot be excised from the human condition, we must search out our way to a life that binds together meaning and justice, dignity and tenderness. For Ramatoulaye, that way unites in one true Quranic discourse and Proustian "sensory time."

The Constraints That Give Rise to Freedom

Ramatoulaye cannot begin to link words to sensations and images until she has discharged the social obligations of her new widowhood. She is forced to endure the presence of her young co-wife and to shower her in-laws with gifts:

"This is the moment dreaded by every Senegalese woman, the moment when she sacrifices her possessions as gifts to her family-in-law; and, worse still, beyond her possessions she gives up her personality, her dignity, becoming a thing in the service of the man who has married her" (4). Patriarchal violence is depicted here in terms equally congenial to Simone de Beauvoir, Kate Millet, and Luce Irigaray. What is distinctive to Wolof and Senegalese contexts is the way that ritual praise enforces a communal fiction that Ramatoulaye experiences as a naturalization of injustice: "Our sisters-in-law give equal consideration to thirty years and five years of married life. With the same ease and the same words, they celebrate twelve maternities and three" (4).[21] At the same time, however, Bâ also suggests that ritual praise can allow people to "say" what cannot be "said." Describing the men lauding Modou with pious epitaphs, Ramatoulaye notes, "They are there, his childhood playmates. . . . They are there, his classmates. They are there, his companions in the trade union struggles" (5). Her own formulaic phrasing seems to acknowledge that social obligations need not always be alienating or inauthentic. Rather than making a blanket judgment (speaking from a culturally constructed "subject position" is either always proper or inherently repressive), Ramatoulaye implies that one ought to assess such forms against their success in translating ethical duty into communal life.

Ramatoulaye is granted the space, the peace, to reconstruct her identity because of the Quranic injunction that a widow must seclude herself for four months and ten days following her husband's funeral. By making obligatory seclusion the occasion of Ramatoulaye's discourse, Bâ challenges the modern West's conception of freedom as necessarily antithetical to constraint. Instead, submission (*islam*) gives rise to form, which in its very constraints enables the rational acquisition of freedom. Ramatoulaye describes herself as living alone, "in a monotony broken only by purifying baths" (8). However, Bâ immediately juxtaposes this image with Ramatoulaye's reflection: "J'espère bien remplir mes charges. Mon coeur s'accorde aux exigences religieuses. Nourrie, dès l'enfance, à leur sources rigides, je crois que je ne faillirai pas" (*USLL* 18) ["I hope to carry out my duties fully. My heart concurs with the demands of religion. Reared since childhood on their strict precepts, I expect not to fail" (8)]. The terms "charges" and "exigences" make clear that Ramatoulaye anchors her identity in responding to demands that come from outside herself. At the same time, her "coeur s'accorde" with demands linked to maternal imagery — "nourrie . . . à leur sources" (lost in the English translation) — that connects

rahma with law. Ramatoulaye's ability to shelter herself in an externally or-
dained form is inseparable from her having an interiority shaped by the co-
implication of *rahma* and law.

Mildred Mortimer argues that Bâ can reveal "the positive aspects of enclosure" because the letter constitutes "an inner journey for the explicit purpose
of lucidity and self-understanding," a journey that replicates metaphorically
the outer journeys of male characters in oral literature and early Francophone
novels. While skillfully tracing how Ramatoulaye's inner journey echoes earlier narratives' outer journeys, Mortimer, like others, assimilates Ramatoulaye's achievement to a modern Western conceptuality: "Challenging the
matriarchy and the patriarchy—for both demand submission and obedience—Ramatoulaye looks within herself to find the courage to break free."[22]
Mortimer makes the unlikely assumption that a piously Islamic author and
character would reject any demand for submission and obedience, in part because she neglects how insistent Ramatoulaye is that what is "within herself"
comes from outside herself.

Immediately after noting that she has plenty of memories to ruminate,
Ramatoulaye reflects, "And these are what I am afraid of, for they smack of
bitterness" (8). Ramatoulaye dreads the taste of bitterness adhering to her
memories because that taste might lead her into self-pity, self-love, and thus
ethical failure. Mortimer notes that Ramatoulaye comes to "forgive her late
husband,"[23] but that forgiveness should not be understood as a therapeutic
gesture necessary to "break free." Forgiveness is an ethical obligation imposed
by God. Noting her memories' bitterness, Ramatoulaye exclaims, "Puisse leur
invocation ne rien souiller de l'état de pureté absolue, où je *dois* évoluer" [my
emphasis] (18) ["May their evocation not soil the state of purity in which I must
[develop]" (9)]. Kristeva argues, "With Proust, forgiveness is turned into a
novel."[24] Despite their vast cultural and thematic differences, Ramatoulaye's
retrieval of identity shares with Marcel's search for lost time the divestment of
bitterness from memory.

Just as Ramatoulaye's ability to write is supported by obligatory seclusion, so
it is initiated by another scripturally enjoined constraint, the *mirasse*. Susan
Stringer notes that this "Islamic practice . . . entails listing the possessions of
the deceased in order to divide the inheritance," which necessarily "involves
the revelation of the most intimate details of the person's life."[25] Mbye B.
Cham has argued that Bâ "extends and adapts the notion of disclosure" in a
way that "legitimises . . . a systematic analysis of some of the most pressing

socio-economic and cultural issues challenging women and society."[26] Obi-oma Nnaemeka describes Bâ's narrative disclosure "subverting the 'truth' which is established by the 'law.'"[27] Uzo Esonwanne argues that Bâ, by having Ramatoulaye "exploit . . . a fissure in Koranic law" (it does not specify which survivor should preside over *mirasse*), creates "an alternative medium for women's speech."[28] Ramatoulaye certainly discovers the depth of Modou's injustice to her: "His abandonment of his first family (myself and my children) was the outcome of the choice of a new life" (9). Economic exploitation accompanied betrayal: the ultramodern house Modou gave his second wife and her mother was financed by a loan using the mortgage on Ramatoulaye's house as collateral. Like Cham and Esonwanne, Stringer argues that the concept of *mirasse* "can be extended to the whole novel," for since feminism "is presented as a matter of consciousness," the novel's "diary form is both a way of exteriorizing . . . inwardness without losing any of its intimacy and a means of creating a strong emotional bond between Ramatoulaye and the reader."[29]

Like the critics above, Mortimer argues that Ramatoulaye "broadens the definition of disclosure to unveil Modou's emotional breach of faith in their marriage."[30] While this is the case, Bâ's text does not simply use indigenous cultural practices strategically.[31] The Quran's authorizing of polygamy comes in a discussion of the duties of guardians to orphan wards, beginning with the declaration, "O people, keep your duty to your Lord, Who created you from a single being and created its mate of the same (kind)" (Sura 4:1). Duty to the Lord is inseparable from recognition that the Other is ultimately kin, and that male and female are of the same (kind),[32] which leads to an articulation of piety in terms of the obligations of the privileged to the marginalized (4:2). Within this context, the Quran declares, "[M]arry such women as seem good to you, two, or three, or four; but if you fear that you will not do justice, then (marry) only one or that which your right hands possess [war captives]. This is more proper that you may not do injustice" (4:3). The imperative to be just in property relations, and just to those vulnerable to exploitation, reflects the broader principle that justice to others "exteriorizes" inward submission to God. Modou's behavior, placing self-love or lust above justice, is pure *fitna*.

Ramatoulaye wonders, "What inner confusion led Modou Fall to marry Binetou?" (11). She poses the question in terms of an abrogation of internal order that issues in deluded wandering, echoing Quranic equations of lust with deviation. Equally significantly, Ramatoulaye experiences her own anger as something to be overcome (11). She tries to imagine the sufferings of those who are blind, orphans, or lepers to escape enclosure in her own pain, but is brought back to the sting of Modou's betrayal, understood not just as a repudiation of his wife, but of the *idem*-identity characteristic of the twenty-five years he spent with Ramatoulaye: "In loving someone else, he burned his past, both morally and materially" (12). He did so to conform to a "choice of a new life" (9). This negative use of "choix" should be juxtaposed with the positive usages Irène Assiba d'Almeida cites: choice is not an absolute good because, as d'Almeida acknowledges, it must be conditioned by responsibility.[33]

Mortimer argues that Ramatoulaye "begins with two false starts: first, a *cri de coeur*, in which she proclaims herself a victim; then, a letter to Modou, . . . in which she remembers with great sentimentality their first meeting."[34] Although her memories are not without sentimentality, Ramatoulaye can only overcome the *cri de coeur* that risks locking her in a debilitatingly reactive, self-centered identity by repossessing imaginatively the very past that Modou disavowed.

As one of the first generation of African women to receive a Francophone postsecondary education, at the teachers' training college at Ponty-Ville, Ramatoulaye is both feared and prized. Along with the intoxicating pleasure of intellectual achievement and social status, her education gave rise to glittering, fragile "dreams" and a delicious but disorienting sense of personal freedom. One might expect Ramatoulaye to view her Western education, in retrospect, much as Alkali portrays Western influences upon Li. Indeed, the conventional negritudinist rhetoric of Modou's letters from Paris put in doubt whether she saw him as he was.[35] However, Ramatoulaye embraces her education just as she embraces the sensuous particularity of the past, recalling the "green, . . . blue, yellow, . . . colours of the flowers [that invaded] the compound" with the same tenderness as she recalls the multiethnic atmosphere, permitting "a fruitful blend [*brassage fructueux*] of different intellects, characters, manners, and customs" (15).

Ramatoulaye declares, "Aïssatou, I will never forget the white woman who was the first to desire for us an 'uncommon' destiny" (15). An account of the headmistress's educational program is immediately followed by a description of her "love": "She loved us without patronizing us, with our plaits either standing on end or bent down, with our loose blouses, our wrappers. She knew how to discover and appreciate our qualities" (16). Because of such maternal solicitude, inseparable from affirmation of the otherness of the Other (she appreciated *our* qualities and *our* African wrappers), the pupils acquire agency in their own lives—most evidently in choosing their own husbands.

The principles underlying Ramatoulaye's education are described in these terms: "Nous sortir de l'enlisement des traditions, superstitions et moeurs; nous faire apprécier de multiple civilisations sans reniement de la nôtre; élever notre vision du monde, cultiver notre personnalité, renforcer nos qualités, mater nos défauts; faire frucifier en nous les valeurs de la morale universelle; violà la tâche que s'était assignée l'admirable directrice" (27–28) ["To lift us out of the bog of tradition, superstition and custom, to make us appreciate a multitude of civilizations without renouncing our own, to raise our vision of the world, cultivate our personalities, strengthen our qualities, to make up for our inadequacies, to develop universal moral values in us: these were the aims of our admirable headmistress" (15–16)]. Esonwanne reads this passage in terms of the colonizing of the African mind: the "echoes of Diderot and d'Alembert's *philosophe*" help create "a new, pliable post-colonial subject" seduced by an "evolutionist ethos . . . always tending toward a European norm."[36] Mortimer reads the same passage as showing that the director's "message is clearly subversive. Urging her students to break with tradition and to affirm their personality, she calls for revolt rather than submission."[37] Bâ juxtaposes escaping "enlisement" (being bogged down or trapped) with learning to appreciate multiple cultures in ways that do not issue in disavowal (*reniement*) of one's own. The enlightenment's critical power—the side of the enlightenment associated with Diderot and d'Alembert—is implicitly balanced by the side associated with Herder (missing from Esonwanne's analysis), which makes a moral good of appreciating difference.

What separates the education Ramatoulaye describes from contemporary pedagogy is not its affirmation of difference but its stress upon building moral character: cosmopolitanism, raising "notre vision du monde," is inseparable from the effort to "cultiver notre personnalité," understood not only in the Rousseauian-Romantic sense of developing the qualities that are peculiarly our own, but also in the Aristotelian-humanistic sense of shaping character through habit, disciplining *ethos* through the good discourse, good example, of others.[38] In this second sense of cultivating personality, the headmistress's program intersects with the Islamic concept of *adab*, a term that, like the Greek *paideia* and the Latin *morales*, involves both intellectual knowledge and personal conduct and that understands the self's coming to freedom as an effect of, rather than a negation of, the formative influence of other people and of speech heard as ethical assignation.[39] Ramatoulaye's Francophone and Islamic education both make reason and language answerable to ethics and encourage a fashioning of the self against the insularity and indulgence of the ego. It is thus not surprising that neither Ramatoulaye nor Aïssatou experience Ponty-Ville as alienating. Indeed, as Cheryl Wall Staunton has demonstrated, Bâ's description of her own education is cast, like Ramatoulaye's, in the register of gratitude, stressing her debt to her father for giving her a Francophone education, and to two French educators—Berthe Maubert and Germaine LeGoff—for instilling in her a humane multiculturalism that included "the appreciation of one's own African heritage and values." At the same time, Bâ expresses gratitude to her grandmother, "who gave her religious faith and a keen sense of virtue and honor," and describes "a traditional upbringing" where the bond between ethical obligation and piety was reiterated daily.[40]

Ramatoulaye's gratitude is tied to her retrospective recognition that "the path chosen for our training and our blossoming [*notre formation et notre épanouissement*] has not been at all fortuitous. It has accorded with the profound choices made by New Africa for the promotion of the black woman" (16). The way chosen by a white French woman under colonial conditions enables (startlingly) African women's feminist emancipation, for the path for "notre formation et notre épanouissement" combines *formatio*, the Renaissance humanist recuperation of the Aristotelian-Ciceronian tradition, with "épanouissement" (blossoming, unfolding)—that is, the Rousseauian-Romantic conception of cultivating one's own interiority, recognizing duties to oneself that make resistance to external imposition (potentially at least) more than *hawa* and *fitna*.[41]

Through assuming the right to choose her own husband, Ramatoulaye brings her best friend, Aïssatou, together with Modou's best friend, Mawdo Bâ. Mawdo, then a young doctor, is a member of the Tukulor nobility, "a Diofene, a *Guelewar* from the Sine" (17). The Tukulor share with the Peul (or Fulbe or Fulani) a history of Islamic militancy and conquest, both ethnic groups participating "in the *jihad* and subsequent state created by El Hajj Umar Tall in the Futa Toro [northwest Senegal] in the mid-nineteenth century."[42] Ramatoulaye and Aïssatou are Wolof, members of Senegal's largest linguistic-ethnic group. But what makes Mawdo's marriage to Aïssatou controversial is not ethnicity but caste. Aïssatou's father is a goldsmith.

Wolof and Tukulor societies share with other West African peoples a long-standing separation of the nobility, farmers, and freemen, on the one hand, from craftsmen—smiths, leatherworkers, praise-singers (*griots*)—on the other hand. Craftsmen and their kinship networks form endogamous communities, for they are believed to consort with empowering but polluting alien spiritual powers.[43] In precolonial Senegal, social stratification involved both the political distinction between free men (*géer*) and slaves (*jam*) and a socioeconomic distinction between noncasted and casted (*géer* and *ñeeño* in Wolof): Leonardo A. Villalón notes that, while "[r]emnants of an original hierarchical stratification remain, . . . the caste system today has largely collapsed into a two-tier distinction between casted and non-casted people. . . . [C]aste status still remains a far more significant barrier to marriage than either religion or ethnicity." Caste divisions persist despite the lack of any "justifying rationale in either the westernized 'modern' system or in Islamic theology, which . . . tends to be hostile to any distinction that is incompatible with the notion of the fundamental equality of all men before God."[44]

In Senegal, the Tukulor are associated with militant efforts to transform local "paganism" into Islam. Villalón notes that the transformation of Islam "from minority religion to dominant faith" involved both "a series of reformist *jihads* launched against pagan rulers or nominal Muslims" and "the imperative of reconstructing social orders in the context of the upheaval" following "colonial conquest." "The *jihad* launched by the Tukulor cleric El Hajj Umar Tall in the 1850s . . . did much to establish the preeminence of the Tijaniyya [Sufi] order in the region." Similarly, the Sine—the Serer-dominated south-coastal region, home to Mawdo's "royal" family—was the site of "the *jihad* launched by Ma Ba Diakhou [also a Tukulor reformist cleric] in about 1861," an effort "both to overthrow the traditional (impious or worse) elite and to resist the advances of the Christian colonizers."[45] Given this context, Mawdo's repudiation of the caste system is consistent with both the influence of Western education and the spirit of a reformist Islam as skeptical of local superstition as any *philosophe*.

Ramatoulaye depicts the professionalism she and Aïssatou share as schoolteachers in terms that connect the radical primordiality of ethics with both maternal tenderness and progressive social transformation: "On ne badine pas avec la vie, et la vie, c'est à la fois le corps et l'esprit. Déformer une âme est aussi sacrilège qu'un assassinat" (38) ["You don't joke with life, and life is both body and mind. To warp a soul is as much a sacrilege as murder" (23)]. Concern for the proper formation of another's soul need not be paternalistic because deformation is sacrilege. Genuine teachers may be likened to soldiers in ways that evoke the militant reformism not only of French republicanism and 1950s–60s African nationalism but also of precolonial *jihads*, with their fusion of missionary zeal and political activism: "Teachers—at kindergarten level, as at university level—form a noble army accomplishing daily feats never praised, never decorated. An army forever on the move, forever vigilant. . . . This army, thwarting traps and snares, everywhere plants the flag of knowledge and morality" (23).

Assuming the cadences of a *griot*, Ramatoulaye find words that do both the immediacy and significance of experience justice.[46] By finding those words, Ramatoulaye revalorizes "noble" (*géer*) so that it includes Aïssatou. To be "noble" is to so care about others that one becomes part of the army "déjouant pièges et embûches" (*USLL* 38). "Déjouer," to baffle or thwart, opposes "jouer," to play, to the extent that play is "badine," levity bound to antisocial self-love. The unconditional seriousness of the army's concern leads to its fusion of messianism and universalism (a combination repeatedly discussed by Levinas).[47] Although the discursive structure in which Ramatoulaye situates both herself and Aïssatou shares the enlightenment's teleological/progressivist model of history, the description of the flag stresses both women's allegiance to only those currents of Western thought consistent with Islamic *ilm*—a "savoir" indissociable from "virtu," from *adab*, for it connotes religious knowledge as well as practical and theoretical knowledge (Aristotle's *phronêsis* and *epistêmê*) and, crucially, "not just intellectual knowing, but knowing charged with feeling."[48] As Ramatoulaye's blending of maternal tenderness and militant activism indicates, the "feeling" that must charge knowing is that of *rahma*.

Locating oneself within structures of piety and civic obligation need not lead to self-denying asceticism. In one of the most Proustian passages in the novel, Ramatoulaye attempts to recapture the two couples' "lost time" vacationing on the beach, employing what Gérard Genette calls "*iterative* narrative," "where a single narrative utterance takes upon itself several occurrences together of the same events," a form that, as Genette notes, Proust gives a new, radicalized textual and thematic centrality.[49] "We would walk along the Dakar Corniche, . . . a sheer work of art wrought by nature. . . . People would undress, without embarrassment, tempted by the benevolent caress of the iodized breeze and the warmth from the sun's rays. . . . Under the wondering gaze of the kids, the live fish would flip up as the long sea snakes would curve themselves inwards" (21).

On the one hand, the sensual specificity of experience is its own justification. Discussing Proust, Kristeva argues, "Forgiveness endows what is infinitely small—or infinitely abject—with signification. It does so not by drawing attention to such phenomena but by breathing new life into them."[50] On the other hand, Ramatoulaye's aesthetic construction of her experience, both at the time and in memory, implies a relationship between enjoyment and separation: she can appreciate the beach because her relation to nature is structured by both a bourgeois urban lifestyle and a Rousseauian-Romantic understanding of nature's restorative effect. Levinas argues that the dialectic of enjoyment and separation links egoism to a sense of freedom from material dependence that allows exteriority to be savored: "In enjoyment throbs egoist being. . . . To be separated is to be at home with oneself. But to be at home with oneself . . . is to live from . . . , to enjoy the elemental."[51]

Such enjoyment might seem ethically suspect. Charles Ponnuthurai Sarvan argues that Ramatoulaye is oblivious to class exploitation.[52] Bâ's novel, written in the late 1970s, does not anticipate the collapse of the Senegalese economy in the 1980s and 1990s. It reflects, instead, the relative prosperity of the 1950s–60s and the latter half of the 1970s.[53] Thus, it confronts neither the implosion of the labor market for the educated nor the role of the Western-educated elite in contributing locally to the economic devastation wrought after 1979 by falling commodity prices and oil shocks. Catherine Boone has argued, for example, that because "the ruling class" in Senegal was "threatened by the specter of an independent accumulating class," feared the political consequences of "changes in rural social relations," and "depended upon existing market monopolies," the regime protected the status quo "at the expense of changes that would have promoted the rise of more dynamic and productive forms of capital, both local and foreign."[54]

Without discounting the privilege that underlies Ramatoulaye's experience, one may nonetheless recognize in her enjoyment more than bourgeois mystification. Sensory experience is converted into beautiful images that we take into ourselves. Such enjoyment might seem vulnerable not only to the criticism that it reflects a bourgeois, westernized sensibility, but also to the view that it demonstrates the dependence of aesthetic delight upon egocentric appropriativeness (in Levinas's terms, the conversion of exteriority into sources of pleasure rather than calls to responsibility),[55] and so partakes of seduction by sensual images—which would constitute, in Islamic terms, idolatry.

Against such objections, Bâ justifies Ramatoulaye's enjoyment by binding

together Romantic and Islamic understandings of how delight in life, affirming the goodness of the Creation, revitalizes ethical agency: "L'air marin nous
incitait à la bonne humeur. Le plaisir que nous goûtions et qui fêtait tous nos
sens, enivrait sainement, aussi bien le riche que le pauvre. Notre communion,
avec la nature profonde, insondable et illimitée, désintoxiquent notre âme. Le
découragement et la tristesse s'en allaient, soudainement remplacés par des
sentiments de plénitude et d'épanouissement" (36) ["The sea air would put us
in good humor. The pleasure we indulged in and in which all our senses
rejoiced would healthily intoxicate both rich and poor. Our communion with
deep, bottomless and unlimited nature refreshed our souls. Depression and
sadness would disappear, suddenly to be replaced by feelings of plenitude and
expansiveness" (22)]. By stressing how "communion" with nature takes away
"le découragement et la tristesse," Bâ evokes such accounts as Wordsworth's of
how joy, "felt in the blood, and felt along the heart," passes into the "purer
mind, / With tranquil restoration." Romanticism thus helps constitute, in
Taylor's terms, both a source of modern subjectivity and a modern moral
good—for to these "sensations" we may owe our "little, nameless, unremembered, acts / Of kindness and of love." At the same time, Bâ couples the
quintessentially Romantic phrase "sentiments . . . d'épanouissement" with
"sentiments de plénitude," which makes Ramatoulaye's "sentiments" consistent with an "Arab Islamic orthodoxy," perceiving "the world as . . . 'a ple-
num.'"[56] Moreover, Bâ describes the effects of joyous sensations from communion with a sublime, transcendent nature in terms of being "healthily
drunk" and "disintoxicated," terms that evoke Islam's reflections upon "intoxication" (*sukr* in Arabic).

The Quranic condemnation of liquor is treated in Sufi traditions not as a
condemnation of intoxication itself but intoxication through false, delusive
means; liquor, like ungoverned desire and idolatrous imagination, creates an
illusory happiness that seduces by parodying real happiness, which comes only
from God. Sufi piety aspires to bring the individual to "be completely absorbed
by God in a state of intoxication (*sukr*) and effacement (*mahw*)": this temporary "unitive" experience with God "leaves an effect on the Sufi which is very
much like the intoxication (*sukr*) caused by drinking." Even in its spiritual
sense, intoxication remains ambiguous: it is the condition for and the effect of
an ecstatic, transitory, mystical union with God, but it can make the Sufi say or
do things that, when "sober," he will amend.[57] Just as the Wordsworthian subject shaped by "joy" may be better able to respond to the ethical call because of

the "unremembered" effects of "joy" upon the heart and mind, so the Sufi believer may be better able to undertake ethical obligations because spiritual intoxication gives rise to a sobriety that is peculiarly "disintoxicated"—he is less likely to be "intoxicated" by the idolatrous and the illusory.

Describing nature as "profonde, insondable et illimitée," Bâ separates what Ramatoulaye experiences from cognitive objectification or consumerist-tourist appropriation. What is profound, unfathomable, and unlimited supersedes the conceptual categories we would deploy to master it, which is how Levinas characterizes the infinity that marks the Other's face and, as David Haney has argued, how Wordsworth characterizes the sublimity of nature.[58] Such resistance also characterizes, according to Ghazali, the divine word. Similarly, while Sufi traditions vary on the exact nature of the soul's intoxicating unitive experience with God, the divine always outstrips and leaves humble, like a guilty thing surprised, the human cognitive grasp; we experience "effacement" (*mahw*), the uprooting of the ego's imperialism before an otherness absolutely Other.[59] Understood within these contexts, aesthetic delight, as well as the literary labor of transforming sensations into images, articulates not a sense of mastery over the world but an opening of the self to all that opposes the incorporation of the Other into an economy of the Same.

It might still be argued that Ramatoulaye's enjoyment is predicated upon illicit bourgeois privilege. Levinas notes, however, that separation is necessary for there to be a separate identity, an interiority, to be called to responsibility.[60] One cannot give to others unless one has something of one's own. Bâ situates Ramatoulaye's evocation of seaside vacations between her articulation of gratitude for the headmistress's educational program and her epic praise of the army of teachers to which she and Aïssatou belong. She refuses to accord her characters the kind of class guilt—as opposed to individual responsibility—that Sarvan suggests Africans who are "national bourgeoisie" ought to feel. On the contrary, Bâ implies that privilege is redeemed through service. Ramatoulaye's capacity for ethical labor and her opportunity for enjoyment are tied together. Both are threatened when the structures of fidelity supporting both are challenged by the disavowals first of Aïssatou's husband and then of her own husband—disavowals that betray not only wives but also the nonarbitrariness of signification, disavowals that are thus atheistic apostasy.

Feminist Rebellion and the Reconstitution of the Pious Ethical Subject

Apostasy begins in paganism and ends in atheism. While Ramatoulaye and Aïssatou were "blossoming," Aïssatou's mother-in-law, mortified that her royal blood was allied with that of a goldsmith's daughter, was thinking only of revenge. As she looks at the countryside outside Dakar, Nabou reflects, "By its very duration, nature defies time and takes its revenge on man" (27), just as she has defied time to take her revenge on Aïssatou. The nature with which Nabou identifies is not interested in Romantic "communion"; instead, all modification from the outside is experienced as violent imposition.

Bâ characterizes such undiscriminating resistance of the Same to the Other as the essence of paganism. The novel's insistent identification of Nabou with the Sine nobility evokes a specific history. The Sine region was unusually resistant to Islamic conversion; the Tukulor cleric Ma Ba's efforts ended in his defeat and death in 1867, and "the protectorate status which the French devised for the kingdom . . . preserved the formal political structures around the figure of the *buur* [the pagan ruler]." Indeed, "no wide-scale conversions to Islam followed directly on French conquest," and even in 1994, while "the vast majority [in the Sine] are at least nominally Muslim, . . . depth of commitment varies, as all local religious leaders are quick to admit."[61]

Christopher L. Miller has pointed out that in portraying Nabou's journey from Dakar to her ancestral home in quest of a young kinswoman she can shape into Mawdo's second wife, Bâ transgresses the generic boundaries of the epistolary novel: "Ramatoulaye uses . . . free indirect discourse to render old Nabou's inner thoughts as she travels alone." Miller sees this not as a fault but as "a peculiar hybrid, . . . a brilliant departure" that empowers Ramatoulaye.[62] But Ramatoulaye's self-consciousness about the ethical status of her discourse makes it unlikely she would seek a mere strategic advantage. Instead, free indirect discourse allows her to explore what she can respect in one she might be tempted to dismiss. By imagining what Nabou must have thought and experienced, Ramatoulaye can probe her own affinities with Nabou. What matters is not that things occurred exactly as Ramatoulaye imagines them, but that they must have occurred *like that*. By allowing us to experience, vicariously, what things must have been *like*, novelistic discourse redeems itself from the charge of being mere fiction—for the substantiality of the Other, exceeding the categories that would contain it, allows imagination to escape subservience to desire or hatred.

Nabou's determination not to allow Aïssatou's "existence" to "tarnish her noble descent" is connected to the presence "in her thoughts" of "antiquated rites and religion," leading her to remember "the milk to be poured into the Sine to appease the invisible spirits." This determination is reinforced by a rural community for whom the precolonial past is a vital presence: "Visitors came from everywhere to honor her. . . . For her, they revived the exploits of the ancestor Bour-Sine, the dust of combats and the ardour of thoroughbred horses" (28). As Sarvan notes, Ramatoulaye "has a grudging admiration" for Nabou.[63] Even as little Nabou receives a Francophone secondary education and then professional training, "Aunt" Nabou takes pains to inculcate in her traditional virtues by traditional means. Ramatoulaye notes, "It was especially while telling folk tales, . . . that Aunty Nabou wielded her power over young Nabou's soul; her expressive voice glorified the retributive violence of the warrior; her expressive voice lamented the anxiety of the Loved One, all submissive. . . . And slowly but surely, through the sheer force of repetition, the virtues and greatness of a race took root in this child" (45–47). Real "virtues" were internalized, which, when united with an education in modern midwifery, cease to be archaic. Ramatoulaye again assumes the cadences of a praise-singer: "[A]ll day and several times over she would go through the same gestures, engendering life. . . . In the midst of life, in the midst of poverty, in the midst of ugliness, young Nabou would often triumph with her knowledge and experience. . . . Young Nabou, responsible and aware, like you, like me!" (47–48).

Little Nabou shares with Aïssatou an ethically constituted subjectivity. By acknowledging this, Ramatoulaye does justice to Aunt Nabou even as she subjects the latter's morality to ethical assessment. Little Nabou's ethical agency weaves together precolonial aristocratic virtues with modern professionalism, but her own ethical failure (acquiescing in being Aunt Nabou's instrument of revenge) arises from her lack of self, from the woundedness of a spirit never encouraged to cultivate her own personality. Aunt Nabou declares, "Je ferai de cette enfant une autre moi-même" (46) ["I will make of this child another me" (28)]. Thus, she teaches little Nabou that "the first quality of a woman is docility" (29), preparing her for the day when she announces to Mawdo Bâ that the girl she has raised is intended to be his second wife, and were he to decline this family offering, she would die of shame. Mawdo yields, and the griots sing, "Blood has returned to its source" (30).

Miller notes that the "oversameness" of this marriage is "just short of incest."[64] Because paganism makes an idol of the same, it does not—any more than postmodernism, though for quite different reasons—distinguish between formation and colonization. Ramatoulaye goes to pains to note that she, Aïssatou, and the headmistress guard against the psychic or cultural colonization of others. By contrast, the aspiration to create "une autre moi-même" for one's son to marry is an incest grounded in what Levinas would call "allergy" to the Other, an incest epitomizing pagan revolt, since the desire to make the other in one's own image usurps the place of God. It is the self-idolatry that, for Islam, underlies all *fitna*, all regression to *jahiliyya*, "the unbridled reign of *hawa*, desire and individual egotism."[65]

Confronted with *jahiliyya*, calling into question the solidity of any symbolic order, or any orientation of the self in "moral space,"[66] Aïssatou disregards communal "choral" voices counseling cowardice and compromise; she chooses a permanent break that is certainly a feminist rebellion, but also a *hijra*, a fleeing of a sociopolitical order that makes impossible, impious demands. The paradigm, the *hijra* that divides Islamic history into two eras, is the Prophet's flight from Mecca to Medina. Writes Villalón: "As articulated in Islamic theology, *hijra* can refer to the literal emigration . . . , or it can involve a figurative flight by seeking isolation and non-involvement with state initiatives." *Hijra* is contrasted with, and sometimes coupled with, *jihad* (holy war, but also "active struggle," as in contesting state authority or rulings).[67] In the Senegalese context, the concept of *hijra* has a particular potency. As Donal B. Cruise O'Brien, supported by later scholarship, has noted, the French conquest of Wolof kingdoms organized around warfare and supported by warrior-slaves (the *ceddo*) imposed a colonial peace that destroyed the old social order by blocking traditional wealth accumulation (warfare and slavery) and hence warlords' capacity to distribute patronage. In the wake of the old order's collapse, three Sufi brotherhoods, the Qadiriyya, the Tijaniyya, and the peculiarly Senegalese Mourides, established sociopolitical structures and ideological systems independent of first the colonial and then the postcolonial state. In practice, the Sufi orders provided both state-independent structures of meaning and state-independent networks of patronage and wealth formation (most spectacularly, the Mourides provided—at the expense of Peul (Fulbe) herders—land and labor for peanut cultivation). The Sufi orders allowed at once for negotiating with, struggling against, and withdrawing from the state.[68] Villalón points out, "[T]he simple refusal to acknowledge state-imposed rules grants a high degree of societal autonomy. . . . In the mid-nineteenth century

El Hajj Umar called on the inhabitants of areas that had been occupied by the French to flee to Muslim areas. . . . And . . . its more figurative sense implying a distancing from illegitimate authority" continues to shape Sufi power.[69]

Aïssatou's letter announcing her termination of marriage describes the order to which Mawdo wants her to conform as a triumphant *dar al-harb* or a reemergent *jahiliyya*: "Princes master their feelings to fulfill their duties. 'Others' bend their heads and, in silence, accept a [fate] that [bullies] them" (31). From the standpoint of both Islam and Western modernity, such an order can have no legitimacy. Aïssatou refuses to accept a social order characterized by "absurd divisions" (*clivages insensés*). Aïssatou rejects nativism because she rejects relativism; the local, the contingent, is answerable to the ethical, and thus to reason (what is "insensé" cannot command allegiance). The word "clivages" connotes the violent cutting apart of what had been whole. It evokes the Quranic word *shiqaq*, "a schism that splits both the community and heaven in two," a word central to the Quranic account (in Sura 38) of the Prophet's *hijra*. When the ruling council at Mecca in 622 realized Muhammad would accept no compromise on God's oneness, they affirmed a *shiqaq* that forced the Prophet into *hijra*: "The Muslim calendar begins at this time, the year 622, when the break between polytheism and monotheism was decisive," and "[o]pposition to the One would forever have a negative color" in Islamic thought.[70]

When Aïssatou declares, "I will not yield to it," she echoes the Prophet in refusing submission (*islam*) to illegitimate authority. In accord with Islamic teachings, Aïssatou argues that accepting *shiqaq* in one sphere leads to its acceptance in all others. She tells Mawdo, in response to his claims that he is only marrying little Nabou out of family obligation, "You want to draw a line between heartfelt love and physical love. I say that there can be no union of bodies without the heart's acceptance." The denial of the oneness of the human community leads to the denial of internal oneness—a pagan reversion to psychic *jahiliyya* separating the self from ethical accountability. Such a "clivage" repudiates the whole tenor of Islamic ethics, which, as in Ghazali's classical work, fuses Quranic revelation and Aristotelian philosophy: "Training the faculties of the soul does not entail uprooting . . . the faculties of the animal soul. . . . It does, however, imply their subordination to the practical reasoning faculty. . . . [G]ood character is achieved when the deliberative faculty of the human soul subordinates the irascible and concupiscent faculties of the animal soul."[71] Aïssatou refuses to accept Mawdo's claim of a schism between his deliberative and concupiscent faculties: "Your reasoning, which makes a distinction [*qui scinde*], is unacceptable" (32). "Scinde," divide, split up, reinforces the relation between *clivage* and *shiqaq*. Before such apostasy, she can only say, "man is one: greatness and animal fused together." Sufi Islam teaches that ethical life should emulate the oneness of God. The "'Transcendent Unity of Being' (*wahdat al-wujûd*) and the Universal or Perfect Man (*al-insân al-kâmil*)" are connected because "man is the only creature in this world who is centrally and axially located so that he reflects the Divine Names and Qualities in a total and conscious manner."[72]

Whereas the Prophet found refuge in Medina, where he gathered his forces for an ultimately triumphant return, in conquest, to Mecca in 630, Aïssatou finds refuge in part through her professionalism and the institutions that support it (her independent salary makes her withdrawal possible), in part through her friendship with Ramatoulaye, but primarily through books. Ramatoulaye delivers an apostrophe to books that, as Miller observes, may make "[a]ntilogocentrists . . . squirm."[73] "The power of books, this marvelous invention of astute human intelligence. Various signs, associated with sound: different sounds that form the word. Juxtaposition [*Agencement*] of words from which spring the Idea, Thought, History, Science, Life. Sole instrument of interrelationships and of culture, unparalleled means of giving and receiving. Books knit generations together in the same continuing effort that leads to progress. They enabled you to better yourself. What society refused you, they granted" (32).

On the one hand, this apostrophe integrates gratitude toward books into Senegalese culture by employing epic cadences to sing their praises; on the other hand, it closely echoes apostrophes to speech or philosophy in classical humanist literature.[74] The difference between Ramatoulaye's apostrophe and those of Cicero and Plutarch is that books, rather than speech or philosophy, are the source of an intergenerational, intersubjective community knit together by shared ethical civic labor, and that the community, the refuge, created by books constitutes an alternative system of empowerment and so works against "society's" totalizing propensities.

As Miller notes, Bâ is blunt in acknowledging that books are unequaled means of giving and receiving: they are "unequaled by *orality*; the letter and the book 'give and receive' best,"[75] apparently because the precision and permanence of print forces us to attend to exact words in ways that work against diluting, fudging, reshaping the otherness of another's word. By being unique instruments "of interrelationships and of culture" (a significant parallelism), books constitute an indispensable defense against tyranny. Mernissi points out that the Quranic word *taghiya* means "'tyrant,' a holder of power that knows no limits. . . . The *taghiya* is the leader who is contemptuous toward everything, including the divine."[76] Books liberate by restoring order, by reclaiming in the arrangement of words the bond between "relation" and "culture" that opposes tyranny with reasoned repudiations of contemptuousness toward everything, a contemptuousness that, for Islam, is epitomized in atheism.

Discussing this apostrophe, Walker argues that the text "seems an act of deconstruction," for while "the passage is very much about the power of reading for all Africans, in context it also suggests . . . the power of writing and the dire need of African women . . . to read books by African women." Bâ certainly hopes her work will be a refuge for others, but Walker's phrasing presents both reading and writing as instruments of the self's unfolding of its autotelic freedom: "Writing is difficulty, effort, struggle, work, and resistance to pre-description and prescription, but above all, it is refuge, freedom, and power 'granted' when a woman writes the letters that correspond to the sounds emanating from within."[77] It is important that Ramatoulaye free herself from the silencing of women, but Walker's description excludes all the positive value Bâ accords both reason and culture, suggesting instead that any word not "emanat[ing] from within" must be oppressive "pre-description and prescription."

By contrast, Ramatoulaye celebrates how Aïssatou's appreciation of the words of others leads her from figurative to literal *hijra*: through success in exams, demonstrating mastery of languages "emanating from without," she is able to study translation in France and then become an interpreter in Washington. Instead of colonizing or disempowering her, Aïssatou's ability to interpret *accurately* the words of others permits her to distance herself from illegitimate power and, ultimately, reconstitute a life ordered through continuous ethical agency (educating her children, helping Ramatoulaye in her distress).

Describing Mawdo's pliancy, Bâ connects Aunt Nabou's archaic, incestuous idolatry with those aspects of the modern West that encourage placing self-love above being for-another. "Faced with this rigid mother, moulded by the old morality, burning with the fierce ardour of antiquated laws, what could Mawdo Bâ do? He was getting on in years, worn out by his arduous work. And then, did he really want to fight, to make a gesture of resistance? Young Nabou was so tempting" (30). Mawdo Bâ is unmanned by a radically masculinist mother. Moreover, the words "rigide," "pétrie," "brûlée intérieurement par les féroces lois antiques" (*USLL* 48) associate her with the bloodthirsty idols whose reign of violence the Prophet's iconoclasm brought to an end. Mernissi notes that the goddess "Manat shares with the other two goddesses, al-Lat and al-'Uzza, the very revealing title of *taghiya*" and that al-'Uzza in particular "represents most strongly the warrior dimension of the divine, linking the reign of the feminine in the collective memory with the age of darkness, when the insatiable deities bathed in the blood of innumerable victims, who were not always animals."[78] Aunt Nabou certainly acts like al-'Uzza in demanding that Mawdo sacrifice Aïssatou and her children to signify his devotion. Mawdo, inverting the conduct of the Prophet, acquiesces in idolatry, gives himself over to unconstrained female power, and so allows the triumph of *jahiliyya*.

Trying to explain how his regret does not prevent him from having children with little Nabou, he reiterates the "schismatic reasoning" that Aïssatou repudiates. Because "instincts" dominate man, there is no choice but to submit: "You can't resist the imperious laws that demand food and clothing for man. These same laws compel the 'male' in other respects. I say 'male' to emphasize the bestiality of instincts. . . . You understand. . . . Truth is ugly when one analyses it" (33–34). Mawdo turns the Islamic ethics of Ghazali on its head, disavowing his own ethical accountability and so (implicitly) God: "Truth is ugly" because it is, "when one analyses it," nothing but the *dar al-harb*. The confusion and disorder of the pre-Islamic era intersect with the confusion and disorder of that side of Western modernity that sees itself discovering the death of God in giving itself over to "laws" of instinct and will to power.

It might seem startling that Bâ would evoke the cultural memory of goddesses and idols who contribute to misogynistic currents in Islam. However, it is crucial to Bâ's feministic ethics that empowerment be connected to *rahma*, that language not be understood as an arbitrary Law of the Father. Aunt Nabou's idolatrous self-love precludes the *rahma* that allows language to help the Other "blossom." In its absence, incest blocks the cultural affirmation of difference that frees interrelationships from the rule of violence (from a vicious cycle of allergy, identification, incorporation, and abjection). Kristeva remarks, "We should recognize the 'civilizing' role that mothers play. . . . Mothers are the ones who pass along the native tongue, but they also perform an important psychological role . . . , a sort of miracle by separating themselves from their children while loving them and teaching them to speak."[79] In *Tales of Love*, Kristeva argues, "The loving mother, different from the caring and clinging mother, is someone who has an object of desire; beyond that, she has an Other with relation to whom the child will serve as go-between. She will love her child with respect to that Other, and it is through a discourse aimed at that Third Party that the child will be set up as 'loved' for the mother. . . . [I]t is in the eyes of a Third Party that the baby the mother speaks of becomes a *he*, it is with respect to others that 'I am proud of you,' and so forth."[80] Aunt Nabou is not a "loving mother" because her self-love precludes "having an Other" in Kristeva's sense; thus, her relation with the Other in Levinas's sense, one who is not "un autre moi-même," can only be "allergic." What alone prevents maternal love from collapsing into metaphorical incest is precedence of the for-another to self-love: "Since [the mother] is willing to set aside all the tokens of her narcissism and masochism because she will be rewarded by this other's growth, accomplishments, and future, she can subordinate herself to the ideal whom she is trying to raise and who will soon exceed her bounds."[81]

Confronted with Mawdo's apostasy, Ramatoulaye repudiates the atheistic terms of his logic: "He was asking me to understand. But to understand what? The supremacy of instinct? The right to betray? The justification of the desire for variety? I could not be an ally to polygamic instincts" (34). Esonwanne has suggested that associating polygamy with instincts, with innate desires, is "counterproductive" to Bâ's feminist project, for to "attribute polygyny to innatism is to surrender the struggle against 'the status quo' to another status quo, namely, biologism."[82] This argument only holds if one assumes, like Mawdo, that because a desire is innate, one has no choice but to follow its dictates. However, Ramatoulaye allies herself with both Islamic and non-Islamic ethical traditions that see the work of culture as indissociable from the educating, the socializing, of desire, so forming the soul that it can and will subordinate the promptings of instinct to considerations of whether "surrender" would do another injustice.

The injustice inherent in modern paganism, mirror image of the injustice inherent in archaic paganism, is exemplified in Modou's betrayal of Ramatoulaye. As Ramatoulaye's eldest daughter Daba is preparing for her "baccalauréat," her classmate Binetou is besieged by the attentions and gifts of a middle-aged "sugar daddy," who pressures her to marry him. The pressure is increased by her mother, who sees such a marriage as the family's path out of poverty. One morning Ramatoulaye is confronted by the delegation of Mawdo, Modou's brother Tamsir, and the local Iman, who, after such dubiously pious circumlocutions as, "There is nothing one can do when Allah the almighty puts two people side by side" (36), announce that Modou has married a second wife. Ramatoulaye is assaulted by stereotypical language designed to force her to acquiesce in injustice, but instead she recalls her mother's warning that the gap between Modou's first two incisors was a "sign of the primacy of love in the individual" (37–38). However questionable dental character analysis may be, Ramatoulaye's recollection contests the official, patriarchal story: it is not God who has placed two people "side by side," but rather Modou's submission to his deepest weakness.

Not only does Ramatoulaye contest the patriarchal story; she recognizes it as an inversion of Islam, the identification of *hawa* and *fitna* with God's will. Never for a moment does she entertain such an impious thought, which empowers her to assess the morality of the Foucauldian "discourse position" or Althusserian interpellation offered her against the "transcendent" claims of the ethical. Ramatoulaye only learns later that her new co-wife is her daughter's friend Binetou.

Modou disavows his past, destroying the structures of fidelity—supported by his own narrative unity of aiming for the good—upon which Ramatoulaye has depended. The violence to the Other intrinsic to such "breaking free" is laid bare. Although she cries incessantly, Ramatoulaye is prepared to accept "equal sharing, according to the precepts of Islam concerning polygamic life" (45–46), apparently because she is reluctant to "[d]raw a clean line through the past" (40). Modou has no such qualms: "He never came again: his new found happiness gradually swallowed up his memory of us. He forgot about us" (46). Bâ's portrait of a religious and social system that complacently countenances the un-Islamic conduct of prominent men is scathing. At the very least, she suggests that de facto religious practices in Dakar so dilute Islam with indigenous and Western idolatries that a *jihad*, an active struggle, and a *mirasse*, a stripping away to the truth, are ethical obligations.

The violence that Modou's apostasy inflicts upon Ramatoulaye is equaled by the violence worked upon Binetou and himself. Binetou seeks compensation for her lost youth in material possessions: "A victim, she wanted to be the oppressor. Exiled in the world of adults, which was not her own, she wanted her prison gilded" (48). Her rapacious demands, her return of contempt for infatuation, are more than matched by her mother's exactions of tribute and her tyranny over Modou's life. Sarvan argues that Ramatoulaye's treatment of Binetou and her mother, contrasted with her treatment of Aunt Nabou and little Nabou, indicates the "harshness and contempt reserved for the lower class."[83] On the contrary, Ramatoulaye has no problem receiving Binetou in her home and supporting her efforts to rise socially through education. What

Ramatoulaye judges harshly is Binetou's willingness to be victimized for a "gilded prison." Binetou's mother is worse than Aunt Nabou because Aunt Nabou does value self-discipline and duty, albeit in misguided ways. By contrast, Binetou's mother places personal rapaciousness above any other consideration.

Modou opens himself to his new mother-in-law's predations and subjects himself to constant humiliation from Binetou. Seeking to hold her captive, Modou resembles Proust's Swann and Marcel at the height of their jealous imprisonments of (and by) Odette and Albertine. By exiling an "enfant" the age of his daughter to "the world of adults," by continual, futile attempts to appease her by catering to juvenile, crassly commercial tastes, by seeking to make himself appear young with hair dyes and tight pants, Modou resembles Humbert frantically trying to keep Lolita entertained, or Aschenbach striving to deny the impossible distance between himself and Tadzio. In his second marriage, as in Mawdo's, pagan idolatry is implicated with incest, but here the desire is not to achieve an unmodified sameness by marrying one's son to a version of oneself, but rather to achieve a radically other self by marrying another version of one's daughter. The difference is between freezing time and abrogating time. The incest integral to modern paganism connects metaphysical rebellion against God (rebellion against one's finite, created status) with what is just short of pedophilia.

By casting Modou's polygamy in such terms, Bâ audaciously invites comparison between Modou's biography and Muhammad's. Ramatoulaye and Modou enjoy a monogamous marriage of twenty-five years, exactly the number of years that the Prophet was married to Khadija, a wealthy Mecca widow and merchant, whose financial and emotional support, figured by the *hadith* (sacred legends) in terms of *rahma* for her younger husband, was crucial to his early career. The marriage ended with Khadija's death, leaving the Prophet devastated. Only then did Muhammad embark upon a polygamous career, marrying fourteen women, "of which nine were alive when the Prophet died."[84] The most important of these, many motivated by political alliances, was with A'isha, who was nine when wed and fourteen when the Prophet died. The *hadith* portrays this relationship as one of intense emotional love and sensual delight, virtually a divine reward for the Prophet's service: "Reportedly, Muhammad asked Abu Bakr for [his daughter] A'isha's hand in marriage only after the Angel Gabriel had shown him a picture of A'isha . . . ; according to another account, Gabriel showed him the infant A'isha in her cradle as his future bride and befitting substitute for Khadija, a divine favor to lessen his grief over Khadija's death."[85] Muhammad's lifelong devotion to Khadija contrasts sharply with Modou's treason to, and forgetting of, Ramatoulaye. If A'isha is understood as a divine reward for Muhammad's lifelong piety, Binetou may be seen as a novelistically plausible but poetically appropriate punishment for Modou's apostasy. Most important, the traditions' stress upon Gabriel's role in facilitating the marriage indicates that the emotional and physical pleasure the Prophet found with A'isha was not the reason for the marriage, that at no time did the Prophet's intense sensual appreciation of women turn him away from submission to God.

While the dissonant evocation of Muhammad's biography in Modou's story may suggest how the Prophet's polygamy and love of a young girl have given rise to, or provided cultural cover for, patriarchal indulgences in self-love and idolatry, that in no way constitutes, for either Ramatoulaye or Bâ, a "subversion" of Islam itself. Nowhere in the novel does either the protagonist or the author question the reality and goodness of God or the legitimacy of Quranic revelation. Describing how her friends advise her to use magic to retrieve Modou and punish Binetou, Ramatoulaye notes, "My mind [*raison*] and my faith rejected supernatural power. They rejected this easy attraction, which kills any will to fight" (49). The parallelism between reason and faith is crucial; both together allow her to reject "magical thinking" and its seductive, delusive comforts. Here, feminist resistance is born of the refusal to dilute the freedom that reason and faith jointly command. Ramatoulaye learns to run a household of twelve, to appear in public as a single, middle-aged woman (a category Senegalese society disallows), and to assume increasing control of her own life, epitomized in her learning how to drive (54).

Just as the co-implication of reason and faith enables Ramatoulaye's increasing intellectual and practical autonomy, so it anchors an increasing cosmopolitanism. She watches films in a way shaped by the headmistress's educational program: "I learned from them lessons of greatness, courage and perseverance. They deepened and widened my vision of the world, thanks to their [cultural] value" (52). Cosmopolitan acculturation increases one's power to meet the obligations of reason and faith. Aïssatou, having fled to a cosmopolitan refuge, saves enough money to buy Ramatoulaye a Fiat (53–54), a gesture that indicates how she can act, rather like a Senegalese Sufi order, as an alternative system of social support to the potentially totalizing "official" order. The gesture also indicates that Aïssatou has not fallen under the sway of idolatrous self-love: "You, the goldsmith's daughter, gave me your help while depriving yourself" (54). Significantly, Modou can never believe that the Fiat came from Aïssatou. "Like Mawdo's mother, he too believed that a goldsmith's daughter had no heart" (54). Bâ unites, as the conclusion of Ramatoulaye's retrospective account, the characters who epitomize archaic and modern paganism (Aunt Nabou and Modou). Both share the "allergy" to the Other that follows from naturalizing will to power in order to idolize desire.

Rahma without *Jahiliyya*: Anchoring
the Cosmopolitan in the Transcendent

During the figurative *hijra* of her widow's seclusion, Ramatoulaye comes to wed, through novelistic prose, sensuous particularity and significance in a way that sheds bitterness from memory. She recognizes that she is temperamentally incapable of finding in single life a personal happiness that can compensate for what she has lost (55–56). This personal (not philosophical or prescriptive) acknowledgment underscores the permanence of the wound Modou has inflicted. But neither his injustice nor its unreasonableness prevents her from both crying for Modou and praying for him: "I have forgiven him. May God hear the prayers I say for him every day" (57). Such prayers exemplify the triumph of mercy, of *rahma*, over the logic of justice.

Like Nwapa and Alkali, Bâ suggests that only in declining to exact strict justice against patriarchal violence can we align ourselves with what sustains spiritual and material life. At the same time, again like Nwapa and Alkali, Bâ does not suggest that the ascendancy of mercy should make women doormats. When Modou's brother Tamsir complacently proposes to Ramatoulaye, her voice breaks "thirty years of silence, thirty years of harassment," denouncing Tamsir's egotism and greed, his mendacity in desiring to appropriate Ramatoulaye's income under the "pious" guise of taking care of his brother's widow (57–58). In a society where the association of God with the uttered word, and public identity with ritual praise, gives extraordinary weight to what is said and what remains in silence, Ramatoulaye's raised voice carries the force of a physical assault.

Ramatoulaye moves from *hijra* to *jihad*, in the sense of active struggle. While rejecting Tamsir assuages justified anger, the marriage offer that comes from Daouda Dieng, Ramatoulaye's old suitor, poses a more subtle challenge. Ramatoulaye was the love of Daouda's life. Unlike Tamsir, he respects her outspoken demand to be taken seriously as a rational human being, although he is somewhat taken aback (59–63). When he proposes, she experiences the pleasure of being desired (65), the temptation of status and wealth, as well as gratitude for a fidelity that contrasts pointedly with Modou's betrayal. She rejects the offer, however, thus achieving the vital feminist good of dissociating self-validation from a man's support. She writes Daouda that she lacks the "accommodating" conscience (68) necessary to marry one she only esteems, especially as a second wife: "Abandoned yesterday . . . , I cannot lightly bring myself between you and your family" (68).

Ramatoulaye's acts of legitimate rebellion need to be distinguished from the kinds of (delusive) self-assertion that emerge from *fitna* and *hawa*. Claims such as Sarvan's, that "Ramatoulaye is a paradox, a conservative in revolt," or d'Almeida's, that Ramatoulaye is "characterized by a certain malaise" attendant to "wanting to keep traditions while, at the same time, wanting to reject what, in society, ties women down," do not confront the philosophical complexity of Bâ's text.[86]

Ramatoulaye is concerned about the tendency of modern goods—valorizing personal "blossoming," cultivating a critical spirit, enjoying material and physical well-being—to give rise to the modern paganisms that ultimately hollow out such seemingly exemplary characters as Modou and Mawdo. Despite the moral weaknesses motivating their second marriages, their professional lives are anchored in being-for-another. As she looks at the younger, post-independence generation, Ramatoulaye does not see their equals. Modernity's promise of material well-being, instead of focusing one upon concrete, effective service for others, insinuates a subtle materialistic transvaluation of values: "The dream of a rapid social climb prompts parents to give their children more knowledge than education. . . . But all four of us were made of stern stuff, with upright minds full of intense questionings that stuck within our inner selves, not without pain. . . . I observe the young. . . . Where is the vigorous pride that guides a whole community towards its duty? The appetite to live kills the dignity of living" (73).

Desire for, habituation to, material ease induces an intolerance for moral unease—and without the solidity that comes from calling oneself into question, one falls under the spell of "the appetite to live," giving oneself over to the concupiscent faculty in making an idol of this world and its (illusory) gratifications. In the same younger generation, however, Ramatoulaye also finds, in her daughter Daba's marriage, the image of the couple "just as I have always imagined. They identify with each other, discuss everything so as to find a compromise" (73–74). The vexing question is how to realize such goods as Daba's equitable marriage without introducing an ultimately totalizing "appetite to live." Ramatoulaye is even worried for Daba, because her marriage rests upon nothing more solid than mutual inclination.

When Ramatoulaye discovers her three teenage daughters secretly smoking, she is torn between guilt for having allowed them too much liberty and discomfort at imposing outmoded norms on a new generation. Her shock reflects traditional acculturation—"A woman's mouth exhaling the acrid smell of tobacco instead of being fragrant" (76)—and her habitual fusion of moral concern with respect for science: "I was aware of the harmful effects of tobacco" (77). But most important, smoking is emblematic of the idolatrous seductiveness of "the appetite to live." Although, after a scene, Ramatoulaye no longer sees her daughters smoking, she smells, or thinks she smells, its aroma everywhere. Exploiting the feminine pronoun in French, Bâ describes Ramatoulaye experiencing the smell as though it were the nearly tangible essence of *fitna* secretly permeating and threatening all she holds dear: "Sournoise, ironique, elle taquinait mes narines, puis s'enfuyait. . . . Mais elle n'osa plus s'étaler, alerte et impudique" (113) ["Sly and ironic, it would tease my nostrils and then disappear. . . . But it no longer dared to expose itself openly, with jaunty shamelessness" (77)].

The question of what sort of morality does justice to the ethical relation comes crashing in upon Ramatoulaye when she discovers that another daughter, Aïssatou (her friend's namesake), has become pregnant. Her neighbor, the *griote* Farmata, articulates the traditional or conventional course: indignation and repudiation. After hearing Aïssatou's story, that she was in love with a university student, Ramatoulaye recognizes the story's truth because she recognizes her daughter in the "whole-hearted gift of herself to this lover who had succeeded in uniting in this heart my image and his own" (82). She perceives ethical character in an act culturally scripted to be read as shameless because, unlike Aunt Nabou, she can accept that the image of another rightfully has a place in her child's heart. At the same time, she is enraged at her daughter's injustice to her, after all her sufferings. But memory again saves her from bitterness. She remembers "like a lifebuoy, the tender and consoling attitude of [her] daughter during [her] distress" (82), which turns her to "God, as at every moment of crisis in [her] life." Recollection of the Other—a recollection that overflows the stereotype she was about to apply—recalls her to the ethical relation, which turns her to God. What Ramatoulaye affirms seems to come out of that turn: "[O]ne is a mother in order to understand the inexplicable. One is a mother to lighten the darkness. . . . One is a mother in order to love without beginning or end" (82–83). The maternal here, as in Levinas, epitomizes ethical transcendence of all that is said, finite, thematizable, because it is anarchic, without beginning, and infinite, unfulfillable, without end: "Maternity in the complete being 'for the other' which characterizes it, which is the very signifyingness of signification, is the ultimate sense of this vulnerability. . . . We have to formulate what the irremissibility and . . . the anguish of this in-itself of the oneself are. . . . It is a recurrence to oneself out of an irreducible exigency of the other, a duty overflowing my being. . . . Responsibility prior to any free commitment, the oneself outside of all the tropes of essence, would be responsibility for the freedom of the others."[87]

Within such absoluteness of obligation, "Le cordon ombilical se ranimait, ligature indestructible sous l'avalanche des assauts et la durée du temps" (121) ["The umbilical cord took on new life, the indestructible bond beneath the avalanche of storms and the duration of time" (83)]. From the materiality of the body, Ramatoulaye is able to retrieve images and sensations of Aïssatou's previous life that make it impossible to abandon her, "as pride would have [her] do": "Sa vie et son avenir constituaient un enjeu puissant qui démolissait les tabous et imposait à mon coeur et à ma raison sa supériorité sur tout" (121) [Her life and future constituted a powerful stake that demolished taboos and imposed upon my heart and my reason its superiority over all else (83)]. The absoluteness of maternal love demolishes taboos and shatters moralities made idols by imposing its superiority over the heart and reason (feelings and judgments we can enclose within a conceptuality). In a gesture at once unreservedly selfless, profoundly religious, and emphatically self-realizing, Ramatoulaye takes Aïssatou into her arms: "Je la serrais douloureusement dans mes bras, avec une force décuplée, faite de révolte paienne et de tendresse primitive" (121) ["Painfully, I held her tightly, with a force multiplied tenfold by pagan revolt and primitive tenderness" (83)].

By describing this gesture in terms of "pagan revolt" and "primitive tenderness," Bâ links the ferocity of Ramatoulaye's maternal devotion to Aunt Nabou's archaic pagan idolizing of her own flesh and blood. The phrase "révolte paienne" stands out starkly against Ramatoulaye's repeated demonstrations of the centrality of Islamic piety to her character. By employing the phrase, Bâ evokes those currents in Islamic thought that have traditionally supported misogyny. M. E. Combs-Schilling notes, "Islam's dominant sexual culture allocates to women the position of being that part of humanity that is closest to nature and hence least able to transcend its natural drives, including sexual impulses, and therefore least able to connect with the divine who exists beyond the natural realm."[88] The story of Ibrahim's readiness to sacrifice his son to God crystallizes these attitudes. In order to establish absolute submission, God asks Ibrahim to sacrifice his deepest natural bond; he agrees, but must leave his wife behind, go to a mountain where "a sacrificial intercourse and birth overcomes the limitations of male-female intercourse and female birth and makes it an all-male event." Combs-Schilling describes asking individual Moroccans about the mother's absence: "If she had known, they agreed, she would have tried to prevent the father from taking the life of the child. As a good mother, she would not, and could not, have understood. They explained that the mother's natural tie to her children makes her a good mother, one whose energies are focused on reproduction and nurturance of individual human beings. . . . [T]he mother could not have performed what was required of humans in order to forge an enduring connection with the divine."[89]

It seems that Bâ challenges all this at its conceptual core, arguing that it is precisely *in* "the mother's natural tie" that humans' "enduring connection with the divine" is forged, for in the absoluteness of maternal *rahma* the unconditionality of God's *rahma*, the excess of mercy and compassion over justice, evident in the very gift of revelation itself, comes to anchor human existence. Ramatoulaye's description of maternal love as that which comprehends the inexplicable, illuminates the darkness, loves without beginning or end, could equally well describe both Quranic discourse and God; indeed, the Quranic word demolishes taboos, puts aside the dictates of pride, and imposes its superiority upon the heart and reason. Moreover, Ramatoulaye portrays maternal love not as a surrender to natural impulses but as an overcoming of rancor, a mastering of self before a higher duty. Because Aïssatou's young man bears the name Ibrahima, is respectful and responsible, and is associated with the law (he is studying to be an attorney), because the sex involved was motivated by neither predation nor vanity, one may see Bâ rewriting the Ibrahim story along the lines of the rest of her novel. She reminds us that God Himself spared the child, putting mercy over law. In doing so, God recognized the strength and ultimately the just demands of natural law, which bind families together. No woman was needed in the Ibrahim story because God acted the mother's part, refusing to put justice (God's right to take the son) before love, mercy, and nature. Identifying the divine with a maternal love "sans commencement ni fin," with a nature "insondable et illimitée," Bâ suggests that divine saying calls every said, even its own, to account, that the reason and justice of any word must be measured against an ethical *rahma* that grounds reason and justice by transcending both. Ramatoulaye's relation to young Aïssatou thus resembles God's relation to humankind each of the times, culminating with Gabriel's messages to Muhummad, that He "embraces" us with his merciful, life-giving word: God has a "stake" (*enjeu*) in humans that only the maternal relation's divestment of love from possessiveness can suggest, a "stake" that overflows comprehension—what accords with a "reason" bound to the calculus of reciprocity.

Ramatoulaye's "pagan revolt" resembles Aunt Nabou's in the sense of being its mirror opposite. The nature Nabou makes an idol is indeed biologism, will to power; her paganism derives from identifying the human with "invading reality like a wild vegetation that absorbs and breaks or pushes back everything around it."[90] The nature Ramatoulaye follows into revolt binds radical immanence, "ligature indestructible," to absolute transcendence: in loving "sans commencement ni fin," the love maternity commands breaks with the imperialistic logic of biologism, embracing the blossoming of an Other's otherness. Here, as in her "Romantic" appreciation of the beach, Ramatoulaye is taken up by nature to the point that nature insinuates into her what overflows conceptuality and finitude, an experience breaching normative categories, in which the sensuous, the immediate, the transcendent, and absolute converge, "désintoxiqu[ant] notre âme" (36).

Through an extreme moral effort, Ramatoulaye subordinates both her personal anger and her investment in conventional notions to the ethical demand of offering young Aïssatou refuge. By making a mother's "pagan revolt" merge with a transcendent, sublime, unitive experience of connection with God's infinite *rahma*, Bâ takes to their radical limits modes of addressing the relationship between ethics and scripture associated with modernist Quranic hermeneutics. "The *modernists* distinguish the pristine faith and way of life of the Prophet and his first community from later manifestations," which introduced historically, culturally contingent notions and practices into the traditions: "To derive the living value system as it was practiced in its sacred origins, modernists require *ijtihad*, individual interpretation of scripture." (Paradoxically, fundamentalists also appeal to *ijtihad* against interpretation through tradition and consensus.)[91] Following modernist hermeneutics, one could easily see "latter manifestations" as a "said" to be assessed by *ijtihad*; certainly, Bâ's condemnation of the Dakar religious community's indifference to the un-Islamic character of Mawdo's and Modou's second marriages fits this model of grounding social reform in a return to the original texts. Erasmus's slogan, "ad fontes" [to the sources], captures the culturally transformative potential of such a hermeneutic.

The implication is that taking any said to be unconditional would be idolatrous; thus, the saying of the Quranic word has precedence over even its own said, the susceptibility of its verbal, syntactic structure to yield "received wisdom." Bâ's position becomes perilously close to Mernissi's, where the idea of "latter manifestations," accommodations to local customs and political necessities, is introduced into the Quranic canon itself.[92] The difference is that, instead of contrasting a pristine message with later accretions, Bâ suggests, in a way that is at once more radical and more orthodox, that the message is the "saying" of mercy, compassion, maternal tenderness animating every one of the "paroles divines."

The transcendence of the ethical does not make all moral determinations equally arbitrary and violent, nor does love's exceeding reason diminish the authority of reason (rather, it frees reason from the violence to which Nietzscheanism would condemn it). After her experience with young Aïssatou, Ramatoulaye decides she must confront "the problem of sexual education" with her younger daughters (87). She finds herself ethically obliged to put into words what her cultural traditions have consigned to silence; thus, the circumstances of material, historical life can alter the substance of the said answerable to saying. But, while subordinating the said to saying may dissociate *fitna* from specific taboos, such as condemning all premarital female sexual experience, it cannot dissociate *fitna* from ethical failure: "The existence of means of contraception must not lead to an unhindered release of desires and instincts. It is through his self-control, his ability to reason, to choose, his power of attachment, that the individual distinguishes himself from the animal" (87). Ramatoulaye does not, as Sarvan implies, refuse to "give her daughters immunity in pleasure" out of unreflective conservativism.[93] Instead, she presents an argument that replicates Ghazali's: the deliberative faculty must subordinate the concupiscent faculty, for human beings are ethical only if the appetites of the animal soul are answerable to justice.

The novel ends with Ramatoulaye anticipating Aïssatou's return and identifying the "active struggle" she has recounted with "the irreversible currents of women's liberation that are lashing the world" (88). The "blossoming" she seeks has no kinship with Modou's metaphysical rebellion; respect for form (order, law, reason) and acknowledgment of one's created, contingent status go together: "I remain persuaded of the inevitable and necessary complementarity of man and woman" (88). Esonwanne sees both a biologism and exclusionary nationalism in Ramatoulaye's insistence, "The success of the family is born of a couple's harmony, as the harmony of multiple instruments creates a pleasant symphony. . . . The success of a nation therefore depends inevitably on the family" (89). He argues that "coherence derive[s] from being associated with the organic: love, monogamous pairs, symphonies, the nation. . . . [O]ther possible units (unpaired or uncoupled) are not viable as constitutive subunits of the nation state."[94] Ramatoulaye does suggest that life as part of a couple and families that derive from and are guided by loving couples are most "choiceworthy," in Aristotle's sense of being the best conditions under which the excellences peculiar to human life can be realized.[95] This does not mean another kind of life cannot be good: Bâ could hardly affirm Aïssatou more forcefully, though the future of Senegal would seem to rest with couples such as Daba and her husband and young Aïssatou and Ibrahima. Similarly, Ramatoulaye does suggest that successful families build successful nations, but her interest in nation-building is not reducible to a nationalism that views the state as an organic collective subject. Rather, the reiteration of moral practices in intimate, everyday life gives rise to a social, public culture that is progressive in the sense of laboring to narrow the distance between the moral and the ethical.

Nonetheless, the connection Esonwanne notes between Ramatoulaye's organic metaphors and her insistence upon the primacy of the couple is important. Bâ would agree with Levinas, "If biology furnishes us the prototype of all these [social] relations, this proves, to be sure, that biology does not represent a purely contingent order of being, unrelated to its essential production."[96] Just as Bâ views not moral discrimination but its absence as violence, so she views biological determinateness not as an arbitrary imposition but as part of the constraint that makes freedom possible. If a teacher expresses *rahma* by caring for the formation of the soul, so God expresses *rahma* by caring for the formation of the body; having a determinate shape does not prevent but enables individual "blossoming." Bâ implies that, whatever justice polygamy may have served in the seventh century, it cannot do justice in the twentieth, for there are not now, for urban, middle-class people, any social conditions that might override the way that the very biological constitution of the human (by means of couples) intersects with the saying of the ethical (in valorizing monogamous marriage).

Bâ rejects the hostility to nature characteristic of much Western academic feminism because she rejects the claim that associating the human with the organic entails assimilating the human into a totalizing metaphysics of presence. On the contrary, the natural is ultimately "insondable et illimitée," and so our embeddedness in the organic anchors us in the unconditional, in love "sans commencement ni fin," which allows us to hear God's saying in ways that command social transformation. Ramatoulaye's "organic" bond with young Aïssatou brings her to redefine *fitna*; her natural tie to her daughters leads her to blend an acceptance of contraceptives with a reiteration of Ghazali's moral discourse (though notably articulated by a woman to women). The organic, so understood, does not naturalize ethnocentricism, but, as Levinas notes, extends its terms to embrace ethical universalism.[97] To be, through the body, part of constraining structures anchors us in transcendence and grants us a freedom, a "blossoming," peculiarly our own because, as Aïssatou tells Mawdo in her letter, the human, as the image of God, is one, at once body and soul, at once determinate, "subordinate" creature and participant, through ethical responsibility, in the absolute transcendence of divine *rahma*.

5

Acculturation and Decolonization in Tsitsi Dangarembga's *Nervous Conditions*

Modern Self-Cultivation and Moral Guilt

Dangarembga's *Nervous Conditions* (1988), an autobiographical novel describing coming of age as a Western-educated Shona woman in Rhodesia in the 1960s and early 1970s, begins with an extraordinary declaration: "I was not sorry when my brother died. Nor am I apologising for my callousness, as you may define it, my lack of feeling."[1] The heroine, Tambu or Tambudzai, does not apologize because there were "reasons" beyond youth that made her unable to feel "sorry," reasons connected to "the events that put [her] in a position to write this account" (1). Her ability to write becomes part of what the story is about, her "escape and Lucia's," her "mother's and Maiguru's entrapment," and Nyasha's perhaps unsuccessful "rebellion" (1). Like *Ulysses* and *À la recherche du temps perdu*, Dangarembga's novel makes its own composition the achievement toward which a central character unknowingly moves. The broadening of imaginative sympathy and the chastening of disillusionment that lead to Tambu's acquisition of identity, however, occur because of her empowering engagement with the very culture that views her own people and their ways with relentless condescension.

Until she is thirteen, Tambu lives on the family homestead with her improvident father, her overworked, undervalued mother, and two younger sisters. Her brother, Nhamo, attends the local mission school through the charity of her uncle, Babamukuru, who is both headmaster and, as eldest brother, head of the extended family. The novel begins with Tambu's description of her inability to understand why her brother disliked walking from the bus stop to the homestead, which leads to a portrait of Tambu's own appreciation of the people and the landscape: "There were always some people with whom to pass ten minutes of the day"; "If you had time you could run off the road into more wooded areas to look for matamba and matunduru. Sweet and sour. Delicious" (2–3). This seemingly idyllic description invites a reading of Western education as alienating Africans from community and nature, which is how some critics frame the issue.[2] Tambu notes, however, that women washed where the river was shallow, because it "was sensibly architectured for doing laundry," but "we were apprehensive about growing so big that we would have to wash there . . . and no longer be able to swim in the deeper, cooler, more interesting pools" (3). Charles Sugnet argues, "Much of the early narrative captures the felt immediacy of the presocialized child; these memories provide Tambudzai with a position from which to judge the adult world."[3] Dangarembga evokes, as Sugnet's phrasing implies, the Romantic trope of "the presocialized child" as "nature's best philosopher," but, unlike in some forms of neo-Romanticism, "felt immediacy" does not stand in opposition to the internal coherence and momentum of rationality. When Nhamo hears his father praise Babamukuru's superior "brains," he repeats conventional platitudes about using intelligence wisely, while Tambu notes, "I was different. I wanted to find out the truth. Did my father mean that Babamukuru was sharp at his lessons?" (5).

Having established a bond between love of freedom, intellectual curiosity, and respect for truth, Dangarembga reveals the impossibility of pursuing such goods on the homestead. Sugnet argues that "Dangarembga explores the specifics of Fanon's insight . . . that the 'native' does not preexist colonization, but is artificially produced by it. Tambudzai's father, Jeremiah, deprived by the British of his ancestral lands, becomes the stereotype of the shiftless 'native.'"[4] Colonization certainly did much economic and psychological violence, but the axiomatic assumption that "the 'native' does not preexist colonization" leads to treating precolonial history and culture as inconsequential in shaping the texture of colonial and postcolonial experience. In Sugnet's reading, the word *Shona* appears only once, in a passing reference to multicultural sources of postcolonial identity, and his bibliography is innocent of any works on African history and culture. By contrast, the historian Elizabeth Schmidt notes, "The origins of African women's subordination are not solely the result of policies imposed by foreign capital and the colonial state. Rather, indigenous and European structures of patriarchal control reinforced and transformed one another."[5] In precolonial Shona society, female labor and reproductive power were controlled by senior men. Since the husband's kin group gave brides-wealth (*lobola*) to the woman's kin group, a wife would address her husband's sisters as *vene* (owners) and after producing a child would not be addressed by her own name but as "mother of — — —."[6] According to Schmidt, the colonial and missionary powers reinforced the internal patriarchy by restricting female financial opportunity, subsidizing low wages to men by exploiting female farm labor, legislating pass laws to restrict female mobility, and promoting a Victorian ideal of the domesticated housewife.[7]

The combined effect of Shona and Western patriarchy shapes Tambu's early life. Like her mother and younger sisters, Tambu must spend hours laboring in the maize fields (7–8); when Nhamo returns, he treats his sisters as servants and disdains the poverty of his home (9–11), yet the family is entirely focused on his future (12). While Babamukuru is in England, 1960–65, family resources are so stretched that Nhamo can continue in school only because his mother makes enough from selling vegetables to pay his fees. As for Tambu, her father asks, "Can you cook books and feed them to your husband?" (15).

Dangarembga takes pains to show why Tambu does not simply internalize the patriarchy: "His intention was to soothe me . . . but I could not see the sense. This was often the case when my father spoke . . . [but] this time . . . I had evidence. Maiguru [Babamukuru's wife] was educated, but did she serve Babamukuru books for dinner? I discovered to my unhappy relief that my father was not sensible" (16). Juliana Makuchi Nfah-Abbenyi argues that, confronted with naturalized gender roles that rest upon "either/or, mind/body dichotomies," Tambu "tries to subvert [patriarchal] ideology" in order to "make both the spheres of home and school *work for her*" [my emphasis].[8] Tambu's ability to contest the patriarchy's designs is linked not just to her memory and experience of "felt immediacy" but also to her capacity to reason: here reason is a means of liberation.[9]

Reasoning, daring to think, finds reinforcement in having available a plurality of models to contemplate. When Tambu's mother declares that to sacrifice and carry burdens is the natural lot of black womanhood, Tambu contrasts her mother with Maiguru: "I decided it was better to be like Maiguru, who was not poor and had not been crushed by the weight of womanhood" (16). While Tambu will come to reconsider this simple view of Maiguru, she is able to assess her mother's words against a more complicated reality. Martha Nussbaum cites the following sentence from Beckett's *Molloy*: "You think you are inventing, and all you do is stammer out your lesson, the remnants of a pensum one day got by heart and long forgotten," and then comments, "This is not a convincing picture either of an individual child's development or of a society's evolution. Children actively select and interpret; and the society around them contains a plurality of active voices, striving to persuade us in new directions. And persuasion, not just manipulation, is at least a part of what explains those changes."[10] When asked in an interview where Tambu's capacity to rebel comes from, Dangarembga replies that it comes from seeing her extended family and from the criticism that follows naturally from regarding her father's actions and words.[11] Dangarembga's delineation of the bond between Tambu's exercise of reason and the example of an educated, comparatively well-off African woman suggests a positive dimension to both reason and modernity. Assuming that Tambu subverts in order to make cultural resources work for her implies that the self's relation to culture should and can only be self-serving; within such an appropriative model of agency, reason can only be "strategic." But equating all reason with instrumental rationality, refusing "any rational adjudicating of competing truth claims because of the inherent undecidability of language," leads to "an irrationalist decisionism" in which whatever *works for the self* becomes, arbitrarily, the measure of all value.[12]

By contrast, Dangarembga, like Bâ, suggests that the acquisition of autonomy, like narrative plot according to Harpham, reconciles law (necessary predication) and freedom. As Riesz documents for Senegal, Schmidt notes that there was considerable indigenous resistance to sending girls to the mission schools because those schools were viewed as breeding "disobedience": "In disproportionate numbers, school girls were refusing to marry the men to whom they had been pledged in childhood."[13] While the mission school sought to inculcate submission and domesticity, some women "used their education as a springboard for resistance to African patriarchal authority—both old and new. Encouraged by their knowledge of alternative values and lifestyles, they insisted upon marrying men of their own choosing or refused to marry altogether. They became teachers, nurses, and domestic servants, using their newly acquired skills to establish independent economic bases."[14]

Tambu's "escape" from the homestead highlights the complex interplay between compromising debts and ambiguous alienations. She feels "unhappy relief" at being able to demonstrate to herself, through reason, her father's lack of sense: relief because she need not see her present situation as inevitable; unhappy because recognizing as conditional contexts that which her family takes to be natural involves a type of impiety or disloyalty. In order to pay the fees for her own education, Tambu cultivates her own maize field. When she discovers that Nhamo has been secretly eating the maize, she attacks him on the Sunday school playground; when the teacher, Mr. Matimba, discovers why Tambu attacks Nhamo, he takes her to Salisbury to sell her maize, where the whites are scandalized to see a girl working rather than in school. Mr. Matimba makes up a story about Tambu being a needy orphan and so receives a donation of ten pounds from a white woman, which he deposits at the school to prevent Tambu's father from expropriating it (20–30). Through a combination of daring self-assertion, "lucky" compassion from a relative stranger (Mr. Matimba) who is linked to Western education, and the presence and colonizing charity of white settlers who had benefited from preferential governmental economic policies,[15] Tambu receives a primary education and so is in a position, when Nhamo dies suddenly in 1968, to assume his place at Babamukuru's mission school. Dangarembga's description of Tambu's delight at her altered fortunes reveals the disquieting connection between the opportunity to gain freedom, nurture intellectual curiosity, and develop her reason and sense of self, on the one hand, and the insinuation of egoism, self-glorification, and instrumental rationality: "My horizons were saturated with me, my leaving, my going. . . . My father, as affably, shallowly agreeable as ever, was insignificant. My mother, my anxious mother, was no more than another piece of surplus scenery to be maintained, of course to be maintained, but all the same superfluous, an obstacle in the path of my departure. As for my sisters, well, they were there. . . . It was up to them to learn the important lesson that circumstances were not immutable, no burden so binding that it could not be dropped. The honour for teaching them this emancipating lesson was mine" (58).

Tambu's aestheticizing of herself recalls Goethe's Wilhelm Meister, Dickens's Pip, and Joyce's Stephen, just as the narrative irony that accentuates the selfishness and condescending alienation implicit in seeing others as "scenery," "obstacles," or audience recalls the narrative irony through which Wilhelm's rebellion against his narrow bourgeois upbringing, Pip's disaffection from Joe and the forge, and Stephen's artful insulation from his family's misery are all presented. Dangarembga follows Goethe, Dickens, and Joyce in challenging an easy conscience about making cultural spheres and material work for an appropriative self. All four writers suggest that moral guilt is justly inextricable from modern self-creation, that such guilt rests in part upon indebtedness to the very people and structures one would move beyond. Just as Tambu's early education depends upon profiting from white settler wealth, so her later education depends upon the wages Babamukuru receives in return for his own assimilation to the colonial order. Likewise, Wilhelm's bourgeois family's wealth finances his initial adventures; Pip's effort at self-making, like Tambu's, has a "tainted" material source; and Stephen grows acutely aware that his education and opportunities come at the expense of his younger siblings. Just as Tambu senses her guilt enough to want to "maintain" her mother, so Pip intermittently resolves to "do something" for Joe, and Wilhelm and Stephen hope to repay others through an art that will raise up their nations (Wilhelm wants to create a German national theater) or "forge an uncreated conscience" that will contest colonizing forces. Dangarembga, again like Goethe, Dickens, and Joyce, underscores the moral guilt intrinsic to the self-creating enterprise without repudiating that enterprise entirely: there *is* something "emancipating" in recognizing that circumstances are not immutable, and Tambu has good reasons for feeling relief, excitement, and anticipation (58).

The Ethical Assessment of Cultural Patterns of Meaning and Value

Sue Thomas usefully notes that the title, *Nervous Conditions*, refers to Sartre's preface to Fanon's *Wretched of the Earth*, in which Sartre links the internalized and "horizonal" violence of the colonized elites to psychopathologies that come from assimilating a culture that denies one's own humanity: "The status of 'native' is a nervous condition introduced and maintained by the settler among colonized people *with their consent*."[16] According to Thomas, consent depends upon the elites' "libidinal investments" in "bewitching master narratives" by which the colonized, like hysterics, "are mastered."[17] As Thomas notes, most of the characters display pathological patterns that can be related to the stress of colonial and patriarchal rule—Babamukuru is a rigid authoritarian workaholic, Maiguru is aggressively self-effacing, Tambu's father is prone to drink, her mother is given to hypochondria, and Babamukuru's daughter Nyasha becomes suicidally anorexic. Similarly, Sugnet observes that characters other than Nyasha "also have trouble eating, and the imagery of eating, digestion, nutrition, vomiting, and excretion provide crucial metaphors for domination and resistance in the novel."[18] These are important motifs. However, there is a danger of oversimplification in treating the narrative patterns that characters invest in as merely oppressive. According to Thomas, Babamukuru and Tambu are psychically deformed by embracing "the myth that an English education represents progress" while Nyasha is anguished because she cannot fit into either "her father's myth of ideal Shona femininity" or "the good compliant 'kaffir' girl" of white Rhodesian ideology.[19] Similarly, there is a danger of oversimplification in treating a character's commitment to narrative unity as predominantly irrational (a matter of "libidinal investment" or an effect of "domination").

Pauline Ada Uwakweh identifies the "liberational quality of voicing" in Dangarembga's novel exclusively with "debunking patriarchy," arguing that Tambu lays claim to her "own" self by making writing a therapeutic form of self-fashioning, "achiev[ing] voice through narration."[20] Sugnet frames the issue in similar terms: "Tambudzai appears destined for co-optation into the educated elite of colonized Rhodesia, but her rising consciousness averts this. . . . Tambudzai's narrative is the story of . . . multiple subordination, antagonism, and politicization; it also narrates the slow unfolding of the many defenses against this process, the hesitations, the fragmentary realizations."[21]

While such a characterization describes well part of what is going on, it discounts any positive aspects of Tambu's engagement with patterns of identity constitutive of Western modernity. It also prevents any evaluation of characters' engagement with indigenous structures of value, either by condemning them as similarly oppressive (Babamukuru's "myth of ideal Shona femininity," for example) or, more simplistically, by valorizing them because they are native. So Thomas would have readers lament Tambu's alienation from Shona culture without discussing anything specific to that culture other than its sexism. Similarly, Nfah-Abbenyi argues that "knowledge of her roots, history, and culture turns out to be the most important and the most rewarding thing in Tambudzai's life," but she explores Shona culture and history not at all; instead, she claims that women "as storytellers and custodians of history" subvert cultural texts "to their own physical, historical, and spiritual advantage," while noting that some women "reject the obvious [Shona?] naturalization of gendered roles, sexuality, and women's oppression" even as others, like Tambu's mother, inexplicably do not.[22] At best, such readings divide indigenous traditions into mastering, patriarchal narratives and repressed, subversive narratives, but even then, the only value of narrative is its disruptive capability.[23]

What is missing, in addition to any Levinasian concern that a self organized around self-justifying freedom might be unjust or colonizing, is any engagement with what Ricoeur describes as the inevitable relationship between "personal identity and narrative identity" that follows from "the *temporal* dimension of the self as well as of action as such," for temporality, no less than embodiment, is integral to the intersubjective constitution of ethical selfhood.[24] Ricoeur notes the paradox that "the interconnection of events constituted by emplotment" permits one "to integrate with permanence in time what seems to be its contrary in the domain of sameness-identity, namely diversity, variability, discontinuity, and instability." Because we cannot evade a narrative identity, the question of *which* narrative becomes inevitably an ethical one, for "narrative, which is never ethically neutral, proves to be the first *laboratory of moral judgment,*" since "[i]n narrativizing the aim of the true life, narrative identity gives it the recognizable features of characters loved or respected."[25]

Interpretative frameworks that treat narrative identity as somehow optional or as invariably oppressive are conceptually inadequate for the task of delineating Tambu's growth, which asks to be viewed as a product of her engagement with *ambiguous* powers of narrative patterns derived from both Western modernity and Shona oral tradition. When Tambu resolves to plant her maize field, to assert herself against circumstances that would deprive her of an education, she "mumble[s] adoring, reverent prayers" to her recently deceased grandmother (17). Schmidt notes that in precolonial Shona culture grandmothers held a particularly revered place and that women acquired influence through their contact with the spirit world.[26] Through prayer, Tambu calls ancestral spirits (*vadzimu*) to her aid. While Dangarembga does suggest that self-discipline can be carried to "hysterical," pathological excess, she also suggests that it *is* desirable to consolidate the predisposition to work into a habit: some degree of cultural formation is empowering, just as is some degree of narrative identification. Tambu's grandmother "had been an inexorable cultivator of land," with whom Tambu spent "many productive hours working." By praising Tambu's "predisposition towards working," the grandmother "consolidated it in [her] as a desirable habit" (17). Because the grandmother fostered in Tambu both the technical skill and the moral habits necessary to produce maize, she really does empower Tambu from beyond the grave.

Tambu's responses to the grandmother's tales, moreover, show that this empowering process of "formation" depends upon the active engagement of the person being formed. Dangarembga relates the grandmother's account of how Tambu's great-grandfather, "rich" in "cattle, large fields, and four wives," was dispossessed by "[w]izards well versed in treachery and black magic [who] came from the south" (18); then Babamukuru "was educated in their wizardry," worked hard, and became "well enough salaried to reduce a little the meagreness of his family's existence" (19). David Beach notes that Shona oral traditions "are full of accounts of poor hunters, cattle thieves, and even refugees from witchcraft accusations arriving in a strange territory and by bravery and cunning becoming the local ruler, dispossessing the existing one."[27] To a degree, Babamukuru's biography is assimilated to this pattern, but with the subversive implications severely muted. Dangarembga carefully modulates Tambu's assessment of her grandmother's narrative so that the young girl's enchantment with "a fairy-tale of reward and punishment" is balanced by the mature woman's recognition that the message "endure and obey" was calculated not to increase one's ambitions "beyond a manageable level" (19). Sugnet notes that "the grandmother's story suggests that surviving by accommodation may sometimes be the only mode of resistance available."[28]

While this is the case, the story presents an ideal of self-empowerment serving ends beyond self-aggrandizement. By learning the "wizardry" of the colonizers, Babamukuru acquires new sources of power, which—like the old sources of power (cattle, fields, wives)—are justified through providing prosperity and security to the kinship network. Similarly, the primary reason Shona women cultivated maize was neither to resist patriarchy nor to accommodate themselves to it, but to sustain their families, to do the work that allows ethical bonds and intimacy to endure. While insisting, in the manner of Shona oral tales of impoverished exiles acquiring power and wealth, that circumstances are not immutable, the grandmother's story crucially portrays wizardry as good or bad depending upon whether it is used in a sociable, generous manner to increase the prosperity of a larger community or to dispossess others, to serve narrow acquisitive or "devouring" interests. In this way, the grandmother draws upon distinctions between good and bad magic, ethical and unethical self-empowerment, common throughout sub-Saharan Africa.[29] Instead of taking the possessive individual or the desiring subject as the point of departure, African moral discourse views both "constructs" as emblematic of dehumanizations the West has embraced in order to gain illegitimate power.

Nevertheless, the story remains problematic. While Tambu must come to recognize what is compromising and misleading in the story, only the experience of seeking to make the story's narrative her own allows her to separate what is a fairy tale from what is not. Because the story has "a tantalising moral that increased your aspirations" (19), it allows Tambu to see her future in an idealized version of Babamukuru's past and thus helps sustain her efforts to grow maize and to study, efforts that ultimately enable her to see the limitations in both the grandmother's account and Babamukuru's "success."

Dangarembga suggests, moreover, that an interactive engagement with narrative entails not only the disruption *and re-formation* of one's own self-perception, but also an ultimately enriching recasting of one's place in the social matrix. Ricoeur argues, "The action-configuration that we are calling life plans stems . . . from our moving back and forth between far-off ideals, which have to be made more precise, and the weighing of the advantages and disadvantages of the choice of a given life plan on the level of practice. It is in this sense that Gadamer interprets Aristotelian *phronêsis.*"[30]

Tambu arrives at the mission school expecting "to find another self, a clean, well-groomed, genteel self" (58–59), and links her entry into a world where she would "be encouraged to consider questions that had to do with survival of the spirit, the creation of consciousness" with her uncle's generosity and wisdom: "I was going to be developed in the way that Babamukuru saw fit, which in the language I understood at the time meant well" (59). Because Tambu's self-esteem in Ricoeur's sense[31] is tied to a narrative in which Babamukuru plays an uncomplicated positive role, she is distressed by Nyasha's lack of gratitude (60) both for an education and for living in material circumstances that at first dazzle her: "Babamukuru was God, therefore I had arrived in Heaven. . . . The absence of dirt was proof of the other-worldly nature of my new home" (70). But just as habituation to middle-class comforts can incline one to forget "how ordinary humans existed—from minute to minute and from hand to mouth," that same habituation allows Tambu, in time, to realize that "the antiseptic sterility that [her] aunt and uncle strove for could not be attained beyond an illusory level" (71). So familiarity with her aunt and uncle allows Tambu to recognize in Maiguru's "fussing, cooing and clucking" (76) a strained imitation of domestic felicity and in Babamukuru's paternalism a disconcerting rigidity and self-importance. Thus we hear both a credulous and a disillusioned Tambu in such passages as this: "[M]y heart swelled with gratitude as he impressed upon me the great extent of the sacrifice he had made in leaving his work to fetch me from the homestead that afternoon, impressing upon me particularly that the work he had left to fetch me was the work that paid my school fees and bought the food that I was to eat in his house" (87).

Dangarembga explores subtly Tambu's efforts to fend off or reinterpret the concrete daily experiences that undermine her preestablished view of Babamukuru and Maiguru and thus her preestablished view of her own story; in particular, Tambu views Nyasha, whose disbelief in her father's divinity involves both daily contact with him and her acculturation to Western modernity (she is reading *Lady Chatterley's Lover* when Tambu arrives), with a mixture of envy and fear: "Everything about her spoke of alternatives and possibilities that if considered too deeply would wreak havoc with the neat plan I had laid out for my life" (76).

On the one hand, Dangarembga explores how much our need for certainty leads us to push aside all that in the concrete, sensuous particularity of life contests our notions. Tambu observes, "But in those days it was easy for me to leave tangled thoughts knotted, their loose ends hanging. I didn't want to reach the end of those mazes, because there, I knew, I would find myself and I was afraid that I would not recognise myself after having taken so many confusing directions" (116). The imagery of following threads of thoughts through mazes again connects genuine enlightenment with *following* the nonarbitrary predication of reason, as opposed to the mere affirmation of desire, difference, or resistance. But we are reluctant to think for ourselves, to allow the self-esteem that follows from our interpretation of our pursuit of our life plan to rest upon "an exercise of judgment which, at best, can aspire to plausibility in the eyes of others," even though our "own conviction borders on the sort of experiential evidence which, at the end of book 6 of the *Nichomachean Ethics*, made *phronêsis* comparable to *aisthêsis*."[32] Precisely because an identity bound to *phronêsis* needs the (always provisional) confirmation of other people and of ongoing experience, we are reluctant to surrender the comfort of secure theoretical demarcations that would seem to free us from dependence upon our own fallible interpretive abilities. Tambu had been educated to believe, and a genuine part of her wants to believe, that sin had "well-defined edges," was "square rather than round so that you knew where it ended" (150). When she feels bereft of that belief, she also feels alienated from herself, doubtful that the self she would be justifies the self-esteem she would feel.

On the other hand, Dangarembga suggests, like Unger, that while we are inevitably embedded in contexts, we are able to grasp their limits and so revise them.[33] Tambu's alienation is not the inevitable consequence of her victimization by Western ideology but another step in her continuing growth. Part of Tambu genuinely delights in the expansion of her intellectual and imaginative powers, a process that links self-development to the full realization of what lies implicit in speech, a capacity for intersubjective rationality, ethical complexity, and friendship passing into love. Tambu's growing friendship with Nyasha is likened to a "long, involved conversation, full of guileless openings up and intricate lettings out and lettings in." For the first time, Tambu declares, "I grew to be fond of someone of whom I did not wholeheartedly approve" (78). Tambu's expanding appreciation of complexities is tied to her affective bonds with particular people. After witnessing a scene in which Babamukuru accuses Nyasha of being a "whore" for talking at night alone to a white boy, and she strikes him after he hits her (110–18), Tambu feels "sorry" for her uncle while remaining "impressed with Nyasha's resiliency, though" (119).

Just as Tambu must negotiate the alienating and oppressive aspects of Western modernity, so she must likewise negotiate negative aspects of Shona traditions. Babamukuru reacts to his daughter's "disobedience" with violence because it threatens the image of himself that he constantly seeks to have reaffirmed in elaborate displays of gratitude and deference. The women likewise tend to locate themselves in rigidly confining identities. After witnessing Maiguru snubbing Lucia, Tambu's mother's sister, after she appeals for Maiguru's help in resisting the efforts of the men to remove her from the homestead because she has been impregnated by another improvident relation, Takesure, and because she has been sleeping with Tambu's father, Tambu reflects that what is needed is "a combination of Maiguru's detachment and Lucia's direction." But that will not happen because "the matter" "stung too saltily, too sharply and agonisingly the sensitive images that the women had of themselves, images that were really no more than reflections," but reflections and myths that the women were frightened not to recognize as themselves because "generations of threat and assault and neglect had battered these myths into the extreme, dividing reality they faced, of the Maigurus or the Lucias" (138). In the cultural imagination structuring, paradoxically, both Maiguru's and Lucia's self-images, there is a polarization between two internally complex models of female identity: on the one hand, self-effacing, obedient, respectable, but genuinely caring, responsible women; on the other hand, women like Lucia, irresponsibly free, self-destructive, but refreshingly self-assertive. Of course, part of this need to identify with narrow, constricting cultural models may be attributed to the psychic violence of colonialism. In his puritanical authoritarianism, Babamukuru resembles the fathers in Samuel Butler's *The Way of All Flesh* and John Steinbeck's *East of Eden*. Colonial oppression may certainly exacerbate his need to be recognized as manly.

Similarly, Maiguru's willingness to "coo and cluck" may be linked to her desire to replicate Western middle-class interior decor.

However, both the narrow cultural images themselves and the desire to reflect them in narrow and self-impoverishing ways also reveal the abiding influence of Shona precolonial patterns of identity and value. As head of the extended family, Babamukuru is in the position of ruler. Shona rulers were "supposed to be physically perfect and to commit suicide" if they ceased to be so; they were supposed to be "hidden from the view of the public, speaking to visitors through a window." Visitors were supposed crawl toward the ruler "through a courtyard littered with cattle dung. Elaborate flattery, *muzvam-barara*, paid to the ruler also implied a link with crawling."[34] Babamukuru expects, and usually receives, ritualistically extravagant flattery, even from Lucia. When, after considerable manipulation by Lucia, Babamukuru offers her a job as a cook and the opportunity to get an education, she kneels and intones, "You have done a great deed. Truly, we could not survive without you. Those foreign places, those places you went, did not make you forget us. No! They enabled you to come back and perform miracles!" (158–59). There is a Bakhtinian, double-voiced, parodic dimension to this speech, but Lucia reproduces the precolonial pattern of offering flattery in return for favors even as she cunningly uses and even mocks that pattern.

The linguistic enforcement of hierarchy through flattery is linked to a spatial enforcement of hierarchy through the ruler's withholding or concealing his presence. Beach points out that the word *zimbabwe* (capital) refers to the stone walls that shielded the living quarters of the wealthy and the elite from the view of ordinary people at the trading cities of Great Zimbabwe (c. 1250–1500), Torwa (c. 1450–1700), and Mutapa (c.1500–1700).[35] Babamukuru asserts his power by literally and metaphorically shielding himself from view. At the mission, he frequently does not appear at dinner and seldom allows anyone to enter his office. Further, though the mission is located within easy driving distance from the homestead, Tambu sees it for the first time when she goes there to live, and the rest of her relatives never see it. Dangarembga's description of the self-impoverishing concern with presenting controlled images to others and the fear of not recognizing oneself in those images suggests that the entwinement of identity and hierarchy, the need for a performative, public reconfirmation of identity and hence a gnawing insecurity and obsession with others performing the roles that confirm one's own position may well be a pathology intensified by colonialism, but one with deep roots in Shona history. Indeed, an elaborate etiquette of precedence regarding the offering of a water dish for hand washing (40–41), ritual greetings (72, 131), sleeping arrangements, and access to the best food (132–36) interweaves identity and hierarchy in ways that facilitate the reproduction of patriarchy. During the Christmas 1969 holidays, twenty-four people's cooking and cleaning needs fall (naturally) to thirteen women, two of whom are pregnant and four of whom are under ten (133).

Tambu's perception of Lucia's and Maiguru's conflict is remarkable not just because she sees them as imprisoned by the images they insist upon recognizing as themselves, but also because she imagines how the best traits of each might be combined. Tambu is the beneficiary of an aesthetic education that allows her to conceive of images different from the ones that have long been naturalized all around her, to visualize ways of living and thinking that she herself has never seen. Because aesthetic experience opens us to the heterogeneity of possible forms, it disrupts the fictive conceptual totalities that would limit formation to what has already been culturally sanctioned or stigmatized. Because aesthetic experience, especially reading narratives, involves encountering the felt immediacy, the demands and choices of an imagined Other, an aesthetic education insinuates into us the question of what kind of formation is most "choiceworthy." The growth of Tambu's imagination, and thus her ability to question received images, is connected with immersion in a world of (Western) reading. In addition to her lessons, she reads in Nyasha's "various and extensive library" "everything from Enid Blyton to the Brontë sisters" and is "filled with gratitude to the authors for introducing [her] to places where reason and inclination were not at odds" (93).

Tambu's reading has usually been seen in terms of "seduction" into "bourgeois feminist individualist leanings,"[36] or "alienation" because of assimilation to "imported educational structures . . . totally unsuitable to African . . . social contexts."[37] Dangarembga does note the escapist and egoistical dimensions of this reading: Tambu likes to think of her transfer to the mission as a "reincarnation." She invests "robust energy in approximating to [her] idea of a young woman of the world." She thinks of reading as "a centripetal time, with [her] at the centre," and Nyasha criticizes her for reading too many fairy tales and not enough history, about "real people and their sufferings" (92–93). While this strand is important, it is not the only one. Tambu's delight in entering imaginatively into other worlds leads to a broadening of (vicarious) experience that involves a broadening of reflection and a movement out of herself: "I was meeting, outside myself, many things that I had thought about ambiguously; things that I had always known existed in other worlds although the knowledge was vague" (93). Because narrative, as Ricoeur argues, "proves to be the first *laboratory of moral judgment,*" Tambu acquires, through the heterogeneity of "images" that reading offers her, an increasing ability to see the calcifying effects upon others and ultimately upon herself of impoverished, rigid self-images, of threadbare or distorted ideals. It is not just, as Nfah-Abbenyi rightly notes, that Tambu is "simultaneously not quite an insider and not quite an outsider" of two cultures, one colonizing the other.[38] Rather, she comes to acquire an increasingly nuanced, reflective capacity for practical judgment, for *phronêsis,* that will ultimately empower her to assume rational direction of her own life's narrative unity by allowing her, in Levinas's terms, to assess the moral within any culture against the ethical demanded of all cultures.

Situated as she is between Western and Shona patriarchy, Tambu might well feel "gratitude" to those who introduce her "to places where reason and inclination were not at odds." Indeed, being able to imagine such a place may be the first step in coming to interrogate critically the contexts in which one is placed. When Thomas cites this passage in support of the thesis that "English education seduces Tambu," she displaces "inclination" with "desire": Tambu "is introduced 'to places where reason and inclination [desire] were not at odds.'"[39] Inclination, however, need not be the same as desire. Desire may be understood as what is resistant to, an adversary of, acculturation and deliberation—if desire is understood as drive, a presocial impulse toward pleasure, gratification, will to power. An inclination, by contrast, may be cultivated by the kind of deliberation that issues from the ethical relation. It may be the product of reflection, conversation, intersubjective experience, and a temporally extended and coherent (i.e., narratively shaped) ethical life. Understood this way, an inclination may be what desire becomes after the Other robs our exuberant, unselfconscious, spontaneous freedom of its innocence. If inclinations emerge from reasoned deliberations about ethical life, from *phronêsis* itself, as Aristotle suggests, then the reading that allows Tambu to imagine "places where reason and inclination were not at odds" may be, even in their utopian dimensions, genuinely emancipatory, allowing her to imagine a political order in which the seemingly irreconcilable tensions of her current life might be overcome.

Similarly, while Tambu's reading is in some ways alienating, alienation can be conducive to perceiving and moving beyond narrowness and oppression. Gadamer points out that understanding other people, other cultures, requires an alienation from familiar contexts that should not be confused with their repudiation: "If a prejudice becomes questionable in view of what another person or a text says to us, this does not mean that it is simply set aside. . . . In fact our own prejudice is properly brought into play by being put at risk. . . . Transposing ourselves consists neither in the empathy of one individual for another nor in subordinating another person to our own standards; rather, it involves rising to a higher universality that overcomes not only our own particularity but also that of the other," which is possible because "the horizon of the present is continually in the process of being formed because we are continually having to test all our prejudices."[40] Gadamer's account draws upon Hegel, the same source that Abiola Irele draws upon to note that the academic convention of lamenting Africa's contact with the West as "alienating" feeds into a "romantic . . . cultural nationalism" that neglects the "positive significance" of alienation as formulated by Hegel: "It is through the active confrontation of matter by mind that culture and thought are produced." Thus "the notion of alienation" lies behind "all becoming": "In cultural terms, it implies a willed movement out of the self and a purposive quest for new horizons of life and experience."[41] Tambu's alienation through reading English literature has, in part, this sort of "positive significance."

This is not to say that it lacks negative significance: Tambu is led to feel superior to her mother, and she feels guilty about that, just as she feels guilty about speaking English rather than Shona (202–3). Irele notes that while every civilization experiences alienation, Africa's alienation is shaped by forced contact with modernity through colonization: "Hence our mixed feelings, the troubled sense of acceptance and rejection, of a subjective disposition that is undermined by the objective facts of our life. There is something of a paradox here, for the intensity of the ambivalence we demonstrate in our response to Europe and Western civilization is in fact a measure of our emotional tribute; it is expressive, in a profound way, of the cultural hold Europe has secured upon us—of the alienation it has imposed upon us as a historical fate."[42] The nuances of Dangarembga's prose both reflect and explore the reasons for these "mixed feelings." The "positive significance" of Tambu's alienation cannot be simply reduced to disreputable motives (a desire to "capitalize" on her education) or irrationalism (her investments in English education "are certainly fueled by matrophobia, that is, fear of becoming like her mother").[43] Since her mother is overworked, unappreciated, constantly pregnant, and cheated on, and she has no prospects of anything better, it is not pathological for Tambu to fear becoming like her.

Even the self-aestheticizing egoism involved in Tambu's reading is complex. She observes, "With the egotistical faith of fourteen short years . . . I expected this era to be significantly profound and broadening. . . . I expected my sojourn to fulfill all my fourteen-year-old fantasies" (92–93). This emphasis on being fourteen raises the question of how much of Tambu's moral egotism and conceptual egoism may be attributed to Western individualism, to the "luck" of her privilege, and how much may be attributed to the ways of experiencing subjectivity common to fourteen-year-olds. On the homestead, the egotism interwoven with being fourteen would be severely discouraged. At the mission, it is indulged to an extent: "It was a time of sublimation with me as the sublimate" (93). The energy Tambu puts into reading, and thus into the expansion of her imaginative and reflective capacities, depends upon believing that her self is important enough to cultivate. For all its limitations and injustices, Western education provides an institutional space within which such beliefs and such capacities may be reinforced. Since Tambu's own narrative calls attention to her own egotism, we know that the limited indulgence of egotism implicit in her adolescent self-cultivation does not leave her permanently self-absorbed. On the contrary, the energy she pours into her own aesthetic education ultimately allows her to portray self-aestheticization as no less narrow an effort to become the "reflection" of an "image" than the selves Maiguru and Lucia would take, like hairshirts, upon themselves. Nor it is ultimately clear that Tambu would have been better advised to follow Nyasha's example and disdain "fairy tales" in favor of "real people and real suffering." Nyasha's rebellion "may not in the end have been successful" (the novel ends with her in a hospital on the brink of death from anorexia).

What is clear is that the opportunity to develop her mind ultimately leads Tambu to a more reflective, and so more valuable, connection with others, and that the best intellectual development is mediated by friendship. When Tambu scores well enough on an exam of general knowledge to receive a scholarship to an elite multiracial high school, she attributes her success to Nyasha: "With [her] various and exotic library to digest, with having to cope with her experimental disposition, her insistence on alternatives, her passion for transmuting the present into the possible; having to cope with all this, which I did at a purely intellectual level, not because I thought it was rational but because it was amusing and I loved my cousin and admired her, having coped with these intellectual challenges . . . , I was far ahead of my peers in both general knowledge and general ability" (178). Friendship, in the sense delineated above, is crucial not just to Tambu's academic success. It is also crucial to her ability to make a potentially egocentric, isolating self-esteem continuous with the development of ethical solicitude. It turns the novel's metaphors of eating ("digesting" a "various and exotic library") in a positive direction, linking "digestion," appropriating external "nutrients" for one's own growth, with "love" and "admiration," with the displacement of egotism into delight in a shared life with someone we justly admire.

Here "to digest" has neither the connotation of being force-fed nor the connotation of devouring predation. What one "digests" through taking into oneself the "various and exotic library" is first of all an appreciation for the "various and exotic," an affirmation of difference. Coming to value difference derives from the concrete experience of how "love" and "admiration" for a particular Other emerge from "having to cope with" the Other's "experimental disposition, her insistence on alternatives," for the friend's discourse and very being disrupts totalities, economies of the Same. But what motivates the disruption—and merits admiration—is a "passion for transmuting the present into the possible," a measuring of the moral against the demands of the ethical.

What we admire in the friend is the constitution of her subjectivity through subjection to the ethical relation, and what we "cope with" is trying to be a worthy interlocutor. Our self-esteem is bound both to solicitude for the one we "love" and to the transformation of ourselves into something other than what we were. Ricoeur argues that solicitude is not "added on to self-esteem from outside"; rather, it "unfolds the dialogic dimension of self-esteem," for "self-esteem and solicitude cannot be experienced or reflected upon without the other."[44] In any discourse on agency, the crucial emphasis is "on the verb, on being-able-to-do, to which corresponds on the ethical plane, being-able-to-judge. The question is then whether the mediation of the other is not required along the route from capacity to realization. . . . It is indeed just this mediating role that is celebrated by Aristotle in his treatise on friendship (*philia* in the *Nicomachean Ethics* 8–9)."[45]

Nyasha plays the "mediating role" that Ricoeur delineates in his reading of Aristotle, where the desire for a good life passes into a concern with justice, because "being-able-to-do" is impossible without "being-able-to-judge," and "being-able-to-judge" is predicated upon the conversation and example of the

Other who rightly inspires love and admiration: "If the good and happy man needs friends, it is because friendship is an 'activity' (*energeia*), which is obviously a 'becoming.' . . . Friendship, therefore, works toward establishing the conditions for the realization of life, considered in its *intrinsic goodness and its basic pleasure.*"[46]

Because, on a small scale, the ideal is made real in friendship, the experience of friendship provides a rational basis for imagining "transmuting the present into the possible," for imagining a community in which such friendship would no longer be the privilege of the lucky few, in which the walls constructed by self-impoverishing, self-imprisoning "images" could at last come down, allowing life "in its *intrinsic goodness and its basic pleasure*" to be experienced as broadly as possible. Both in Dangarembga's novel and through the community it would establish with readers, what George Eliot calls the "incalculably diffusive" effect of "unhistoric acts," of individual lives shaped into ethical, rational practice, reveal themselves to contribute mightily to what "growing good of the world" there is, to things being "not so ill with you and me as they might have been."[47]

Good conversation and good reading lead Tambu to be able to imagine more than the given, for, as Wolfgang Iser has suggested,[48] the fictive and the imaginative together allow us to figure alternatives, to nurture an "experimental disposition." Through an education of the imagination that is simultaneously an education of the critical facilities, Tambu cultivates a practical rationality that allows her to recognize the self-defeating rigidities of received identities and dogmatic thinking, and so allows her to recognize and contest the colonizing dimensions of that same education.

Sugnet acknowledges that even after locating "sources of Tambudzai's strength in women's solidarity and childhood's 'deep places,'" he suspects "there's something about the level of consciousness she achieves that's unaccounted for in the text of her narrative," which leads him to speculate that the context of "the national struggle," "available to Dangarembga in 1984 [when the manuscript was completed] (but not to Tambudzai in 1974) [when the narrative ends]" may help account for the difference.[49] We are arguing, on the contrary, that the text accounts for the narrator's *later* "level of consciousness." First, the narrative shows how what Sugnet calls the "felt immediacy" tied to bodily materiality grounds a capacity for autonomous and ethically constituted reasoning, irreducible to desire or interest, that allows one to contest the justice of cultural prescriptions and assumptions. Second, the narrative shows how the positive effects of an aesthetic education, alienation, and friendship—interacting with and building upon what "felt immediacy" engenders—stimulate imagination, encourage the ethical evaluation of moral practice, and thus help constitute a practical rationality quite capable of a "transcendent" level of consciousness.

Overcoming the Collapse of Decolonization into Self-Loathing

In developing a "transcendent" practical rationality, Tambu is not "alienated" from Shona forms of thought at their most productive, but rather reconnected with them. Tambu comes, with extreme reluctance, to question Babamukuru's unequivocal rightness and thus the "image" she would recognize as herself. But she is brought to do so after Lucia breaks into the meeting of senior males, the *dare* (136)—literally, public meeting place for men[50]—that would decide her fate, and there rebukes all the men and especially her sometimes lover, Takesure. Babamukuru decides that Lucia's outrageous self-assertion falls within a pattern of family disasters which he attributes to the failure of Tambu's father and mother to have a church wedding. He then proposes such a wedding, the others comply, and Tambu is assigned the role of bridesmaid. As the wedding day approaches, Tambu finds herself horrified at the thought of a ceremony that would make "such a joke of my parents, my home and myself" (149). Sally McWilliams implies that what Tambu objects to is Babamukuru's colonizing insistence that "a Christian wedding" will "right the wrong of only having had a traditional Shona ceremony," which makes her resistance a matter of affirming the culture of the colonized against the colonizer.[51] Sugnet describes the episode in similar terms.[52] Dangarembga, however, specifically situates Babamukuru's action within a Shona cultural context and shows that, at the time, Tambu has little use for Shona customs. After Lucia's public attack on male authority, Tambu's father links her conduct to other family misfortunes and declares that these misfortunes "are coming from somewhere. It's obvious. They are being sent. And they must be made to go back. . . . It is a matter for a good medium. A good medium to do the ceremony properly with everything—beer, a sacrificial ox, everything" (146). Babamukuru objects to a ritual cleansing by witch doctors, but he picks up the idea that their misfortunes are being "sent" and comes up with the church wedding (146–47). Babamukuru puts a Christian gloss on Tambu's father's self-serving, "magical" explanation for family misfortunes; in effect, he accepts his brother's logic.

Just as the ceremony has both Shona and Christian roots, so the women's resistance to it draws on both Shona and Western traditions. A "practical" avoidance of theoretical rigidity was part of precolonial Shona culture: Beach notes that the rule "of avoidance of one's totem was generally observed, . . . but in cases where avoidance might mean serious hardship there were ways around it. . . . Aspiring spirit mediums were tested severely before being accepted as genuine. . . . [T]he only Teve ruler known to have been asked to commit suicide (because he had lost a tooth) refused on the grounds that this was a silly custom. . . . [M]uzvambarara, flattery, was also known to mean deceit and hypocrisy."[53] The irrationality of both Tambu's father's proposal and Babamukuru's is evident to all the women. A senior aunt, Tete, exhibits skepticism by asking, as she shakes with laughter, "And now shall we have a cleansing or a wedding? . . . Tell us, Maiguru, which is the better cure for [Tambu's father's] self-indulgence? Those men, aiwa! Those men!" (148). She regards both suggestions as a wonderful satire on male folly. Tambu, meanwhile, explicitly rejects the cleansing ceremony for Western reasons: "The more I saw of worlds beyond the homestead the more I was convinced that the further we left the old ways behind the closer we came to progress" (147). It is notable (and surprising to Tambu) that Nyasha, the most westernized woman, expresses the most disapproval of alienation from the old ways: "It's bad enough . . . when a country gets colonised, but when the people do as well!" (147).[54]

Nyasha is the lone female defender of "the old ways," not because she believes in them but because she accepts the logic of what Irele calls "cultural nationalism," the idea—derived, as Irele notes, from Herder, Fichte, and other modern Western sources—that "culture" expresses a people's national "spirit,"[55] and so, Nyasha reasons, to fail to give what she takes to be Shona tradition public deference would be to accept being colonized. Missing from such "cultural nationalism" is any sense of how heterogeneous any culture's traditions are, and how practical skepticism about cultural claims can itself be among the traditions a culture transmits. Dangarembga suggests that Western cultural relativism's uncritical valorization of "folkways"—which Nyasha articulates, paradoxically, in the cause of resisting a colonization of the mind—actually ignores indigenous critical traditions (to say nothing of the "native's" capacity for practical rationality). Nyasha seems to participate in Western ignorance by perceiving in Tete's irreverent laughter only an effect of colonialism. Although the condescension in colonially educated Tambu's resistance to the ceremony is evident, the congruence between Tambu's and Tete's attitudes suggests that the critical spirit in Western rationalism is not foreign to Shona culture. In fact, that critical spirit empowers Tete to see how the men are using cultural beliefs (indigenous and Western) to reinforce their authority while evading answerability to others. Tete's laughter, the indifference to her satire of whether they will "have a cleansing or a wedding," implies that cultural practices are not self-justifying. The joke, from Tete's point of view, is that neither a cleansing nor a wedding can do more than reinforce the patterns of ethical evasion that have "sent," and so will continue to "send," disasters to the family.

Moreover, the skepticism, or practical reasoning, that Tambu arrives at, in part through her Western education, is already implicit in Lucia's cunning manipulation of Babamukuru's self-image, in the women's laughter at the schemes of Tambu's father and Babamukuru, in Maiguru's use of her time in England "accompanying her husband" to earn a master's degree (101–2).[56] This does not mean, however, that Shona culture can be bifurcated into standard postmodern oppositions between the dominant and the subversive, the accommodating and the resistant. Tambu's critical understanding is linked to a loving understanding and honoring of her family. Tambu perceives, like Tete, the irrationality of thinking that any ceremony might cure what is wrong at the homestead. While there may indeed be rational insight implicit in traditions of calling upon the aid of one's ancestors, this thinly Christianized cleansing ceremony represents, for both Tete and Tambu, magical thinking at its worst—an evasion of moral responsibility that will ensure the reproduction of "misfortunes." Such a critique implies, on both Tete's and Tambu's part, a recognition of the primacy of the ethical: nothing can substitute for its absence. Tambu thinks, "[T]he whole performance was ridiculous. The whole business reduced my parents to the level of stars of a comic show, the entertainers. I did not want to see them brought down like that" (163). Significantly, Tambu does not want to see her parents "brought down" even though neither parent has shown her particular affection or contributed to the realization of her aspirations. Dangarembga, like Nwapa, Alkali, and Bâ, goes to pains to make clear that the ethical relation is not predicated upon reciprocity or solidarity; rather, it is, as Levinas insists, asymmetrical because it is unconditional. Again like Nwapa, Alkali, and Bâ, Dangarembga insists that the ethical is articulated bodily, somatically, because it is anarchic, prior to conceptualization. Tambu's body refuses to get up the morning of the wedding despite Babamukuru's commands and against her conscious will (166–68). Tambu's "hysterical" breakdown suggests that the body conveys moral knowledge that contests unjust cultural demands.

This "hysteria" is usually seen as physiological resistance to colonization, an analogue of Nyasha's eating disorder. Sugnet argues that the novel would teach that it is "better to have symptoms than to digest your Englishness too easily," for the symptom manifests "an involuntary inability to succumb completely to oppression," even as he warns against tendencies in McWilliams's similar reading to view "these forms of resistance as consciously controlled heroics. Nyasha may well die of her bulimia."[57] The symptoms certainly express involuntary bodily resistance, but what is being resisted is not simply, or even primarily, what is done to oneself, but what is done to those one loves. Sugnet acknowledges Nyasha's love for her father, and so her symptom, like Tambu's, reflects the precedence of being-for-another over self-love. Part of what she cannot stomach must be what colonialistic oppression has done to, and made of, him—and he is for her emblematic of all the others psychically brutalized by power relations whose legitimacy she cannot, with an increasingly pathological literalness, swallow. A visceral, bodily articulated concern for others, rather than just or mainly a chafing at restraints placed upon oneself, gives rise both to the symptom and to critical, skeptical insight. Because her love of her parents allows her to see what is ethically indefensible in Babamukuru's conduct in organizing her parents' wedding, Tambu begins to see him as less than ideal. Similarly, when he brutally punishes Tambu for "disobedience," Maiguru leaves him for a time (significantly, she does not leave because of what he has done to *her*—habitually patronizing or ignoring her), and she returns assertive enough to challenge his reasoning when he would have Tambu decline the scholarship she is awarded to an elite high school (180–81). Maiguru acquires a degree of self-empowerment not because her own oppression becomes too much but because she cannot be ethically indifferent to the injustice done another. It is not in making cultural material *work for* oneself, but in responding to the ethical call that a resistance disentangled from self-love and self-aestheticization becomes possible.

Of course, the narrative link between Tambu's resistance and Maiguru's self-assertion might be viewed as suggesting an infectious quality to modern destabilizations of patriarchal power. Likewise, Tambu's "hysterical" refusal to participate in the wedding might be read as a form of self-violence that fits into the patterns of internalized violence or "horizontal" violence among the colonized elite as described by Sartre. Sartre argues that self-violence and violence against one's fellow colonized will pass into "le troisième temps de la violence: elle revient sur nous, elle nous frappe" [the third stage of violence: it turns back upon us, it strikes us].[58] Sartre maintains that only by participating in violence against the European colonizer can the colonized undo the psychic violence done him. Thus violence becomes a productive, psychically and communally healing activity: "Abattre un Européen c'est faire d'une pierre deux coups, supprimer en même temps un oppresseur et un opprimé: restent un homme mort et un homme libre; le survivant, pour la première fois, sent un sol *nationale* sous la plante de ses pieds" [To assault a European is to kill two birds with one stone, suppressing at the same time an oppressor and an oppressed: leaving a dead man and a free man; the surviving, for the first time, feels the *national* soil under the weight of his feet].[59] Since the novel ends in the early 1970s, just before the beginning of the guerrilla campaign that would lead to the end of white minority rule,[60] one might ask whether Dangarembga implies that the psychological violence she portrays will have to issue in political violence before the underlying pathologies can be cured; certainly, her novel explains the reasons, including ethical ones (the impossibility of being indifferent to the brutalization of those one loves), for that future violence.

But violence is not the last word, nor is it clear that Dangarembga agrees with Sartre that killing the oppressor confers genuine freedom. For Sartre, the circulation of violence is explicable in terms of a psychic economy organized around desire (desire for pleasure, freedom, recognition). Colonizing violence becomes personally unbearable to the colonized individual, so he seeks relief by inflicting violence upon himself and his fellow colonized, until he is able to transfer that (personally therapeutic, healing) violence to the "right" object: the colonizer. Obviously, this egocentric account of the symptom is at odds with Dangarembga's correlation of the symptom with asymmetrical ethical relations in both Tambu's and Nyasha's cases. Critics tend to read the novel as a feminist supplement or modification of Sartre not only because of the title (added during the four-year interval between the book's completion and its publication), but also because they tend to take Nyasha as Dangarembga's mouthpiece, especially in her "violent" speeches when, after Tambu has gone to the elite high school, she descends into anorexic self-destruction: "Their history. Fucking liars. . . . They've trapped us. But I won't be trapped" (201). Tambu is seen as moving toward Nyasha's insight at the novel's end: "Quietly, unobtrusively and extremely fitfully, something in my mind began to assert itself, to question things and refuse to be brainwashed, bringing me to this time when I can set down this story" (204).[61]

However, this passage recalls the novel's beginning, the linking of escape with being able to write the story, and with questioning the success of Nyasha's rebellion. The ending is complex. On the one hand, Tambu's mother warns her against "Englishness," and though this is somewhat undermined by her mean-spirited attribution of Nhamo's death and Nyasha's anorexia to the ancestors' revenge for the Englishness that, in her view, Maiguru has brought to the family,[62] Tambu also begins to suspect that she had been "too eager to leave the homestead and embrace the 'Englishness' of the mission" (203). The implication that self-fashioning involves a betrayal and abandonment of one's mother recalls Stephen Dedalus's guilt toward his mother. By ending the novel with the mother's reproaches, Dangarembga recalls the end of Camara Laye's *L'enfant noir* (1953), where similar maternal protests about the son's Western education are registered.[63] On the other hand, the last we hear of Lucia, the other person who "escapes," is that she has just "passed her Grade One so well that they were moving her into Grade Three" (196), which suggests that Western education, female self-assertion, and Shona identity might be compatible in ways that Tambu's mother, paralyzed not just by patriarchal and colonialist oppression but also by a cultural insularity evident in her demonization of Maiguru, cannot imagine.

But the contrast between Tambu and Nyasha is most important, because Nyasha is not the heroine of the narrative, and one should ask why. When Babamukuru brings Lucia to the mission, Tambu "could not stop admiring him," while Nyasha, situating his subjectivity—like a good postmodern critic—in its historical, cultural contexts, sees him as "a historical artefact" (159, 160), a phrase Sugnet adopts for the title of his essay's section on the novel's males.[64] When Nyasha asks Tambu if she should take her place as bridesmaid, Tambu thinks, "As far as I was concerned, she belonged to Babamukuru and his beliefs, whereas I did not. Yes, Nyasha, I thought bitterly, we can change bridesmaids' dresses because it's all a joke" (167–68). Within the space of a few pages, Nyasha is described as viewing Babamukuru through a seemingly enlightened, anticolonial analytical framework *and* she is described as so belonging "to Babamukuru and his beliefs." Given Tambu's love and admiration of Nyasha, this description of her viewing the cause of Tambu's unbearable pain as a joke is startling. What both seeing her father as "a historical artefact" and taking the cause of Tambu's pain as "all a joke" have in common with Nyasha's final, angry speeches about being trapped by them is that they reveal her penetrating insight and clarity of analysis to be both "far-minded and isolated" (1): she sees the truth as yielded by Western postcolonial thought, but Dangarembga firmly suggests that to see only this truth is to be reduced to despair. Truth must be softened by love, by the binding of clarity to charity. Otherwise, "it's all a joke" in senses that lead not to anticolonial liberation but to despair and suicidal self-loathing.

Nyasha's anorexia is, in part, an effort to impose perfection on her necessarily imperfect humanity; it is the internal equivalent of an external demand for perfect justice. Nfah-Abbenyi observes that while Nyasha "rightly confronts women's oppression," there is an "intransigent and almost chaotic streak embedded in her rebellion," leaving "no room for dialogue and gradual reconciliation. . . . She expects radical changes and when they do not happen, she seems to blame herself."[65] Here, visceral ethical concern lapses into a perverse self-love: self-loathing emerges from disappointment in one's lack of messianic power, in one's own "contamination" by finitude, embodiment, ambiguity, enjoyment. Dangarembga implies that the self-loathing such isolated absolutism engenders (one hates the colonizing and colonized Other and so wants to "spit out" everything that one might have "ingested" connected with both, subtly shifting the locus of the symptom from concern for the other to preoccupation with the self) issues, quasi-logically, in a repudiation of femaleness. Sugnet notes that "Nyasha's anorexia is a way of refusing her femaleness, stopping menstruation, reducing female curves."[66] Nyasha certainly imagines perfection as emulating corrupt Western models of female beauty, as Sugnet argues—which makes her disease a rather chilling form of anticolonial resistance. But as he also points out, her rigidity destroys her fertility, her capacity to reproduce and nurture life. The problem is not simply or primarily that Nyasha loses "sight of living, of being a child, of being a teenager" in ways that could be healed by regaining "faith in her mental capabilities" through seeing that power is not monolithic but "a system of overlapping contradictions" and that sexuality is "a contested terrain."[67] Her problems could not be solved by simply taking Foucault's ideas as her own. What is needed is not a "flexible" manipulation of diverse means of giving the self power, but displacement of a pathological fixation upon the self into loving, forgiving regard for others. Through her portrayal of Nyasha's anorexia, Dangarembga reveals how the "sterile" rigidity that consumes social and physical being turns against the very continuance of life. The way to life, as opposed to a death through a theoretical rigidity, involves recognizing that one's imperfections, and so one's guilts and debts before others, no less than the bodily imperfections that have become the focus or displacement of Nyasha's murderously lucid self-loathing, cannot be entirely done away with, nor can one's relations with other people, with Shona culture, with the West entirely do away with an injustice that involves both "lucky" benefits and searing victimization.

The final word is not Tambu's promise of greater suspicion and resistance but an acknowledgment that identity, like liberation, is found in an understanding that what we are is bound to our love for concrete, flawed others, and so what we are is "indebted" to the complex, ambiguous, unjust history that has shaped them, a history whose wrongs must be acknowledged and redressed, but for whose ultimate injustice—Tambu's identity is tied to Nhamo's death—it is bad faith to apologize: "The story I have told here is my own story, the story of four women whom I loved, and our men, this story is how it all began" (204). By calling attention to her novel's formal characteristics, that the narrator's identity is tied to her love of four women, and that this love has been articulated through her story, the story of acquiring an outside position from which to see each of the women with clarity and charity, Dangarembga suggests that the relation to others and self enacted in and by the novel is the achievement toward which Tambu unknowingly moves—an achievement that, like the novel itself, is based upon the strengths of both indigenous and Western cultures. Indeed, in an interview, Dangarembga notes that her first goal in writing the novel was to capture "a real taste of life," and the models that allowed her to imagine such an achievement were "all the English classics."[68]

Sugnet notes that Tambu's growth involves a similarly appreciative relation to multicultural sources of meaning and value: "[Her] reinvention will doubtless include the 'old deep places,' but will also continue to reach beyond her mother's binary oppositions to employ 'Englishness' (the language itself, ideas from the Brontës, feminism from London, etc.) *where it serves her*" [my emphasis].[69] Sugnet's recognition that Tambu's relation to Western acculturation is not merely a matter of negative alienation constitutes an advance over earlier criticism, but the description of her using multicultural resources "where it serves her" is problematic. Were Tambu really to view, at the end of the novel, all that was outside herself—other discourses, the world's cultural riches, by implication other people—simply or primarily as material that could "serve" her "reinvention," she would have made no ethical advance beyond her attitude, upon leaving the homestead for the mission school, of seeing "horizons . . . saturated with me," of viewing others as "props" and "scenery." To view what is exterior to the self as material to serve the self is what Levinas describes as the imperialistic, appropriative, colonizing aspect of intentional cognition, which leads to the "complacency of subjectivity, a complacency experienced for itself," which is "its very 'egoity,' its substantiality."[70] Such an appropriative stance, such a focus upon the self and a "reinvention" whose lack of definition or "aim" suggests that it is only a synonym for spontaneous, self-justifying freedom, bears moral characteristics Shona discourse associates with "evil wizardry."[71]

The multicultural resources available to Tambu are significant not because they will permit her to reinvent herself through a self-aestheticizing postmodern *bricolage*, but because they will help empower her to do better justice to others. Tambu's novelistic representation of her own story, the story of four women she loved, and their men, provides the best evidence that she may realize such a life, for the justice her depiction does the characters achieves what Newton calls "a representational ethics" that "ties acts of representation to responsibilities," which suggests "not only that fiction can operate as a kind of 'knowing,' but also that fiction's modus vivendi—its power to represent—at some level gives way before the more severe and plenary power of ethical responsibility."[72]

Tambu comes to see, and so comes to represent, her mother, Maiguru, Lucia, and Nyasha from the outside in ways that dispute theories that realistic fiction invariably "colonizes" its subjects.[73] Dangarembga portrays Tambu achieving what the early Bakhtin calls "sympathetic co-experiencing": "Love-like sympathy accompanies and permeates aesthetic co-experiencing. . . . A sympathetically co-experienced life is given form not in the category of the *I*, but in the category of the *other*. . . . In other words, a sympathetically co-experienced life is the life of another human being (his outer as well as his *inner* life) that is essentially experienced *from outside*."[74] Dangarembga's novel traces the conditions of possibility for Tambu's sympathetic co-experiencing the story of the four women she loves, and the novel itself enacts that sympathetic co-experiencing, which suggests that to the extent that the novel can gather us into this activity, it can—as a genre—help establish and broaden a genuinely decolonized moral community.

Tambu's sympathetic co-experiencing is tied to her recognition of indebtedness to others: "The child begins to see himself for the first time as if through his mother's eyes, and begins to speak about himself in his mother's emotional-volitional tones. . . . I feel an absolute need for love that only the other is capable of internally actualizing from his own unique place *outside* of me."[75] Both human subjectivity and life itself are sustained by a love in which, as Kristeva describes maternal love, solicitude divests itself of possessiveness. The good autobiographical novelistic narrator, like the good mother, recognizes the other as constitutive of herself at the very moment that she loves the other in her difference from herself. Genuine identity is inaugurated by an ethical life in which we return to others the love we have received, in which we become "the other" who can respond, from our "own unique place *outside*," to the "absolute need for love" of those who call us to ourselves by calling us away from an immersion, however reinventive and self-serving, in "horizons saturated with me."

6

Ambiguous Freedom in Ama Ata Aidoo's *Changes*

Modernist Indirection and Akan *Abutia:*
Aidoo's Sympathetic Reticence

From its title on, Ama Ata Aidoo's *Changes: A Love Story* (1991) is marked by laconic reserve. The sparse title leaves unresolved how "changes" should be viewed, which leaves open how one should view the protagonist, Esi Sekyi, a data analyst for the Department of Urban Statistics in Accra, Ghana, who (unlike less privileged African women) *chooses* the changes that constitute her narrative. Similarly, the subtitle, *A Love Story*, raises the question of whether "love" should be read descriptively or evaluatively. Is it a sign of empowerment or an affect of colonization that a young African professional woman allows "a love story" to change her life?

Interpretation is further complicated by Aidoo's prefatory "confession-apology," in which she notes that when she "was a little older than [she is] now," she had promised not to write a love story because Africa presented so many "more important" matters; thus, composing *Changes* was "an exercise in word-eating!"[1] This is the first of many references to eating in the narrative. Aidoo's promise occurred in a 1967 interview.[2] The tone of her "confession-apology" implies mature reconsideration of youthful certitudes. Aidoo describes her novel as "not meant to be a contribution to any debate, however current." A debate totalizes in the sense of treating the particular as important only as a contribution to something larger. By suggesting that literature insists upon the significance of what is recalcitrant to totalization, it might seem that Aidoo is endorsing a negative ethics of destabilizing disruption consistent with Derrida's claims that "making the *archê* tremble" is the only way language can circumvent its own complicity with onto-theology.[3]

Aidoo, like major modernist Western writers, is motivated by an ethical (and thus stylistic) imperative to avoid the moralistic on the one hand and the sentimental on the other. To see the moralistic as immoral (as the novel tends to do, at least in its high form, from Fielding, Sterne, and Austen on) is to see simplification as the "polite" modern face of violence, a social equivalent of the capitalist economy's techniques of indirect coercion. Antipathy to the sentimental likewise rests upon seeing it as a modality of effacement, but the intensity with which modernist writers such as Conrad, Joyce, and Mann guard against the sentimental derives in part from knowing that many of their most sympathetic readers are tempted to poeticize themselves by taking subversive characters as affirmations of all they long to be. In Aidoo's case, vigilance against the sentimental is inseparable from awareness that women's writing is expected to be "sweet."[4] Refusing sweetness involves exposing the subtle mechanisms of masculinist violence, but also exposing as sentimental the desire for "feminist" stories to be easily "consumed" as contributions to a debate.

Aidoo deploys now canonical modernist techniques allowing authorial comment without a normative narrating voice: the arrangement of scenes, juxtaposition of details, orchestration of characters' voices, reiteration of phrases and images, use of significant omissions. It has become a standard postmodern critique of modernist literature to charge that masterfully coherent indirection "naturalizes" a particular hierarchy of values precisely because the artist, as Stephen Dedalus would have it, "remains within or behind or beyond or above his handiwork, invisible, refined out of existence, indifferent, paring his fingernails."[5] Modernism might reply to such critiques, as Aidoo's novel effectively does, that indirection need not naturalize, unless one assumes that value and meaning can only be the effect of "impositions." Such an assumption entails a view of human nature that African cultures in general, and Aidoo's Akan culture in particular, emphatically reject.

Aidoo links modernist techniques of indirection with those of Akan oral discourse. Articulating painful truths subtly is a skill (and a value) central to Akan acculturation. Kwesi Yankah notes, "Indirection, through the use of *kasakoa* (metaphor), *akutia* (innuendo), or an *ebe* (proverb) is one frequently used mode of controlling the potency of the spoken word. The ambiguity of indirection, in which there is often a shift from one domain of experience to the other, prevents the easy assignment of malicious motives to its user."[6] Criticizing while avoiding eye contact (*akutiabo*) and criticizing behind the impersonality of proverbial discourse deflect confrontation while calling upon the ethical sense of the person addressed to grasp the contextual import of what is being said: "*Akutia wo ne wura* (*Akutia* has a known target), the Akan say, implying that *akutia* always aims at someone—and that its target is expected to be aware of the subliminal frame of interpretation."[7]

For such indirection to work, the ethical relation must be the precondition for communication.[8] Kwasi Wiredu notes, "The first axiom of all Akan axiological thinking is that man or woman is the measure of all value (*Onipa na ohia*)," and the Akan conception of human personhood perhaps goes "beyond Aristotle's maxim that human beings are political animals," for "a human being is already social at conception, for the union of the blood principle [*mogya*, from the mother] and the personality principle [*sunsum*, from the father] already defines a social identity." Moreover, a person, *onipa*, is the possessor of not only *mogya* and *sunsum* but also *okra*, "the speck of God in man" that links "all human beings together in one universal family."[9] The indirection of *akutia* addresses another *onipa*, someone whose constitution as human places her in nonarbitrary ethical and social relationships. By blending modernist indirection with *akutia*, Aidoo brings to the novel a mode of communication that Akan women exercise masterfully in private domestic discourse.[10] The paradox of *akutia* is that it empowers one to articulate cutting observations and judgments, while its very use implies that one is addressing an *onipa*. Thus, the very reticence of *akutia* is sympathetic, insofar as it acknowledges the ethical humanity of the person it "targets."

Victimization, Opportunism, and Empowering Self-Definition

Changes begins by inviting the reader to construct Esi as a victim: she feels "angry with herself" for driving across town to perform a secretarial errand. Since she is a woman, such tasks "naturally" fall to her. Because her car stalls periodically, she is honked at and stereotyped as a woman driver (1). Aidoo situates Esi within sexist cultural, institutional contexts,[11] making her the potential victim of an impersonal ideological "gaze" that would "fix" her in a disempowered position.[12] However, Esi's very ability to reproach herself indicates that she is too conscious of duties to herself to accept the subservient identities assigned her. Duty to oneself, as Charles Taylor notes, becomes a crucial "good" for the modern West through the influence of Rousseau: "Rousseau frequently presents the issue of morality as that of our following a voice of nature within us. . . . [S]elf-determining freedom . . . is the idea that I am free when I decide for myself what concerns me, rather than being shaped by external influences."[13] Esi's anger reflects awareness that she has let external influences determine her conduct, despite her strong feelings that she should decide for herself.

Her willingness to do secretarial errands, however, allows her to meet Ali Kondey, the owner of the travel agency arranging her office's participation in a conference. Ali is charming, considerate, and flirtatious. "Esi became aware that something quite new and interesting was trying to make itself felt in that room. . . . She was not quite sure *she wanted* to welcome it or even identify it" [my emphasis] (3). The language of obligation is displaced by the language of desire. Although she declines Ali's offer of a ride home in his much better car, her manner induces him to view the meeting as "a gift from Allah": "If it was His Will, things would right themselves in the end" (4). Ali's Islamic piety, quite different from that articulated by Alkali and Bâ, gives him an easy conscience about viewing this chance encounter as an opportunity. Aidoo seems to imply that Islamic traditions of viewing sensual pleasures as legitimate rewards for the pious encourage masculine, predatory self-indulgence. However, the immediate chemistry that he and Esi share suggests affinities between his traditional masculine self-assurance and her feminist sense of personal aggrievement.

Just as the "love story" of the subtitle is being engendered, Aidoo abruptly calls her reader's attention elsewhere—to Esi's six-year-old daughter, Ogyaanowa. In a pagelong passage beginning the second chapter, Ogyaanowa's pain and confusion witnessing the breakdown of Esi's marriage to Oko is poignantly depicted. Then the second chapter begins again, describing Esi's and Oko's marital frustrations. While Ogyaanowa appears repeatedly in the novel as a problem for Esi, Ogyaanowa as a center of consciousness never reenters the text. Her marginality to Esi's love story has led to her marginality in criticism on the novel. Although Gay Wilentz notes that Esi lacks "a relationship with her own daughter whom she mostly ignores," she treats this only as an instance of Esi's alienation from tradition. Juliana Makuchi Nfah-Abbenyi argues that there is "a selfish streak in Esi," but mentions the daughter only as one of a number of people from whom she "alienates herself" by becoming "an Other within the context of an ever-changing post-colonial world in which she struggles to lay down her own rules."[14] Elizabeth Willey refers to Ogyaanowa only in the context of a list of wrongs done to Esi: "She is patronized by her male colleagues at work, abused by her husband, misunderstood by her friends and family, made to feel guilty about her benign neglect of her daughter, and finally abandoned by her second husband."[15]

Willey places so much more stress upon Esi being "made to feel guilty" than on Esi's "benign neglect" because she assumes the novel must be about whether Esi attains what she desires: "Neither of these [monogamous or polygamous] forms of marriage *works for Esi*; both seem to be maladjusted to the realities of Esi's life as a career woman who wants a family as well as a job" [my emphasis].[16] While recognizing Esi's "selfish streak," Nfah-Abbenyi argues that the novel affirms her because she is "the agent of her own self-destruction, self-reconstruction, and self-determination." She "realizes that her marriage cannot work *on her terms* and calls it off" [my emphasis]; nonetheless, Esi needs to "tap into" traditional history and knowledge "to fuel and regenerate *herself*" [my emphasis].[17] Sally McWilliams mentions Ogyaanowa once in passing while praising Esi as a rebel against "society's heterosexual mandate for women," arguing that she, along with her friend Opokuya, break "the culturally and socially imposed silences concerning female sexual, personal, and social desires."[18] Claiming that the novel "celebrates the modern woman's new status, her self-determining and independent spirit," Pauline Onwubiko Uwakweh discusses Ogyaanowa not at all (though she is mentioned once in a long citation). Ogyaanowa never appears in Miriam C. Gyimah's discussion of how Esi lays "claim to her subjectivity."[19] Only Vincent O. Odamtten, maintaining that Aidoo follows oral storytelling techniques in "giving us the personal histories of each of the principal characters" to keep "us from indulging our prejudices in the process of interpretation," suggests that Ogyaanowa might have value beyond her effect upon Esi's feelings and projects: "Perhaps the most important character and victim of this love story is the one from whom we hear the least—Esi's daughter, Ogyaanowa. . . . [W]hat kind of world are we leaving for those unable to articulate . . . their concerns, when we so often and so blatantly refuse to consult them? . . . [W]hat about the children . . . ?"[20]

Odamtten calls attention to the thematic significance of what is not portrayed. Not a single conversation between Esi and her daughter is recounted, nor is there any occasion when Esi is described as delighting in her daughter for her daughter's sake. It would be a mistake to assume that the novel's registering of Esi's consciousness demarcates the limits of Aidoo's. *Changes* is dedicated to Aidoo's daughter, Kinna, and in response to a question about who influenced her writing, Aidoo cites her daughter immediately after her mother: "Not only in terms of having a child with you, but because when one communicates, one has to be very careful. You and I [Abeola James, the interviewer] come from traditions which don't even recognize people, their intelligence or their contribution, until they start growing gray hair. So it is good to have Kinna around."[21] Aidoo alludes to what Wiredu describes as Akan "traditions" of restricting and dismissing the speech of young people.[22] Esi's inattention to Ogyaanowa derives in part from an excessive, westernized individuality, but also replicates, in novel forms, patterns rooted in Akan cultural practices.

The tendency of critics to marginalize Ogyaanowa reflects legitimate concerns that discourses of maternal obligation can be used for emotional blackmail. Indeed, Aidoo notes, "Traditionally, a woman is supposed to be nothing more valid than a mother."[23] However, Aidoo also describes how her previous novel, *Our Sister Killjoy* (1977), took five years to write because she was "teaching, mothering, and doing some other things." She has often been "too busy teaching in the university, too busy being in government, or making a baby." At the same time, she observes, "I did not set out to sacrifice family life for my writing. It just happened. Those you care for, and who care for you, come into collision with you as a writer."[24]

Being a writer, having any sort of modern, professional career, involves a high degree of focus upon oneself and one's projects. Just acquiring the education to be a professional demands, as Dangarembga illustrates, making the broadening of one's own horizons an abiding, defining preoccupation during adolescence and young adulthood. Oddly, being pampered by social and institutional environments organized around the enrichment of the self becomes the prerequisite, under the conditions of modernity, for any professional "success" distinct from the gratifications of making a good living, making a name for oneself, enjoying agreeable (nonmanual) labor—that is, the professional success of being genuinely for-another in the highly specialized but also (potentially at least) revolutionarily efficacious ways that professionalism allows.

Modernity holds out the hope that a radically expanded capacity to serve others will emerge from, and thus justify, the radically intensified focus on self that "having a career" presupposes and demands. However, this radically intensified focus on self creates a professional "you" who inevitably comes to experience "[t]hose you care for, and who care for you" as being "into collision" with the self so organized. Both the habits of mind that modern professionalism cultivates and the working conditions necessary for professional "productivity" accentuate the allergy to the other endemic to human consciousness, our "natural" inclination to enjoy the world free from interference. At the same time, paradoxically, professionalism becomes ethical activity, as opposed to an exercise in opportunism, only if the focus upon self converts itself into a very high order of service to others, and—more paradoxically—that conversion actually requires us to become "open" to constant, insistent, ethically imperative disruption. While Aidoo's daughter, Kinna, "collides" with Aidoo's writing self, her work is indebted to "having a child with [her]." The proximity of the child calls one out of oneself, forcing upon one a being for-another that "collides" with, but also simultaneously enriches, the being for-another of one's professional life.

Aidoo forces the reader of *Changes* to encounter Ogyaanowa as a "collision," placing the sketch of her consciousness between the story of Esi's meeting Ali and the story of Esi's break with Oko. On first encountering the passage, the reader does not know who Ogyaanowa is. Odamtten suggests that Aidoo follows in her narratives the patterns of "*nutinyawo* (a collection of prose-poetry narratives)," where judgments are complicated and deferred by a sequence of tales commenting upon, modifying, reversing those that go before.[25] Odamtten associates such infinite deferral of closure with "interminable palavers" produced by oral discourse, which, he argues, Aidoo transfers into a written discourse "disrupt[ing] normative Western generic compartmentalization" in ways that demand "polylectical" criticism, criticism acknowledging "the *interdependencies*, even as it recognizes the *overdeterminate autonomies of writer, text, audience, and social whole.*"[26] While Odamtten's attention to indigenous contexts is valuable, his account of polylectical criticism leaves unresolved the relationship between "interdependencies" and "autonomies," giving rise in practice to a valorization of multiple voices, heterogeneities, and disruption not very distinct from standard postmodern ways of valorizing literature. Our argument here is that Aidoo problematizes judgments not to engender "interminable palavers" but to render moral discrimination more acute by impressing upon us, through insinuation, *akutia*, what is uncomfortable and complicating but morally necessary for us to confront.

What is confronted in the Ogyaanowa passage is, first of all, the reader's nascent identification with Esi's and, to a lesser extent, Ali's perspectives; the disorientation that Ogyaanowa's abrupt appearance occasions underscores parallels between reading a narrative, in which we "concretize" a fictively unfolding "world," and our intentional structuring, in everyday life, of the phenomenological "world" or "worlds" we find ourselves "being-towards."[27] The reader's initially comfortable intentional structuring is rebuked by the presence of the Other in ways theorized by Levinas.[28] Notably, there is no "bridge" between the first chapter and the portrait of Ogyaanowa at the beginning of the second: while Esi is concerned about her errand lengthening her day and about getting home before dark (2), nowhere in the first chapter is Ogyaanowa's existence registered upon Esi's consciousness.

In his account of "Vulnerability and Contact," which he closely associates with maternity, Levinas observes, "Contact is not an openness upon being [as in Heidegger], but an exposure of being."[29] The reader makes contact with Ogyaanowa through the text's evocation of her gnawing loneliness: when much older, she "was to ask herself what she would have preferred if she had been consulted"—watching her parents fight or hearing them while she pretended not to notice (5). She wishes she were elsewhere, wishes she were unconscious. While this depiction indicts both parents, it ought to call the reader's attention to the absence of Ogyaanowa from Esi's thoughts in the previous chapter, where all her attention is fixed upon slights and inconvenience to herself.

As abruptly as the reader is exposed to Ogyaanowa, she drops from view. Although Ogyaanowa is never "consulted" again, Aidoo forces the reader to be aware of what is missing from the rest of the novel, which should prevent a comfortable consumption of what might otherwise seem enjoyable—identification with Esi's empowering determination to end her marriage for reasons that are valid only for her, Esi's liberating pleasure in her own sexuality, Esi's satisfaction in concentrating without distractions upon her career. These feminist goods are served up for the reader in ways that suggest not that they are illusory or unworthy but that to follow Esi's example of enjoying them without reserve requires us to follow Esi in forgetting Ogyaanowa—whose name combines Twi words signifying "something left behind" and "something originating elsewhere." As an epigraph to *Otherwise than Being*, Levinas quotes Pascal, "'That is my place in the sun.' That is how the usurpation of the whole world began." Contact with Ogyaanowa should cast a shadow over the reader's participation in Esi's enjoyment of her "place in the sun."

Aidoo does note the coercive pressure Esi is under to produce more children. Oko's mother and sisters have reproached him about "the unsafety of having an only child" (8). The prominence of his mother's and sisters' voices in Oko's consciousness reflects the matrilineal structure of Akan society: "In [its] outermost dimensions a lineage becomes a clan. Its innermost circle comprises the grandmother, the mother, the mother's siblings, her own children, and the children of her sisters."[30] By seeming to devalue her duty as a mother,

Esi seems to Oko's relations to be depriving him and Ogyaanowa of a lineage that can function as a system of social support. Addressing such cultural pressure, Aidoo has, in essays and interviews, defended the right of African women not to marry, not to be pressured into considering "higher education . . . an unfortunate postponement of [female] self-fulfillment" in marriage,[31] a fulfillment inseparable from motherhood, since raising children is the presumptive reason for marriage.[32] Later in the novel Aidoo suggests that Esi was socially bullied into marriage, "made to fear that in fact she would never marry" (41), for the prevailing opinion was that "any successful career outside the home is naturally for men and a few rather 'ugly' women."[33] In a society restructured by feminist goods, Esi might not have been led to feel for Oko "in the first years of their married life . . . gratitude more than anything else. Gratitude that in spite of herself he had persisted in courting her and marrying her" (41). Persecuted by a sexist environment, Esi confuses gratitude with love and so produces Ogyaanowa.

But, however ill advised our marriages, our obligations to our children remain. Both Akan culture and Levinas treat the maternal relation not merely as an ethical relation but as the paradigm (conceptually and experientially) for all other ethical relations. The mother is "the principal personage" because she nurses newborn children: "The Akan have an acute sense of the dependency of a human being. On first appearance in this world, one . . . [has] the greatest need . . . [and so] right to that help. But this right never deserts a human being, for one is seen at all times as insufficient unto oneself. . . . The right to be nursed, then, is the first human right. In the fullness of time it will be transformed dialectically into a duty to nurse one's mother in her old age."[34] The right of the infant to be nursed extends itself metaphorically to the right of humans to nurture, to kindness, which converts itself into duty to particular others (such as one's own mother) and to the community at large. Oddly, as with modern professional identity, a world centered upon the self's needs and growth makes possible the self's acquisition of ethical humanity. At the heart of the system is the notion that maternal ethical care is the precondition—materially, psychologically, socially—for the next generation's ethical disposition and activity.

Oko's relations see Esi threatening all this. Ogyaanowa's unhappy isolation underscores how Esi does not provide her with the resources—emotional, psychological, and social—that human beings need in order to be genuinely "cared for." She has no inclination to provide Ogyaanowa with siblings, and she can ignore any "amount of reasoning and pleading" (8) on the part of Oko and his relations, deciding alone, thanks to the Western technology of birth control pills, whether there are going to be any more children.

Both Oko's feelings as Esi makes her toilet and these labors themselves emphasize her power and suggest its sources. Esi adorns herself for the day with "some cream for her skin, a deodorant stick, a very mild toilet spray" (6). Such pampering of the body reflects Esi's urban, bourgeois social status. At the same time, it recalls the personal habits of the precolonial elite in Asante, the imperial center of Akan power in the eighteenth and nineteenth centuries. Robert B. Edgerton notes, "Men and women of the higher orders bathed every morning with soap and warm water, wore scrupulously clean clothes, and ornamented themselves profusely. They . . . shaved armpits to reduce body odor, which they found repellent."[35] Such meticulous care of the body differentiated the elite from the lower orders, *ahiato*, reputed to be "small in stature, filthy, ungrateful, insolent, and licentious,"[36] and was a direct consequence of the elite's self-empowerment through Western technology. Asante assumed hegemony over other Akan polities and conquered non-Akan neighbors by exchanging gold for European weapons to equip an army that produced slaves for gold mines, land clearing, and transatlantic export.[37] Implying a connection between Esi's strong sense of self and her care in personal grooming, Aidoo suggests that Esi, as a government technocrat, may be heir to the sense of entitlement that distinguished not only the British colonial bureaucracy but also the precolonial Asante civil service, the *nhenkwaa* (sing. *ahenkwaa*). T. C. McCaskie notes, "Licit or not, the proprietorial assumptions of the *nhenkwaa*—towards food, drink, and much else—are fully documented."[38] Indeed, the house Esi and Oko live in comes with her job.

Esi, of course, is not the only subjectivity structured by proprietorial assumptions. Oko clings, unconsciously, to the notion that he should remain the pampered center of a phenomenological and social world. Oko enjoys gazing upon a naked woman who retains "schoolgirl looks . . . [and] ways" (6). He then "scold[s] himself" for associating the erotic with schoolgirls, noting that he is about to become a headmaster; instead, he focuses upon what is distinctive to Esi, especially "the little protrusion" of a "sassy navel" (6). Gyimah argues that Oko "positions Esi as a schoolgirl" in an effort to "occupy a safe ground for himself where his authority and stature are not threatened."[39] While Oko's arousal upon noting Esi's schoolgirl manner does introduce the important theme of male interest in young girls, Oko rebukes himself and thus is shown to recognize that not everything encountered may be construed in terms of opportunities for enjoyment. Moreover, Oko's "positioning" of Esi may reveal something about her no less than about him: perhaps there is something schoolgirlish — unaware, immature — about Esi.

On the other hand, Oko's focus upon Esi's navel in the matrilineal Akan social context recalls the strong Akan emphasis on the mother-infant bond. Aidoo observes that Esi's mother could have told Oko that the "sassy navel" he so admires "had nearly killed her daughter," for instead of healing normally, it had almost gone "septic" (7). By interjecting the mother's voice here, Aidoo implies that whatever we enjoy involves a cost of some kind to someone. Similarly, Ali is "there" for Esi to enjoy because his fifteen-year-old mother died giving him birth.

Oko's desire for Esi is complicated by his sense of aggrievement. Knowing "how much he had invested in the marriage with Esi," he feels a "little angry" (7) for the same reason that Esi felt angry driving to Ali's travel agency: he has fallen short of sufficient duty to himself. At the same time, he is "a little embarrassed" because he "had always loved Esi," which ill accords with African notions of male dignity and self-protection.[40] What particularly aggrieves Oko is that he has received nothing in exchange for his love: "No affection. Not even plain warmth. Nothing except one little daughter!" (8). He sees Esi's unstated decision to have no more children as emblematic of this lack of reciprocity.

Esi comes to find "Oko's attentions so suffocating" (41) because they seems expressive of immature dependence. Nonetheless, Oko's perception of Esi as lacking reciprocity and warmth need not be without foundation. He is not a typical chauvinistic villain. He would be happy for "even one more girl." The thought of other women has long "left him quite cold" (8). Because Esi is the focus of his erotic and familial concerns, it disturbs him that she "definitely put her career well above any duties she owed as wife," that, while "a great cook," she "complained endlessly" about entering the kitchen. Reflecting on her career as a data analyst with the government's statistical bureau, he asks himself, "Good God, what on earth did that mean?" and notes her frequent travel to "all those conferences" (8). There is a strong current of whining in all this, but Oko raises a series of specific charges — that Esi's careerism reflects a habitual placement of her own desires and convenience "well above" any regard for others; that her work is something unreal; that "all those conferences" are emblematic of an unrelenting fixation upon self.

By offering, early in her novel, Oko's reading of Esi's character, Aidoo invites the reader to do what Elizabeth Bennet does when, in *Pride and Prejudice*, she assesses the justice of Darcy's depiction, in his letter to her, of Wickham's character: "She tried to recollect some instance of goodness, some distinguished trait of integrity or benevolence, that might rescue him from the attacks of Mr. Darcy. . . . But no such recollection befriended her."[41] Elizabeth rakes her memory, whereas the reader of *Changes* must look forward, scouring each successive scene for some proof of the injustice of Oko's perceptions. Because we are so understandably predisposed to discredit Oko's interpretation, the novel's ultimate refusal to "befriend" us with any such evidence is as devastating and chastening as the absence of Ogyaanowa from the text.

Making the acceptance of Oko's reading even harder is his brief but brutal perpetration of sexual violence. Oko attempts to engage Esi in conversation by noting that his friends think he is not "behaving like a man" (8). Of course, this observation is intended to put her on the defensive, but when she deflects it, he replies, "Opokuya is a good woman" (9). This remark could imply that Opokuya is good because she has four children, because she does not put her career "well above" her duties as wife and mother. However, we learn that Opokuya is in fact outspoken and devoted to her work as a midwife (14–15). That Oko praises Opokuya, as opposed to some self-effacing woman, suggests that he might be trying to change the subject or tone in ways Esi might find agreeable. Aidoo's refusal to make clear his intent or tone underscores how in a bad or dying marriage each partner interprets the other partner's every word and action in the most negative way. But Esi does more than that; she yawns and looks at her watch. The novel reveals aloof inattentiveness to be Esi's peculiar mode of antisocial violence. Each instance is a small matter (who does not, to concentrate, block out others with some regularity?), but the invariability of Esi's practice suggests a fundamental allergy to other people. In response to being ignored, Oko forces himself upon Esi: "[H]e went on doing what he had determined to do all morning. He squeezed her breasts repeatedly, thrust his tongue into her mouth, forced her unwilling legs apart" (9).

Sexual assault is usually understood as an effort to objectify and so "shut up" the other: Lovelace's rape of Clarissa is novelistic discourse's paradigmatic example. But Esi understands Oko's action as indicative of "rage," "frustration," and "deliberate provocation" (9). To "provoke," as the word's etymology suggests, is to seek a response. Of course, children habitually rage with frustration to obtain maternal acknowledgment, which further underscores Oko's psychic immaturity. But there is something childlike in the emotional neediness of every human being, just as there is something maternal in every ethical relation. Oko's sexual violence is inattention raised to the level of assault. When Esi seeks to be acknowledged, he ignores her, "pounding and just pounding away" (9). Oko's and Esi's forms of antisocial inattention are not morally equivalent, but the violence of tuning out others so that we can concentrate on what we want finds its most radicalized, revelatory manifestation in marital rape.

As soon as the encounter is over, Oko feels like apologizing, but he is "also convinced that he mustn't" (10). He knows, behind and before cultural constructions, that he has done wrong, but believes that to acknowledge this would disempower him. Later, in her office, still feeling unclean after a second bath, Esi realizes that she has undergone a marital rape (11). She immediately imagines how that claim would be dismissed, as an imported Western feminist concept, since there is no equivalent in African languages. Cultural relativism underwrites a moral relativism that would position her within patriarchal scripts: "Sex is something a husband claims from his wife as his right" (12). To reject such arguments is to discover the ethical anterior to cultural constructions of moralities. The ethical "comes to us," impresses itself upon us bodily, as in Esi's feeling of being "still dirty" (12), with an immediacy no sophistry, no "regime of truth" can undo.

The reader might expect Esi's ability to define Oko's assault as marital rape to constitute a step toward feminist consciousness. Surprisingly, Esi's view of the encounter shifts as soon as she regains her composure. One month later, she believes that, having "decided to feel assaulted . . . , her mind had seized on her 'assault,' and held it. Part of its fascination for her was its legal usefulness. She was clever enough to know, if only subconsciously at that stage, that it could come in handy should she ever decide to apply for a proper divorce" (36). For her, the incident is no longer marital rape but an opportunity about which she "decides to feel" a certain way. Why would Esi want to "de-essentialize" Oko's assault? Actually "feeling" assaulted would serve her ends as much as, if not more so, than, "deciding to feel" assaulted.

If intentional consciousness is called into question by the ethical, then we displace from the center of ourselves the kind of freedom that comes with taking ourselves to be co-extensive with our projects, taking exteriority, all that we can encounter, as "an experience of . . . , a consciousness of . . . ," that is, as phenomenological "worlds" always already shaped by intentionality: "When interpreted as openness of disclosure, as consciousness of . . . , sensibility would be already reduced to sight, idea, and intuition, a synchrony of thematized elements and their simultaneity with the look."[42] The very language of "positionality" structures subjectivity in terms of seeing something from a somewhere that might easily be an elsewhere. The appeal of absorbing the immediate into "consciousness of . . ." (rather than allowing the unconditionality of the immediate to put in question all manner of sexist, oppressive cultural mediations) lies in the freedom it gives us to "position" ourselves as *we want*, the way it seems to set us outside the world whose meaning for us is ultimately the work of our own projective consciousnesses. By contrast, in the ethical relation, we are *discontinuous* with intentional subjectivity: "Contact is not an openness upon being, but an exposure of being. In this caress, proximity signifies as proximity, and not as an experience of proximity."[43] Reducing assault to an experience of assault, Esi defines herself as a particular kind of agent, an agent who welcomes the opportunity that her chance encounter with Ali presents.

Making the World Work for Us:
Empowering and Appropriative Enjoyment

A month after deciding to leave Oko, Esi meets her friend Opokuya by chance at the Hotel Twentieth Century. At the beginning of each of the two successive chapters, Aidoo calls the reader's attention to what lies immediately next to the elegant oceanside hotel: fishermen "were wondering . . . whether the government would fulfil its promise to help them get motorised boats and better nets" (31); as the hotel "blaz[ed] with light," the fishing villages went without electricity, even though "massive cables passing over the roofs of their homes . . . bore . . . electricity to the more deserving members of society" (43), such as the novel's protagonist and her friend. These brief passages, like the Ogyaanowa passage, alert the reader to what is sacrificed by focusing upon Esi and her problems.

When Esi wants to buy her friend a cocktail, Opokuya protests that were she to drink that early, she would want to go to bed as soon as she got home, to which Esi responds, "So what?" (34). Opokuya is "shocked" because with "a fully grown man, a young growing woman and three growing boisterous boys to feed," she cannot sleep any time she desires. This exchange raises the question of what is the "target" of Aidoo's *akutia*. Does the exchange reveal that Opokuya is a mystified victim of the patriarchy, or that Esi has embarked on a career of self-indulgence? Once Esi announces, with strained breeziness, that she is leaving Oko, a "sadness . . . descend[s]" that is not "easy to get rid of." Sadness here has an independence of the immediate intruding upon "consciousness of."

Esi hopes to gain "understanding" (38) from Opokuya because she has received none from her mother or grandmother. Esi recalls an earlier discussion in which the grandmother, Nana, had declared that "we all marry to have children" and "to increase the number of people with whom we can share the joys and pains of this life" (42). Esi had asked about love, which Nana had dismissed as "fine for singing about" but "when we need to count on human strength . . . love is nothing." On the one hand, love (in the sense of love songs) is not an ethical relation, whereas marriage, as the sharing of joys and pain, might be; on the other hand, the grandmother's dismissal of all love as illusory may suggest a hard-edged, contracted vision, reflective of her own slender opportunities.

Opokuya responds to Esi's story much as her mother and grandmother did; she calls her "mad" and is "surprised" to find Esi "beginning to sound childish and petulant" (44). Opokuya's insistent concern about others and her lack of enthusiasm for Esi's choice do not make her a dupe of the patriarchy: she notes that men do not really want intelligent, independent women and that the few who do want their wives to give up demanding jobs to devote more time to the family, which leads to the contraction of the women's "vision" (45). What Opokuya outlines, as Gyimah notes,[44] is later illustrated in the story of Fusena, Ali's first wife (57–67). Similarly, Opokuya knows that her husband, Kubi, is not always "reasonable" (46) and that women who refuse to sacrifice independence to men are habitually stigmatized and "branded witches" (47). Significantly, the first appearance of witchcraft in the novel makes clear how it has served as a disciplinary mechanism to normalize conduct and intimidate women—a characterization that diverse studies well support.[45]

Because Opokuya's feminist consciousness is made clear, her refusal to endorse Esi's conduct and reasoning is striking. She tells Esi, "You just can't have everything your way," and observes that whatever Oko's "other faults," he "loved [her] and wanted [the] marriage to work" (49). When Esi protests that he wanted the marriage to work on his terms, Opokuya remarks, "Why are you now being so childish, eh?" She laughs when Esi suggests that men "naturally" assume that women will be the "fools" who let marriages work, but she loses "her patience" (50) when Esi complains that doing more than she did "as a wife and a mother" would have hurt her career: "How can I do more than I'm already doing and compete effectively for promotion, travel opportunities, and other side-benefits of the job?" (50).

Opokuya's loss of patience reinforces the questions that Oko's reflections on Esi's career raise. Esi describes her job's importance exclusively in terms of opportunities for herself. She desires to have more time for it so that she can exploit more fully what it might do for her. She prepares statistics for ministers, but nowhere in the novel does she exhibit any concern about what those statistics are used for. When she complains that she works harder and is rewarded less than her male colleagues, Opokuya will not have "any of her self-pity" (50), remarking that life is much harder for poor, nonprofessional African women and admonishing her to "remember it is always harder for some other women somewhere else" (51), which reinforces what the fishing village passages insinuate.

Through this exchange, Aidoo juxtaposes two kinds of feminism. Each has a substantial downside: if Esi's focus on self engenders a "childish petulance" and "self-pity" that is simply unethical in its inattentiveness to others, Opokuya's maternally capacious attentiveness to others opens her to imposition, to bearing injustices, to working her life away without proper support or gratitude. Significantly, at the moment when these two roads are laid out for the reader, Esi catches sight of Ali. She tries "not to stare too hard" (51).

In an effort to distinguish Esi's staring from a Sartrean or phallocentric gaze, Gyimah argues that Esi engages in what bell hooks calls "an oppositional gaze," in looking as a means of rebellion by subordinates against oppressors: "She is not simply an appropriated sexual object, but an aggressive woman consciously claiming her sexual agency." As though aware that this characterization might nonetheless affiliate Esi's gaze with a phallocentric one, Gyimah adds, "Nevertheless, Esi approaches her sexual relationships with men as one of reciprocity."[46] Opokuya, however, has just insisted that, *like men*, Esi does not want "reciprocity" but things "on her own terms," and Esi's discussion of her job reveals—as Opokuya again notes—"childish" egocentricism. Discussing Akan theorizing of the gaze, Yankah points out that "one's gaze . . . can be used as a form of attack. The concept of *anibone*, evil eye, is believed by the Akan to be capable of altering reality." Children are taught "gaze avoidance," for staring at an adult while being rebuked is taken "as a sign of juvenile insolence."[47] Because gaze avoidance acknowledges a person's subordinate position, one might indeed read Esi's staring as involving hooks's oppositional gaze, but one might also take it as suggesting a measure of antisocial aggressivity. Akan contexts for interpreting the gaze underscore the difficulty, and necessity, of discriminating between oppositional self-assertion and predatory self-aggrandizement.

The reader is put in the position of Opokuya, of learning just now the dimensions that Esi's love story has already assumed. Hearing that Ali has been bringing her "all sorts of gifts from his travels," Opokuya declares, "I just caught you out" (53). After asking if there is a wife, and receiving no direct answer, Opokuya notes that if Esi is lonely, there is something she can do about it: "I don't blame you. He looks good enough to eat" (53). In Twi, the Akan language, the same word, *di*, indicates eating and sex. Eating as devouring, as consuming the substance of others—both their own physical and spiritual substance and their property and kin—constitutes the central trope of Akan conceptions of witchcraft.[48] Akan studies was pioneered by R. S. Rattray, who, though a colonial officer writing in the 1920s and 1930s, is described by Kwame Gyekye in 1987 as "perhaps the most perceptive and analytical researcher into Ashanti [Asante] culture."[49] Rattray's 1927 account of Asante witchcraft (*bayi*) accords in its essentials with contemporary research: "The majority of witches are women. . . . The great desire of a witch is to eat people, but she will not do this so that any one may see; they suck blood. . . . All witches know one another and are in league. . . . Witches walk about naked at night. . . . They eat all together, each supplying the feast in turn. A witch can only kill in her own clan."[50]

Witchcraft as a moral discourse is double-edged. On the one hand, the concept persecutes "transgressive" individuals. On the other hand, it describes rapacious self-aggrandizement as an alienation of the self from its own humanity. As Jean and John Comaroff note, because witchcraft repudiates unrestrained selfishness, it becomes in colonial and postcolonial contexts a way of critiquing modernity, the West, and those Africans who seek to be initiated into the "magic" of Western acquisitive individualism: witches "travel across broad horizons, take up residence in towns, become mistresses of money, markets, and motorized transport, wear makeup and modish attire. . . . They also become the personification of capricious commodities, the sirens of selfish desire. . . . [Witches] embody all the contradictions of the experience of modernity itself, of its inescapable enticements, its self-consuming passions, its discriminatory tactics, its devastating social costs."[51]

By joining the depiction of Esi's eyes following Ali's movements with

Opokuya's description of Ali as "good enough to eat," Aidoo raises the question—soon pursued by characters in the novel—of whether there is something witchlike in Esi's consciousness and conduct, and whether she herself has been bewitched by forces and values that alienate us from goodness in the Akan sense of *papa*, which Gyekye defines as "the welfare or well-being of the community," concern for actions' "consequences for human well-being," which leads to valorization of "deeds, habits, patterns of behavior" such as "kindness (generosity: *ayamyie*), faithfulness (honesty, truthfulness: *nokwaredi*), compassion (*mmôbrôhunu*), hospitality (*ahôhoyê, adôe*)."[52]

As Gyekye points out, Akan morality resembles the Aristotelian tradition in its association of ethics with character: *onni suban* connotes at once, "He has no morals" and "He has no character"; being a bad person, *onipa bône*, and having bad character, *suban bône*, "are considered identical."[53] Wiredu notes that *onipa* has an evaluative as well as a descriptive sense. Someone who has "demonstrated an ability through hard work and sober thinking to sustain a household and make contributions to the communal welfare" is an *onipa*: "In this sense, personhood is not something you are born with but something you may achieve, and it is subject to degrees."[54] This roughly corresponds with the Aristotelian-humanistic notion that we become more or less "truly" human depending upon our ethical disposition. Clearly, witchcraft describes absolute alienation from *suban*, forfeiture of *onipa*, through giving oneself over to a pattern of desire, deliberation, and conduct divested of *papa*.

Aidoo folds the two chapters describing Esi's conversation with Opokuya between two chapters describing first Ali's youth and then his wife Fusena's life. We learn that Ali's singular mobility—he carries passports of eight countries—and relentless charm derive from his father's success as both a traveling salesman and a "devourer" of young girls: "Like most men everywhere and from time immemorial . . . Ali's father preferred his women young and tender" (23). Described this way, Aidoo suggests that an element of predation is constitutive of male sexuality, but in the cultural world depicted in the novel that instinctive predation has been accentuated or licensed by social practices. Ali's mother, fourteen when wed, died in childbirth at fifteen. A verse interpolation declares, "She sat / quietly and bled to death" (23). In a few brief strokes, Aidoo describes gender relations in terms analogous to those of witchcraft: the young girl is eaten up and her blood sucked away. Ali is at once the product and victim of this violence: "In the commotion that had followed that catastrophe, Ali had been nearly forgotten. Indeed, the only one who seemed to have remembered his existence had been himself. He yelled and kept yelling until someone had picked him up, cleaned him and found him some breasts with milk in them. He never forgot the experience ever! And for months he never really stopped crying, completely convinced that if he stopped, he would be forgotten again" (23).

The implication is that by naturalizing the "devouring" of women, a culture breeds in its own posterity an elemental insecurity. Ali's ingratiating charm, his insatiable ambition, his relentless womanizing are all ultimately effects of having "never really stopped crying." Ali is at home everywhere because he has no real home; he charms and seduces everywhere because he is ultimately detached from everyone. He can adeptly intuit how others will see him because he bears a spectator's relation to himself. In his extraordinary mobility (borders mean nothing to him), in his almost magical ability to manipulate circumstances and people to enrich and empower himself, in his constant seduction of others through gifts of modern consumer goods, Ali bears the major attributes of a postcolonial witch. While most witches were female (*obayifo*), the Akan culture recognized male witches or sorcerers (*bonsam*) as well.[55]

By evoking a child's devastation over maternal abandonment, Aidoo casts a harsh light on Esi's treatment of Ogyaanowa, suggesting that the absence of an anchoring maternal presence leads to the loss of a basic trust in others upon which, as Erik Erikson famously argues, elemental psychic security depends.[56] Similarly, Ali's ultimate detachment from others suggests that he is afflicted by an inability to love that Kristeva has traced to the breakdown of "primary narcissism" in the small child's self-constitution: "A not-yet-identity (of the child) is transferred or rather displaced to the site of the Other who is not libidinally cathected as an object but remains an Ego Ideal. . . . If narcissism is a defense against the emptiness of separation [from the mother], then the whole contrivance of imagery, representations, identifications, and projections that accompany it on the way towards strengthening the Ego and the Subject is a means of exorcising that emptiness."[57] To attain an identity capable of love, we must know ourselves as beloved by the mother in relation to a Third Party the mother desires, so that we can bear "the emptiness of separation" by investing in an image of ourselves we love because it is symbolically evocative of what she desires beyond ourselves: "Possibly the most radical atheists are those who . . . remain prisoners of the archaic mother, for whom they mourn in the suffering of emptiness"[58] because they lack an image of themselves endowed with meaning to replace an original dyadic fusion with the mother. Ali is consciously no atheist. Seeing himself as the pampered center of Allah's care is a way of unconsciously making up for the mother's loss. Nonetheless, his insatiable need to bewitch people, to confirm his hold over them, suggests that, instead of assuaging his mourning and anxiety, his mode of piety ultimately only facilitates his pursuit of substitutes forever inadequate to still the hunger within. If losing one's mother induces a witchlike insatiable hunger, then Esi's neglect of Ogyaanowa cannot be "benign."

The predatory context of Esi's love story is forcefully underscored in the chapter that follows the conversation in the cocktail lounge, which portrays Fusena's friendship with Ali while they were both training to be teachers and her sacrifice of her own teaching career to "look after the children" (67). By the end of the chapter, Aidoo has articulated fully an individuated subjectivity characterized by thwarted feminist aspirations. While the chapter reveals how devastating Ali's largely unconscious manipulation of others can be, it simultaneously calls attention to the solidity of the other who, aside from Ogyanowa, is the most obvious sacrifice to Esi's appetite.

To be bewitched may entail being devoured, losing one's life's substance—blood, *mogya*, which is associated with breast milk, maternal nurturing, the warmth of loving human contact—or it may entail being seduced into witchcraft oneself. The first effect of Ali's charms upon Esi is her acquiescence in letting Ogyaanowa stay permanently with Oko's mother: "It had seemed to Esi that the older woman was getting ready to use the child as some sort of weapon to fight her with, and she had secretly sworn not to let that happen. So one day, and much to her mother-in-law's surprise, she had suggested to her that Ogyaanowa could stay on" after the end of the summer holidays (68). Aidoo's phrasing leaves unclear whether any concern for Ogyaanowa herself motivates Esi's choice. It *is* clear, however, that she is determined to shield herself. "Just like any mother, she found it difficult to accept that her child could be happy in any environment other than the one she had created." This is "difficult to accept" because it is a blow to pride. The next sentence begins, "However, the truth of the matter was . . ." A reader might expect the "truth" revealed in the next clause to be something that would balance wounded maternal pride against real concern for her daughter. Instead, the "truth of the matter was that if Ogyaanowa had been still at the bungalow, she would have felt at least a little funny bringing in Ali so soon after virtually throwing Oko out" (68–69).

Esi's delight in Ali is contrasted with Oko's anguish. He first tries to win her back. When that fails, he buries himself in work: her absence and "the sense of loss . . . assailed him mercilessly, and cruelly ruined his mornings. . . . And he missed his daughter terribly too" (71). Oko's female relations can account for his abiding obsession only in terms of bewitchment. They "call her a semi-barren witch" (70), and Oko's mother deposits "a breathing parcel on his door-step, in the form of a very beautiful and very young girl" (71). If Oko really did want a schoolgirl, he would be pleased. Instead, he struggles "not to think of her as too stupid to take Esi's place, even remotely" (71), and even after Esi divorces him, he tells her "without the slightest trace of irony and cynicism" that if she ever wishes to return, he will welcome her back (72).

On the other side of the ledger from such pain, Aidoo presents Esi's exuberant happiness. She enjoys "walking around naked after love-making," and Ali enjoys watching her ease with her own body (75). Esi's comfortableness in her own nakedness is frequently viewed as a feminist good,[59] but the voice in the novel that articulates an ideological critique of female modesty is Ali's: having "slept with a great number of women in his time," he knows that there are very few "who even tried to be at ease with their own bodies," which he attributes to traditional, Islamic, and colonial cultural repression. The context of this "affirmation" of Esi might give a reader pause: it seems doubtful that Ali, with his womanizing and infidelity, would validate feminist goods and feminist cultural critiques. Perhaps Ali appreciates a genuine feminist good but for proprietary reasons of his own; perhaps the dual cultural significance of nakedness—something a woman who affirms the female body and female sexuality will enjoy, and something characteristic of witches—comes into play. On the one hand, Ali recognizes a kindred, witchlike spirit. On the other hand, the misogynistic strand in the discourse of witchcraft might well indicate that most women have been alienated from their bodies in ways that are illegitimate; thus, the novel might be seen as recoding nakedness, allowing it to be understood in ways that need not signify evil.

However, what it signifies in Esi's case remains a question. In addition to making love and watching her body, Ali enjoys Esi's splendid cooking (76–77). The narrative closely links the sensual pleasures of food and sex. "Feasting" with Ali alternates with sex as a source of delight. An account of Ali's frequent absences leads into a description of Esi missing her daughter, but she is not portrayed as missing her "terribly," as Oko is. Indeed, because there are "some tensions" when she visits Oko's mother's house, she thinks "that if she could only stop herself from missing the child so much, she would just stop going to that place," but a "test of her willpower" fails, and so she visits once a week (80). Although Esi is not indifferent to Ogyaanowa, indeed is persecuted by an involuntary need to see her periodically, the text makes clear that she would like to have no such need, even as it raises the question of how much that need is the product of Ali's absence.

Esi's relation to Ogyaanowa does not contrast favorably with Ali's relation to Fusena and his children: "He loved Fusena his wife and tried not to hurt her deliberately" or "leave her feelings unnecessarily bruised. . . . He was also too sensitive a father" (78). Without actually letting consideration for others curb his pleasures, Ali is sufficiently attentive to their feelings to maintain a certain aesthetic decorum. But both Esi and Ali willingly, knowingly, adjust the lives of others to accommodate their consumption of one another. Aidoo's descriptions of sex are unusually frank, breaking traditional silences. Those descriptions are, however, integral to characterization: "And then he was inside her, feeling his way into a cave that was warm, of uneven surfaces, wet and dangerously inviting. . . . On her part Esi felt somewhat cramped on the couch. . . . But . . . she would rather not be comfortable if it would mean having to give up all those different kinds and levels of sensation she was enjoying without shame. She wanted to scream, and scream and scream" (85). The passage might be seen as celebrating the right of independent, professional women to enjoy really good sex, but just as the narrative stresses the cost to others of this pleasure, the passage itself stresses that what Esi and Ali share here is only self-absorption, an all-consuming delight in their own individual sensations: "It was not possible to feel like this on this earth, she was thinking. And nothing is as sweet as being inside a woman, he was thinking."

Although Esi exhibits no unwillingness to go on as Ali's mistress, he wants her to become his second wife, insisting that she accept a ring, because a ring lets "the rest of the male world know that she is bespoke," that—as Esi puts it and he readily agrees—"she has become occupied territory" (91). McWilliams and Gyimah note that Ali's likening of a woman to occupied territory reveals the chauvinism beneath his sensitivity,[60] but it also reveals what is at stake for Ali in his campaign to charm and bribe both his family and hers into condoning his marriage to a woman he already enjoys fully. The phrase "occupied territory" suggests military conquest to Western ears, but it has another equally important connotation. Throughout Africa, until recently in some areas, there has been abundant unoccupied land, the bush, but scarce labor resources and weak means of controlling labor.[61] As a result, political and economic power

accrues to those who show themselves capable of occupying territory, of bringing under their control sufficient human resources to clear the bush and establish farms. This was especially an acute problem in the dense forests of Asante
and other Akan polities.[62] Wilks notes, "Those who controlled the production
and sale of gold were those able to procure a supply of unfree labor. Those who
procured unfree labor were those able to create arable land within the forest.
Those who created the arable were those who founded the numerous early
Akan polities. . . . These entrepreneurs were known as the *aberempon* . . . ,
literally 'big men.'"[63] Thus, private accumulation and the expansion of the
state were united in the activities and the persons of the *aberempon*. Both
Wilks and McCaskie have documented how material accumulation in Asante
brought enormous social prestige.[64] The most obvious beneficiaries of system,
and ideally allies, were the *aberempon* (the big men, the nobility of wealth),
the *nhenkwaa* (the civil service), and the *adehyee* (the nobility of officeholders). Paul Nugent has traced how these precolonial patterns continued
into the colonial and postcolonial eras, where the alliance and mutual enrichment of big men, the civil service, and officeholders was tolerated, even celebrated, as long as private accumulation was seen as flowing into benefits for
the larger society, which, Nugent argues, was called into question only with
the collapse of Ghana's economy in the late 1970s.[65]

Despite his Islamic background, Ali is as much a contemporary variant of
the *aberempon* as Esi is a descendant of the *nhenkwaa*. McCaskie notes that in
the nineteenth century "some confirmation of the uneasy tension between the
moral economy of lineage or descent and the world of the accumulator of
wealth is to be found in the contrast made between the concept of *papa* . . . and
the individualistic behaviour and even hubris that might ensue from enjoying
favoured access to the mechanisms of accumulation."[66] Nugent argues that the
moral legitimacy of the elite's right to accumulation collapsed with the
economy in the 1970s and that moral collapse was signified by the sudden
prominence of the word *kalabule*, denoting "profiteering, either by manipulation of the state machinery or merely by evasion of official controls." The
Rawlings rebellion of 1979 and revolution of 1982 were conceived as revolts by
the "small boys" against domination by "big men" and their enrichment—
through privileged access to (state-controlled) means of accumulation—at
everyone else's expense through *kalabule*. Seen in these terms, the "big men"
were no longer benefactors of the state and community, but "parasites" suck-
ing away the life-substance of the people.[67] "In Ghana, those who are corrupt

are said to 'chop' (literally, eat) money. This kind of metaphor was especially resonant in the era of grand *kalabule*, when feeding a family became a genuine predicament for the average Ghanaian. . . . To continue with the gustatory metaphor, Ghanaians imagined that [*kalabule*] enabled a minority to grow fat on illicit pickings, while the majority of citizens were impoverished as a direct consequence thereof."[68] The metaphoric proximity of this discourse to that of witchcraft should be apparent. Ali hopes to get Esi's and his own lineage groups to legitimize socially what he has accumulated and thus to confirm that he is indeed an honored big man.

In portraying Ali's success, Aidoo depicts a postcolonial social world in which traditional constraints upon rapaciousness have fallen apart. When she sees the ring, Opokuya startles Esi by asking if she can imagine becoming friends with Fusena, noting that "in a traditional situation, it was not possible for a man to consider taking a second wife without the first wife's consent. In fact, it was the wife who gave the new woman a thorough check-over" (97). McWilliams argues that Esi, buying into Western heterosexualist ideas, cuts "herself off from the support that could have been exhibited from her co-wife."[69] But McWilliams's own description of Esi's project—"to create for *herself* a space in which *her* sexual desires, *her* need for companionship, *her* counter need for freedom and *her* career ambitions can all coexist" [my emphasis]—would make it unlikely that the first wife's "thorough check-over" could yield any other conclusion than that the husband was enchanted by a witch. Ali cannot present himself as a prospective husband to Esi's people unless he is accompanied by his people, but they refuse unless Fusena consents (106). However, this check to the desire of a son who has made it big is only formal; the women of Ali's family meet with Fusena, and, convinced there is no choice, she puts on a mask of compliance (107). Here the negative side of postcolonialism's cross-cultural, cosmopolitan "openness" comes into view: Fusena can rely upon neither ethnic nor religious difference to function as obstacles to the realization of Ali's desires. Nor does the genuine respect that Ali's people have for Fusena matter. The combination of polygamy with a "modern" cultural context produces a social world where people like Fusena are defenseless against being devoured by people like Ali and Esi. No amount of fidelity and hard work can shield one from predation by those who cleverly manipulate a hollowed-out shell of a "system." Fusena's position is analogous to that of an ordinary Ghanaian's of the 1970s victimized by *kalabule*.

When Esi informs her family of her intentions, she receives an extended dressing-down by Nana, the grandmother. Tuzyline Jita Allan argues that Nana provides a "double-voiced narrative that both affirms and subverts the military metaphor of woman as 'occupied territory.'"[70] McWilliams sees Nana presenting a "counter mythology" where the apparent "primacy of the devouring gods (men) is undercut" by women's ability to "hold the power of oration and the vision of change."[71] Gyimah finds in Nana's words a confirmation of "the theoretical concepts of Western philosophers such as Michel Foucault and Jacques Lacan," showing how "sexual politics . . . (always) indicates one group's domination over another" through control of language and the gaze.[72]

Nana's discourse is complex, but about one matter there is no ambiguity: she disapproves of Esi's decision to marry Ali. She tells Esi that "in a world where lies are pampered like the only children and nephews of queens and kings, all we can do is to hold to our own truths. . . . These days, we are getting used to people . . . [who] talk of pretty things when they intend ugly, and carry dangerous deeds home that properly belong to the bush" (109). What characterizes people nowadays is that they say "big things when they mean so little or nothing at all," which well describes the radical dissonance between high-minded public rhetoric and the covert practice of *kalabule* that marked Ghana from Nkrumah's First Republic to the brief Third Republic.[73] What is "double-voiced" in the passage is the dual political and personal reference: it describes the self-aggrandizing activity of the political elite *and* of people like Esi and Ali, both pampered only children, who "talk of pretty things," such as marrying, when they "intend ugly" — such as pursuing their desires at whatever cost to others.

By linking public and private predation, Nana suggests that both are marked by a failure of character (*suban*) exemplified by "carry[ing] dangerous deeds home that properly belong to the bush." The distinction between home, or domestic, civilized space, and the bush, the world of the raw, the violent, the unsocialized, is crucial throughout sub-Saharan Africa.[74] Both by appearing to value constraint and by affirming the legitimacy of the social containment of desire, Nana's discourse would seem consistent with Akan morality. Nana's *akutia* has Esi as its target, which implies that if Esi has any sense at all, she ought to recognize herself as the predator Nana describes in general terms.

It is within this context that Nana presents her "counter-myth," telling Esi that her reasons for rejecting Oko and embracing Ali have cheered "the heart of an old woman who has not found anything in this life amusing in a long time" (109). She tells Esi that she can "pick and choose" because she is privileged, but "the best husband you can ever have is he who demands all of you and all of your time" (109). She then launches into a discussion of consumption that does indeed seem subversively double-voiced. "What is a good man if not the one who eats his wife completely. . . . A good woman was she who quickened the pace of her own destruction. . . . I have had four children, and I know that each time a baby came out of me, I died a little. . . . Men were the first gods in the universe, and they were devouring gods. The only way they could yield their best—and sometimes their worst too—was if their egos were sacrificed to: regularly. The bloodier the sacrifice, the better" (109–10).

Here the language of witchcraft merges with a description of social life. When men are compared to "devouring gods" needing "bloody sacrifice," Aidoo evokes the precolonial annual Asante *odwira* (yam harvest, cleansing ceremony), where the elite, led by the king, did indeed present themselves as "devouring gods" to whom bloody sacrifices were made.[75] By placing predatory violence at the heart of socialization, Nana would seem to undermine her own home/bush distinction as well as reiterate the central tension of Akan history, that individualistic accumulation underwrote the acquisition of socialized space.

However, Nana's discourse bears a cynical, rather than subversive, relationship to Akan morality. Nana's declaration that every time she gave birth, she "died a little," resonates with an Akan recognition that if one refuses to die a little by having children, the community will die completely. By extension, the care we bestow on others does involve something like giving over our life-substance to be sucked away, but without a willingness to give of oneself, would any home be distinct from the bush? But Nana implies that women are simply "swallowed up" so that "societies" can prosper (110). She posits no alternative to being one of the devourers or the devoured. In dismissing, as emblematic of the sacrifice-demanding egos of the Europeans, the moon landing—"[A]mong other things, they can build strong machines of fire to burn us all and then go to the moon. . . . Ah, ah, ah, let me spit!" (110)—Nana reveals insights into the arrogance that often goes with technology, but also a cynical narrowness. As when she dismisses any possibility of love that is not a song-and-dance delusion, Nana seems unable to value what goes beyond her own experience. It is within this context of cynicism that Nana advises Esi, "My lady Silk, remember a man always gained in stature through any way he chose to associate with a woman. And that included adultery. Especially adultery. Esi, a woman has always been diminished in her association with a man" (109–10). A woman should be wary of men out of self-interest, to avoid being eaten.

Even as Nana paints the alternatives of eating and being eaten, the tone of her discourse indicates disapproval of profiting from predatory power relations. The accents of indignation in her voice would seem to contest the cynicism of her account. True, there is a certain relish to Nana's tone, which suggests that she sees herself as having been eaten and gets a measure of malicious pleasure in the conviction that Esi will get hers, too. Nonetheless, Nana also acknowl-edges, "They say it was not always like this" between men and women, and she professes that "[l]ife on this earth need not always be some humans being gods and others being sacrificial animals" (111).

Either Nana's discourse is incoherent (being consumed is the inevitable condition of social life; being consumed is a cultural-historical affliction sub-ject to remedy) or its "vision of change" collapses into cynicism (people *may* once have been different but that was long, long ago; people *could* change, but they will not). While her advice is about how to forestall being devoured, her biting tone seems to entertain the prospect that modern women can — through Western ideas and education — become themselves devouring gods. By col-lapsing being "eaten" in ways that sustain human and communal welfare (ways that correspond to *papa*, which finds its first instance in the baby's "eat-ing" the mother's milk) and being "sacrificed" to the ego of "devouring gods," Nana dismisses Akan moral ideals, much as earlier she dismissed any possibil-ity of nonillusory love. At the same time, her discourse ends where it begins, in moral condemnation of Esi: just as she insinuates that Esi is among those who "talk pretty" but "intend ugly," so she insinuates that she may be among those who would be gods to whom others (such as Fusena and Ogyaanowa) are sacrificial animals. For all her malicious glee and celebration of cunning, she does not find this prospect acceptable. After Esi remarks that Ali's lack of close relatives nearby was "the main reason why she was thinking of agreeing to marry him," Nana "nearly fell off her short stool" and her mother "stared hard at Esi and called her a witch" (111).

The trope of witchcraft appears in the cocktail conversation with Opokuya as a misogynistic way of controlling women; then it is applied by Oko's female relations to Esi; then it is applied to her by her own mother. After this conver-sation, Esi overhears Nana scolding her mother for having called Esi a child; she equates such naming with "many things these days" she does not "approve of," not because "they are new and [she's] old, but because they are just bad" (112). She insists that Esi not be pampered by being seen as a child. Children are not ethical agents—which is why among the Akan "a non-adult cannot be a witch."[76]

Esi hears in Nana's rebuke only a closeness between mother and daughter that she cannot share and for which she blames others: "Why had they sent her to school? . . . Who had designed the educational system that had produced her sort?" (114). She reflects that both she and the country are in a state of "dangerous confusion." The wound that colonialism and the West inflict upon Esi is analogous to the "catastrophe" that Alasdair MacIntyre describes befalling moral philosophy in the modern West. He begins *After Virtue* with painting a picture of an imaginary calamity that destroys modern science, leaving people with a few disconnected fragments of a lost tradition.[77] MacIntyre claims that such a disaster has actually befallen moral philosophy, so that people argue in seemingly irresolvable or arbitrary ways because they are dealing with half-understood fragments of lost structures of meaning. Esi's relation to Akan moral discourse is similar. Nana, her mother, and Opukuya all lose patience talking with her because her reasoning, unmoored from concerns for duties other than duties to herself, seems to them a parody of reason—childish, petulant, mad, witchlike.

Esi imagines that while her life is full of "serious personal, and not so personal questions," the answers "could not come from her," but would have to come from "a whole people": "In the meantime she would listen to her grandmother. . . . She would just relax and flourish in her mother's and her grandmother's peace" (115). The reader can see that she will do no such thing, for the grandmother's art of insinuation, except as it relates to cunning, is lost on her. She embraces the image of "just relax[ing] and flourish[ing] in her mother's and her grandmother's peace," which is a child's aspiration, not an adult's. If mothers and grandmothers provide peace, then surely it is her obligation to provide that peace for a real child, her own daughter.

As is frequently the case with selfish people, the attainment of their desires brings them a world of grief. Esi spends her wedding night alone, for Ali must "make up" for time he spent away from Fusena attending the multicultural wedding ceremony (116–17). Ali, who has a long-standing family ritual of coming home early on New Year's Eve, is torn between a sense of duty to Fusena and guilt at neglecting Esi, and so attempts to make a quick visit to her bungalow before going home from work. When he arrives, he and Esi say nothing but start "eating one another up," for Esi feels shame about her emotional dependence on a man "too preoccupied for other matters to ever be with her," while he feels "several shades of guilt," especially because as he is "so busy pumping into Esi," he is "also busy ruining a tradition" (120). While Esi's shame involves seeing herself as vulnerable, at risk of being devoured, Ali's guilt involves a sense of himself as ethically positioned in ways that he cannot evade. At this moment, Oko suddenly arrives, and a pathetic, farcical altercation ensues (120–21). "Then a child began to cry. It was Ogyaanowa" (122). By startling the reader with the revelation of Ogyaanowa's presence, Aidoo again calls attention to her habitual absence from her mother's thoughts. Leaving the two men fighting, Esi takes Ogyaanowa and seeks refuge at Opokuya's.

Opokuya is feeling especially tired—"Tired from being too conscientious. Tired of being too mindful of other people's needs and almost totally ignoring her own" (123). During the holidays, everyone at the hospital where Opokuya works wants time off. Opokuya, having fifteen years' seniority as a midwife, could manipulate the work schedule to her advantage. "However desperate she may have felt, she kept telling herself that it just wasn't right that she who fixed the rota should also give herself the best part of the timetable. . . . Obviously, when the ancients had said that 'who shares the meat doesn't eat bones,' they hadn't counted people with her kind of conscience, had they?" (123). Allan insists that Opokuya's apparent maternal concern for others is really a "maternal mask": "The self-serving motives underlying Opokuya's maternal attitudes should not be overlooked." For example, her own relations are not close, so caring for her nuclear family "is simply a matter of survival."[78] One might question whether it is actually a better feminist good to put on a "maternal mask" for "self-serving" reasons than to be genuinely concerned about others. In any event, the passage above is inconsistent with such a reading. Out of a maternally structured "mindfulness of other people's needs," Opokuya deliberately does not exploit her position to serve herself. She refuses to engage in *kalabule* because a maternal ethic of being for-another gives rise to a civic ethic of not treating one's status in a hierarchy as a vehicle to make the world work *for us*. By contrasting Opokuya's conduct with a proverb echoing the "eat-or-be-eaten" cynicism of Nana, Aidoo implies that beyond the logic of what Levinas describes as the collusion of being and self-interest, beyond the appropriative rapacious of "big men" and women who would imitate them, there is the "otherwise" of the ethical and maternal, the "kind of conscience" embodied in someone who does not conceive of her career primarily in terms of extracting "side-benefits."[79]

Opokuya is particularly exhausted because she is cooking for New Year's Eve, the children are greedy, and numerous relations of Kubi arrive (124). Into this situation, Esi arrives. When she first hears that Ali and Oko are fighting, Opokuya wants to laugh, but "check[s] herself" because we cannot be "rude or unkind" to our friends: "[S]he kept quiet and gently rocked her friend as though Esi was a baby" (125). Once again, Aidoo gives the ethical, here in the form of female friendship, the face of the maternal. Opokuya actually does get something out of her kindness: "Esi's invasion" becomes for her "a real boon" (129). They chat, and laugh, and Esi helps cook. The real companionship experienced by both Esi and Ogyaanowa at Opokuya's contrasts sharply with the resumption of the life Esi has made for herself. Soon after the holidays, Oko and a male relative come "to collect the child" (132). Ogyaanowa, "thoroughly fed up with" having only a housekeeper around while Esi is at work, shows "such an eagerness to go" that Esi feels "rejected," but lets her go, regaining a life where the concerns of others need not bother her.

The Bewitching Self-Impoverishment of Contemporary Goods

Ali's absences, excuses, and gifts increase, but at first Esi finds satisfaction in being able to focus exclusively on her projects. She discovers that "she actually enjoyed working. She enjoyed working with figures—co-ordinating them, correlating and graphing"; she is also able not only to attend "all the important office meetings" but also to participate fully (138). This passage is often cited as showing that Esi realizes the feminist good of valorizing her career.[80] Although the novel does present this as a genuine good, it also presents Esi's relation to her career as entirely self-centered. There is nothing inherently wrong with enjoying mastery over numbers; indeed, such labor may have great social usefulness. But her work's value for others occupies no space in Esi's consciousness. Just as she enjoys numbers, so she enjoys not feeling "harassed" by the need to make time for "her role as a mother, a wife and a home-wife." Aidoo adds, "Of course, when she thought of her daughter, she felt a little bad too. But there was no doubt at all that she enjoyed the fact that she was free to attend all the conferences, workshops, seminars, and symposia on her schedule, whether they were held inside the country or outside." Phrased this way, the narrative information is an *akutia* devastating in what it implies: "*when* she thought of her daughter," which we have seen is remarkably seldom, "she felt *a little* bad *too*." But, for her, the effective removal of her young daughter from her life is counterbalanced by her freedom to enjoy "all the conferences, workshops, seminars, and symposia" she wants.

Delineating the tension between the way professional life consumes adults' time and the way "children, especially young children," need the sheer material presence of their parents, Hillary Rodham Clinton notes, "And inconvenient as it is to admit, they don't need or appreciate 'quality time' so much as 'quantity time.'"[81] Esi seldom admits what is inconvenient. When she thinks that she misses Ali because he was "supposed to be her husband," she reflects that "Ogynaanowa was her daughter and she missed her. The comparison worked for her although she knew they were not exactly the same type of relationship" (139). Esi will not think through the difference, but Aidoo's phrasing invites, almost begs, the reader to do so. Esi's relationship with Ali is structured around what she gets—good sex, a charming companion, expensive gifts. Her relationship with Ogyaanowa ought to be structured around what she gives—which is quite little. To think of her career, Ali, and her daughter as competing goods betrays a fundamental egotism. All of these should not be construed as simply goods *for her* to be mixed and matched.

Aidoo is frequently most eloquent in her silences. Esi's career as a government data analyst might actually have a great social value, depending upon exactly when the novel's action takes place. Aidoo offers few clues. We are told that Ali began his travel agency soon after independence (20). That would be around 1960, which would suggest that the narrative present is the 1970s, which is also suggested by Nana's remark about moon landings, the scarcity of consumer goods, and government regulation of prices (31). On the other hand, the level of traffic might suggest the mid-1980s. The very inability to be sure from Esi's reflections upon her career is telling. If the narrative present is the 1970s, Esi's work is entirely useless, since a variety of mostly military governments would be driving the economy into the ground, inflicting great material hardship on the vast majority of the populace, while *kalabule* would be ensuring the flourishing of the elite.[82] On the other hand, if the narrative present is the mid-1980s, Esi's work might indeed be crucial to the Rawlings government's ability to improve the Ghanaian economy through a series of liberal economic reforms (that had the effect of reducing government control of the economy, and so structural opportunities for *kalabule*), instituted, incongruously, by the Marxist economic theoretician, Dr. Kwesi Botchwey.[83] Central to the Rawlings government's economic success was the emergence of a new class of technocrats, who gained increasing political authority and personal self-confidence as their economic policies began to bear fruit.[84] Nugent cites Botchwey's response at a 1986 press conference to complaints from the left that he used statistics to obscure what everyone "knew to be true": "I get bemused when people bemoan statistics. When the statistics are bad, they quote them; when they are good, they don't want to hear them. Now, if you don't want statistics, how are we to measure the improvement or deterioration in this economy? Do we take a vote of everybody? Subjection? This man says it has improved, that man says it has not improved. Isn't it science, whether it is social or natural, based on some quantification?"[85]

If the narrative present is the mid-1980s, the statistics Esi prepares might contribute to a new, positive direction for a Ghana and an Africa impoverished materially and morally by statist regimes of both the right and the left.[86] In that case, the ethical goods of her career would show that science and analytical rationality matter in ways that her grandmother cannot comprehend. In fact, the effect of economic recovery in Ghana was to displace the "eat-or-be-eaten" world of *kalabule* with a system where accumulation, doing well personally, need not come at the expense of the community: by the early 1990s, "Apart from exposing fresh veins of accumulation, the Rawlings regime had rehabilitated the sociability of wealth. That is, it was once again possible to distinguish 'legitimate' wealth from that which had been acquired illegally, a boundary which had become extremely blurred during the heyday of *kalabule*."[87] The inability to tell, from the way Esi thinks of her career, whether the context is the 1970s or 1980s underscores how little she thinks about her career at all, except in terms of what it can do *for her*.

Esi's enjoyment notably is short-lived. Ali's absences increase as he acquires a pretty young secretary (139–40). When Esi sees Ali only twice briefly between the end of October and the middle of December, she tries to assuage her loneliness by asking Oko's mother for Ogyaanowa for Christmas, to which Oko's mother responds, "What ever for?" (141), a question certainly mean-spirited but a reasonable indictment of Esi's understanding of what having a daughter entails. She spends Christmas alone in her bungalow and decides by New Year's Eve to take tranquilizers (143–44). Waking from a drugged sleep to the honking of a car horn, she discovers Ali presenting her with a new, expensive sports car (145–46). Although she tries, Esi cannot "experience any joy," because she understands that the car is a "very special bribe" that, like his presents, substitutes for his attention (147). Since Ali has to leave, Esi is left alone with the car and nowhere to go. Finally, she goes to Opokuya's (151–52). When Opokuya sees the car, she is crushed (152).

That Esi receives such a reward for organizing her life around her own desires seems to make a mockery of Opokuya's life of daily sacrifices. Once Esi learns that Opokuya wants to buy her old car, Esi reluctantly agrees to sell it to her, for as small a price as Opokuya's pride will allow, but only after deciding to take it to a garage where it will be reorganized "completely with spare parts manufactured by" the self-styled engineers themselves (155). The need to manufacture spare parts locally, and the fact that new cars have "completely disappeared" (147), suggests that the narrative present is the 1970s, for by the mid-1980s there was a "sudden availability of consumer goods and spare parts."[88] That would place Opokuya's envy of Esi's car in a particular poignant context: because endemic corruption "cast doubt on virtually all forms of accumulation," Ghanaians "coined the term 'bottom power' to describe the success with which certain young women . . . were able to gain possession" of privileged access to mechanisms of accumulation, of which new cars were the emblematic fruit.[89]

Esi's willingness to sell her old car and her concern that it be made as safe as possible are frequently viewed as evidence of feminist solidarity. It involves, however, little inconvenience: she would have gotten rid of the old car in any case, and helping Opokuya affords her the pleasure of exercising the powers of her position to serve a friend. She exhibits a form of "generosity" central to how big men articulate power. Ali helps educate his foster mother's children and instructs his local office to make "regular remittances" to the family (134).

But being able to help Opokuya and attend all the conferences on her schedule cannot prevent Esi from sliding into a depression. Ali's dwindling visits lead Esi to proclaim their marriage over (159); when Opokuya comes to take delivery of the car, she notices that Esi is in the habit of drinking alone with rapid refills (160). When Opokuya drives off, Esi is only "aware of . . . desolation" (162). Forgetting to lock the iron gate that has become emblematic both of Esi's self-enclosure and a predatory outside world, Esi awakens from a stupor to find Kubi at her door, looking for Opokuya. When he sees her disorder, he begins making love to her, which suggests that Opokuya has long received an ill return for her concern for him.

Esi's hesitant but ultimately firm refusal of Kubi's advances is frequently cited as a redemptive moment. McWilliams argues that "her grandmother's words keep her from capitulating and highlight the enduring importance of female friendship."[90] Uwakweh claims that Esi "realizes that friendship is also a fulfilling choice."[91] Gyimah sees Esi "reclaim[ing] her subjectivity" by learning from her grandmother "to resist dominance."[92] However, Aidoo's depiction does not support such readings. Esi is, first of all, tempted to yield, thinking that "maybe this might be an answer to the great question of how to get one's physical needs met, and still manage to avoid all attachment and pain" (163). This "great question" defines a predatory, witchlike relation to others. Of course, the question reflects Esi's sense of betrayal, but as we have seen in the psychological portrait of Ali, as well as in Nana's discourse, one of the violences a predatory, oppressive culture inflicts upon people is disposing them to cultivate witchlike sensibilities.

When Esi begins to reconsider, Aidoo's phrasing might well be taken to support the readings above: "She remembered that there is something called friendship. And hadn't her friendship with Opokuya been, so far, the most constant thing in her life? . . . And to maintain a friendship is a choice? . . . Opokuya's ample face came into view, beaming . . . humorous" (164). Were the passage to end here, it would suggest that Esi has finally been decentered from an egoistic structuring of identity. To remember that "there is something called friendship" returns to the theme of words having a meaning not contingent upon desires, convenience, or cultural-historical contextualization. By noting that friendship with Opokuya has been "the most constant thing in her life," the text suggests that Esi, in this crisis, is thrown back upon the one current in her life that might be construed as a narrative unity of pursuing the good. When Opokuya's "ample face," "beaming . . . humorous" comes "into view," Esi seems at the edge of a paradigmatically Levinasian moment, when the face of the Other rebukes the spontaneity of our freedom. The one anomalous element here is thinking of friendship as a "choice," something at the disposal of a self-creative subjectivity.

Construing friendship as a choice turns out to be the pivot that moves Esi sharply away from the ethical. As soon as Opokuya's face comes into view it has, incongruously, Nana's voice and declares, "My lady Silk, remember that a man always gains in stature any way he chooses to associate with a woman — including adultery. . . . But, in her association with a man, a woman is always in danger of being diminished" (164). Opokuya's face ought to ground a moral economy irreducible to self-interest. But Esi cannot hear Opokuya's own (ethical) discourse; instead, all she can hear is a discourse of self-serving cunning. Aidoo concludes the passage, "In any case, wasn't the need to maintain that friendship greater on her part? Maybe Opokuya could shed her. She, Esi, could not afford to shed Opokuya" (164). Ultimately, the reason why Esi does not sleep with her best friend's husband is that she calculates that she could not afford to shed Opokuya. Esi is motivated by neither female friendship nor feminist solidarity. Perhaps she understands that she cannot alienate herself from sociability altogether (she needs a friend), but she conceives the value of that friendship only in the witchlike terms of what it does for her.

Startlingly, the passage indicates that Opokuya has a level of power hitherto unrecognized. Her habitual being-for-another has paradoxically empowered her, giving her several layers of community with whom she can share the joys and pains of life, as well as an identity of such solidity and resources that potential predators, like Esi, back off. By contrast, the self-impoverishment that has accompanied Esi's predations leaves her vulnerable enough to curb her appetite when it might threaten the support she receives from Opokuya.

The implication is that because the ethical relation resembles the maternal relation, good people will open themselves to being imposed upon and used up, but this very asymmetry of the ethical relation makes the building of a just community a moral imperative. Arguably, such a world emerged, out of the ashes of *kalabule*, in the course of the 1980s that was indeed an answer on the part of "a whole people" to the problems the novel delineates, but that answer would not come from people like Nana, locked in the zero-sum logic of "eat-or-be-eaten" analysis, nor would it come from people like Esi, although she is professionally positioned to make a contribution. Rather, it would come from people like Opokuya, clever enough to recognize structures of oppression, but ultimately unwilling to allow themselves to be bewitched by the goods that making *kalabule* work *for them* would provide—for other goods, inseparable from a maternal, sociable care for a future beyond and larger than their personal future, would matter more.

Just as the novel suggests that real changes will not come from Esi, so it implies that real changes will not come *to* her. Her marriage with Ali never formally ends, but they become "just good friends who found it convenient once in a while to fall into bed" (164). Esi, so enchanted with her own freedom, learns never to wonder where Ali is "when . . . not with her" (165). Aidoo remarks laconically, "Given the nature of her job, it was only natural" that Opokuya heard the most "gossip about Ali." But, kind to the end, she tells Esi the least of all those close to her. Still conceiving the world as somehow made for her, and meeting her personal needs as the overwhelming object of life (Ogyaanowa is not mentioned in the novel's final section), Esi is left—like any self-absorbed baby-boomer—querying her own self about her own lack of satisfaction, taking solace in the commercialized vague hopefulness of the Highlife singer romanticizing about the day when fulfillment will finally come *to us* (166). All Nana's predictions are realized about Esi being devoured, being lonely, being gulled by a song-and-dance image of happiness. Levinas entitles an essay on Judaism, "A Religion for Adults." By insisting, through the details of her plot and the nuances of her phrasing, that Esi is too self-centered to be ethically mature, Aidoo articulates a feminism for adults, one that recognizes that while it may be hard to "resolve" the many roles "a woman with high education" must play, and while it may be "a good thing" to dare, to risk being unconventional,[93] no good life, no life that genuinely realizes feminist goods, can emerge from subjectivities that are childish or witchlike in their constitution.

7

Self-Assertion, Piety, and Ethical Responsibility in Buchi Emecheta's *Kehinde*

Abortion, Individualism, and Cultural Articulations of the Good

Emecheta's *Kehinde* (1994) opens with Kehinde's husband, Albert, after eighteen years of marriage in London, wanting to return to Nigeria, in part to participate in the 1970s oil boom, in part to become the patriarch of an extended family, in part to avoid dependence on his wife's higher salary as an assistant bank manager.[1] When Kehinde, who has two teenage children, announces that she is pregnant, Albert fears that it will endanger her promotion. Since he is counting on her money for "his home-going" (22), he pressures her into an abortion, telling a coworker, "This is not the right time for another one. I know abortion is wrong but we are in a strange land, where you do things contrary to your culture" (15). When Kehinde insists that she should also have her tubes tied, Albert tells himself "that if doctors could tie up women's tubes, surely they could untie them again whenever he and Kehinde could afford another child" (22). Albert imagines that Western technology has made narrative causality optional: Whenever it is convenient, actions can be undone, stories can be unwritten, consequences can be erased.

John C. Hawley notes that some Western readers "may feel uncomfortable with Emecheta's portrayal of Kehinde's abortion as the token of her servitude" to her husband.[2] In her autobiography, *Head above Water* (1986), Emecheta, the mother of five children by the time she was twenty-two, notes that she "would never have aborted a living embryo. I am not saying that this is the right decision, but this is me. I don't believe in abortion."[3] Emecheta's position reflects neither sentimentality nor a sheltered life. Her husband, always improvident, abandoned the family, leaving Emecheta destitute with four small children and pregnant with the fifth: "I was virtually raped for Alice to be conceived, though, looking at her now, I'm glad it happened." By treating Kehinde's unexpected pregnancy as an inconvenience, Albert carries to its logical conclusion the allergy to the Other that marks intentionally structured egoism. In Emecheta's own life, the antisocial violence inherent in such self-involved egoism was brought home by the conduct of her husband, Sylvester, who wanted her to put the children up for adoption because "he did not wish to be saddled with five kids."[4]

Although Emecheta notes that abortion is a practice consistent with the assumptions and values of the modern West, she does not therefore locate it within a register of cultural relativism. Even as Kehinde agrees to Albert's demand, her body resists in ways that suggest that bodily sensations convey moral knowledge derived from the realm of "saying." On the way to the hospital, her legs are "like jelly, scarcely able to carry her weight"; she longs for Albert to relent, but when he does not, she walks "like a zombie to the front door" (22). The nurse has "a strictly commercial smile" (23); her roommate, a young white girl, Leah, "convulsed in spasmodic sobs" (25), explains that she cannot afford to keep her baby, isn't sure she "loves David," doesn't want to "trap him," for that would be "unfair," then adds, "What makes me angry is this. Why am I feeling so sad about it all?" (27). The nurse's "commercial smile" is linked to her "honeyed words" and her technological mastery: she closes the curtains electronically and gives the women a sedative so that "Kehinde's mouth" is "unable to say what her heart [is] thinking" (27).

While Albert declares that "abortion is wrong" and then implies that it is simply "contrary to [his Igbo] culture," Emecheta suggests through Leah that remorse over abortion is not culture-specific, that the sadness one feels is in no way ameliorated by having culturally approved "reasons" for an abortion, and her portrait of the nurse links abortion to technological, institutionalized dehumanization: "commercial smiles" and "honeyed words." Indeed, this institutionalized dehumanization suggests the nurse's need, and the institution's need, for stylizations that prevent human contact. The "saying" implicit in Leah's inarticulate anguish and in Kehinde's inability to say what her heart is thinking condemns all that is "said" to serve as a sedative for the conscience. While Emecheta does not argue that abortions should be illegal, she does argue that efforts to dissociate abortions from moral guilt are dehumanizing. In so doing, Emecheta is able to use abortion not simply as a token of Kehinde's servitude to Igbo patriarchy but as a means of insisting, through communicating the shared desolation of Kehinde and Leah to the reader, that ethical responsiveness to the Other (Kehinde's, Leah's, the reader's) articulates a moral sense that transcends cultural differences. That Leah cannot say why she feels so sad no more demonstrates that the moral significance of abortion is merely culturally constructed than the absence of indigenous African terms for marital rape indicate that it is merely an "idea" imported from the West.

While Leah has no cultural resources in which to place or interpret the moral intuitions implicit in her "unaccountable" sadness, Kehinde is able to experience her husband's conduct as violence to both intrinsic humanity and social rights because Kehinde locates identity within human and spiritual networks of affiliation and obligation. Kehinde's compliance with her husband's demands meets the internal resistance of her recognition that he has "brought her to the level" of a prostitute; both, to him, were "just bodies, convenient vehicles which, when they took an inconvenient turn, could be emptied" (17). Like Efuru, Kehinde experiences ontological reduction as a violent obliteration of social distinction: Efuru resents being treated like a slave, and Kehinde resents being treated like a prostitute. At the same time, Kehinde experiences a voice "interrupting her thoughts, . . . the same voice she often heard when she was lonely or confused. 'Our mother died having you. I too died so you could live. Are you now going to kill your child before he has a chance of life?'" (17). We learn that this voice comes from the spirit of Kehinde's twin, Taiwo, who died in the womb, and that Kehinde's mother died giving her birth (17–18).

Emecheta narrates Kehinde's story in the third person, but has Kehinde describe her past, and thus her relation to the spirit world, in the first person. Bakhtin argues that in everyday life we experience "inner self-activity" as exceeding "both nature and the world" while we experience others as "connatural with the outside world and thus . . . woven into that world"; for this reason, "idealism is intuitively convincing from the standpoint of self-experience, whereas, from the standpoint of my experience of the other human being, materialism is intuitively convincing."[5] In the third-person narration, the reader sees Kehinde embedded in an outside world, conditioned by her socioeconomic, historical, cultural contexts. But the first-person narration allows the reader to experience Kehinde's "inner self-activity," that is, a standpoint distinguished by an intuitive sense that what we are and can be exceeds the sum of contexts into which we are placed. Just as Ricoeur argues, in temporal terms, that an interplay between *idem*-identity and *ipse*-identity is constitutive of a self resolvable into neither narrative continuity nor rupture alone, so Bakhtin argues, in spatial terms, that the self is at once "woven" into contexts, into multiple positionalities, and exceeds, through its "inner self-activity," all the contexts of "nature and the world" to which it would otherwise be totalized. While Bakhtin maintains that narrative art can combine these standpoints in ways that real life never entirely does, Emecheta's dual mode of narration emphasizes their "lived" separation, forcing the reader to balance the knowledge of one against the truth of the other. At the same time, Emecheta's first-person narration articulates a different sort of materialism from that generated by applying to humans the ways of knowing characteristic of natural science. The first-person narration grounds spiritual life in material, biological networks of dependence, revealing, in Ricoeur's terms, that *ipse*-identity is itself predicated upon "a dialectic of *self* and the *other than self*," so that "the selfhood of oneself implies otherness to such an intimate degree that one cannot be thought without the other."[6]

Following Kehinde's account of her internal life, we learn that her earliest trace of herself involves sensations of "no will of our own. We followed the rhythm of everything around us. Our food came from mother, and in return, we passed our waste back into our mother's blood" (17). A primordial oneness is broken by asymmetrical exchange—receiving food and giving back waste— that locates one's "own" being in guilty dependence; however, when "[e]verything was becoming short and cramped," "we started to talk to each other, sharing as best we could for survival" (17). On the one hand, Emecheta suggests that injustice, an invasive taking over of space and resources for ourselves, lies at the heart of our being; thus she connects, in ways explored by Levinas, the essence of being to self-interest. The unfolding or expansion of ourselves (literally as well as metaphorically) is inseparable from appropriation.[7] On the other hand, Emecheta suggests that "talk[ing] to each other" leads to sharing, that the recognition of the other as kin, a recognition mediated through speech, allows one to move beyond what materialist-egoist modes of analysis can grasp.[8]

Just as Levinas argues that the recognitions of the other embedded in speech have their roots in a "pre-original language" where "being's *esse* is inverted" through "the responsibility of one for the other" (a prelinguistic discourse grounding subjectivity upon and within intersubjectivity, which is explored in Bakhtin's account of "emotional-volitional tones"),[9] so Emecheta notes that Kehinde's prenatal "talking" took the form of "touching and kissing," "communicat[ing] . . . by touch and by sounds," sounds the twins alone "could understand" (18). Kehinde's earliest "becoming" involves, nearly simultaneously, a separation tied to aggressivity, an enjoyment bound to the experience of a "free" appropriation of "outside" material, *and* an intimacy, a responsibility, an obsession with the Other opened up by that very separation: "Egoism, enjoyment, sensibility, and the whole dimension of interiority—the articulations of separation—are necessary for the . . . relation with the Other which opens forth from the separated and finite being."[10]

Emecheta presents as equally or nearly equally anterior both a "violent" use of others as means to one's own being (thus, Kehinde and her sister "laid siege" to the "skin wall that kept [them] enclosed," "banged and . . . shouted, . . . kicked and . . . cried") and a need for mutual love, companionship, conversation (thus, when her sister dies, Kehinde "called her, but there was no answer. I cried for her in my now lonely tomb. . . . I hugged her, held her to myself, so tightly that the wetness from her body started flowing into mine"). Kehinde, like Tambu, benefits from the demise of others: "As she dried, I had more space. I grew bigger. . . . Our mother, poor soul, must have gone through hell giving birth to us" (18).

Of course, not everyone is the surviving twin of a dying mother, just as not everyone gets an education through a brother's "convenient" death, but Emecheta and Dangarembga locate their heroines' identities within these situations to underscore, through fictional intensification, how the networks of kinship and dependence intrinsic to human identity make impossible any "innocent" becoming, how the egoism at the essence of our being makes self-consciousness "inseparable from a consciousness of justice and injustice. The consciousness of any natural injustice, of the harm caused to the Other, by my ego structure, is contemporaneous with my consciousness as a man." But the very consciousness of the "natural injustice" of "my ego structure" also makes "natural" an ethical sense irreducible to culturally imposed "guilt feelings." Kehinde's understanding of her prenatal experience suggests that "[s]elf-consciousness inevitably surprises itself at the heart of a moral consciousness. The latter cannot be added to the former, but it provides its basic mode," for "I begin to ask myself if my being is justified, if the *Da* of my *Dasein* is not already the usurpation of somebody else's place."[11]

By contrast, Western postmodern theory tends not only to place violence first, to give it a radical priority, but also to see it as remarkably uncontested by any competing or conflicting principle of equal or nearly equal anteriority:

even if the world is assumed to be characterized by plurality, multivalence, and *différance*, human cognitive and cultural activity is described as invariably driving toward violent occlusions of otherness.[12] Even studies such as Katherine Fishburn's recent book on Emecheta, a work that criticizes Western readers of African novels for not examining assumptions embedded in Western modernity, and that aspires "to let the Other speak to and through us—and to let ourselves be changed by the conversation," is hobbled by axiomatic postmodern assumptions. Accepting that "the world is our text and all people in it are texts, too—unstable, contested selves that have been, and are continually being, constructed in discourse," leads to rejecting "notions of Truth, Beauty, and Justice" while affirming "with Foucault the conjunction of power, truth, and knowledge."[13] In Emecheta's portrait of Kehinde's prenatal relationships, an emphasis upon the material, biological context of identity does not deny an unstable, contested dimension to selfhood, but does suggest that an exclusive focus upon that dimension occludes much that makes us human, and much that helps explain how "[l]anguage is born in responsibility"[14] in ways that allow us to discuss "notions of Truth, Beauty, and Justice."

By discounting cross-cultural rationality and universalizing the priority of will to power, Fishburn is led to view any text, even her own, as largely an act of aggression: "Given my own desire to dismantle the Western regime of truth, I often position myself in opposition to its teachings. At the same time . . . I acknowledge (and yet hope to undermine) the will to power behind what I claim."[15] On the one hand, Fishburn criticizes Gadamer's use of "tradition" in hermeneutical understanding because she collapses all possible determinate cultural notions into the single category of "camouflaged essentialism." She does so because she follows Peter Winch in taking "as a given that 'standards of rationality and intelligibility' vary from culture to culture." On the other hand, Fishburn exempts Foucault's "conjunction of power, truth, and knowledge" from this general relativism; she quotes approvingly Mark Poster's advice that "all theorists" should "acknowledge the will to power behind and within the truth claims of [their] discourse.'"[16] In a manner that is symptomatic of much postmodern discourse, relativism rests upon totalization; discourse is always only a drive for power.

In fact, Gadamer applies Aristotle's distinction between practical rationality (*phronêsis*) and theoretical knowledge (*epistêmê*) to distinguish the use of tradition in interpretation from "camouflaged essentialism." Gadamer argues that Aristotle does not say "that the nature of the thing—e.g., the ideal of bravery—is a fixed standard that we could recognize and apply to ourselves. Rather, Aristotle affirms as true of the teacher of ethics precisely what is true, in his view, of all our men: that he too is always already involved in a moral and political context and acquires his image of the thing from that standpoint. He does not himself regard the guiding principles that he describes as knowledge that can be taught. They are valid only as schemata. They are concretized only in the concrete situation of the person acting. Thus they are not norms to be found in the stars, nor do they have an unchanging place in a natural moral universe." Similarly, in hermeneutics, "application did not consist in relating some pregiven universal to the particular situation. The interpreter dealing with a traditional text tries to apply it to himself. . . . In order to understand [what the text says], he must not try to disregard himself and his particular hermeneutical situation."[17]

Fishburn's relativistic hermeneutics seems to permit readers to take from African fiction only an intensification of the relativism it already assumes, reducing that fiction's value to "calling into question how we [Westerners] perceive the world and ourselves."[18] Emecheta begins *Kehinde*, however, by explicitly disputing the assumption that will to power is, in a significant degree, anterior to sociability, sharing, and responsiveness to the other; further, by representing Kehinde and Leah as sharing a common moral intuition, Emecheta disputes the notion that, at the most fundamental level, we are the constructs of different cultures, and so no shared rationality or intelligibility is possible.

Kehinde, who is Igbo, is sent to Lagos to be raised by her aunt, who is Christian, in a largely Yoruba community. As a toddler, she shares her food with her Taiwo, even though she is ignorant of the circumstances of her birth. After having seen a Yoruba mother of twins dancing, she asks her startled aunt where her twin, her Taiwo, is, whereupon the aunt tells a fellow market woman, "I always thought when she divided her food in two before eating that she was giving it to her *chi*" (21), that is, the personal god who is at once intrinsic to but not identical with an individual's self. The other woman replies, "Her second [the twin, Taiwo] and her *chi* are the same" (21), a statement which suggests that both the Yoruba celebration of twins (which contrasts sharply with the Igbo dread of twins) and the Igbo reverence for one's *chi* articulate metaphorically shared experiences of identity and value. Donatus Ibe Nwoga observes, "The individual depends on his *chi*. He prays to his *chi* for favours, for life and good fortune. He thanks his *chi* for his achievements and successes."[19]

Kofi Asare Opoku points out that for the Yoruba, "The souls of the twins are believed to be inseparable and when one of the twins dies, a little ibéji statuette is carved to serve as the abode of the dead twin."[20] What both the Igbo notion of the *chi* and the Yoruba notion of twinness suggest is that, as in Ricoeur's analysis of Aristotle's theorizing of friendship, the other than self is integral to the self's identity and empowerment. While one may speak of a dimension of discursively constructed selfhood in Yoruba and Igbo versions of the relationship between spiritual indebtedness to others and one's "own" identity, Kehinde's spontaneous mingling of aspects of spiritual indebtedness from both cultures while living in a Christian home suggests that the two notions can "speak" to each other, and be understood by the Christian aunt, because both speak to a level of experience that cannot be reduced either to arbitrary cultural impositions or to mere instability or contestation. In fact, Leah's unsureness about the source and nature of her spiritual pain ("Why am I feeling so sad about it all?"), as well as her spiritual and physical isolation, strongly suggest that to circumscribe human identity within the arbitrary or unstable alone connotes an extraordinary degree of cultural impoverishment, an impoverishment that will leave us bewildered and helpless in the face of our own moral intuition — and thus, like Leah, open to victimization.

Through recognizing her affiliation with Taiwo, through locating herself within networks of dependence and obligation, Kehinde is able to assert herself: upon her insistence, her aunt allows a Yoruba *ibéji* (twins) carver to make her a Taiwo (wooden image of the deceased firstborn) and begins to call her by her "real name, Kehinde" (Yoruba for secondborn twin), rather than by her Christian name, Jacobina — a name that associates identity with sibling rivalry (Jacob and Esau) rather than with sibling interdependence. Brenda F. Berrian argues that Emecheta uses Yoruba ideas about twins to allow Kehinde "a transcendence of the Igbo limitations of traits which constitute a good mother and wife. . . . Neither defeated by indigenous Igbo gender definitions nor constrained by Western gender definitions, Kehinde conjures up her own self-definition with the aid of her spirit twin Taiwo and embraces only those values which are the most beneficial for her lifestyle."[21] By knowing herself through her bond with the Taiwo, she names herself "Kehinde." Naming oneself often implies a bid for self-creation: the self-naming of Defoe's heroines, Melville's Ishmail, Dicken's Pip, Fitzgerald's Gatsby announce their ambiguous projects of self-making. But what makes such projects ambiguous is that one cannot — either practically or ethically — simply use what lies outside the self, in a mixing and matching manner, to serve the self without becoming, like Modou, idolatrous or, like Ali, witchlike. Berrian treats multicultural sources of value and meaning as significant only in so far as they can serve as material for the self's generation of its own spontaneous, self-justifying freedom.

By contrast, Emecheta not only suggests that Yoruba and Igbo beliefs arise from cross-cultural experiences of an interdependence of self and other; she also insists, as do the Yoruba and Igbo beliefs themselves, that our primordial bond with the other than self takes forms of indebtedness and obligation. As a child, Kehinde habitually shares her food with the other. Already as a child, she experiences the attitude of naive enjoyment—simply delighting in the expropriation of exteriority (the goods of the world) for our own benefit—as unjustifiable, antisocial, inhuman. Indeed, while multicultural contexts for identity empower both Albert and Kehinde, the difference is that Albert really does choose whatever values seem most beneficial for his lifestyle, whereas Kehinde experiences the power of multicultural contexts not as "positions" to be assumed when convenient but as voices to be heard, as interlocutors who make us answerable to more than ourselves. Kehinde's Taiwo, who ultimately guides her to a self-assertive, multicultural freedom, is first heard immediately after Albert is described as exemplifying the modern West's conviction that freedom involves liberation from narrativity, from the "law" of plot and consequentiality. In striking contrast, Taiwo's first words address Kehinde as one whose identity is inseparable from concrete bonds, from obligations that cannot be evaded: "Our mother died having you. I too died so you could live. Are you now going to kill your child before he has a chance of life?"

By carefully showing that Kehinde's experience of her Taiwo need not be seen as doing violence to a sense of reality shaped by modern science, Emecheta allows the culturally specific elements of Kehinde's identity to assume cross-cultural significance. While the aunt is unnerved by Kehinde's knowledge that she had a twin when that knowledge was deliberately kept from her, Emecheta has Kehinde note, "Some people who knew had made hints in unguarded moments about my past, because they felt my birth caused a disaster, and those hints must have entered my subconscious" (21). At no point in the novel does Kehinde's relationship with her Taiwo take on the dimensions of magical realism. In warning against "a new orientalism" within postcolonial theory, Spivak singles out the attribution of magical realism for scrutiny: "What are the implications of pedagogical gestures that monumentalize *this* style as the right Third World style?"[22] Whereas the paradigm of magical realism is García Marquez's *Cien años de soledad*, in which a mimetically plausible social-historical novelistic world is disrupted by magical events, such as when José Arcadio Buendía's death is followed by a rain of yellow flowers so thick that sleeping animals are suffocated or when Remedios the beauty ascends from the garden into the heavens,[23] Kehinde's experience of divine or supernatural sources of self-understanding might have subconscious sources consistent with novelistic realism. Rather than reiterating magic realism's insistence upon the actuality of supernatural events, the narration allows events that produce empowering self-understanding or moral insight to be read either as visitations by supernatural forces or as psychological experiences interpreted fruitfully through the cultural categories of supernatural forces.

Such a staging of interpretive ambiguity allows an author not to dispute the "realism" that comes with an acceptance of natural science and a respect for the "logic" of ordinary life, even as she suggests that the full significance of a world depicted through "novelistic realism" may require the reader's voluntary assent to a religious frame of reference that goes beyond what a novel may affirm as certain. The great paradigm is Manzoni's *I promessi sposi*. When the previously lawless aristocrat, the "Unnamed," refrains from sending the heroine, Lucia, to her would-be ravisher, Manzoni's phrasing allows the Unnamed's decision to be seen in terms of either secondary causes alone or a divine force that *genuinely* works through secondary causes: "Ma un *no* imperioso che risonò nella sua mente, fece svanire quel disegno" [But another voice within him replied to this (scheme) with a resounding "No!" and that idea faded from his mind]. Similarly, Cardinal Fredrigo treats the Unnamed's coming to him as evidence that God has moved him: "Che Dio v'ha toccato il cuore, e vuol farvi suo" [That God has touched your heart, and would make you his].[24] While Manzoni permits a reading in terms of psychological and historical causality alone, his phrasing implies that the elimination of a religious reading would constitute premature closure and thus gratuitous dogmatism. Emecheta's staging of interpretive ambiguity suggests that a similar premature closure and dogmatism occur if readers take varying cultural interpretations of experience to indicate only that we live in "alien" realities. What seems most "alien" actually discloses shared human experience of the ethical relation. Emecheta remarks in a 1992 interview, "I think my writing isn't English or African as much as more international, more universal. . . . I try to write for the world."[25]

In a chapter entitled "The Dream," Kehinde, unconscious during the abortion, has a vision of approaching her father, then being blocked by her mother with her Taiwo. The mother declares, "Your father was coming to you, but you sent him back. He was coming to look after you because he feels guilty about not looking after you the last time. But you have refused to receive him" (31). Kehinde is seized with longing and affection: "I suddenly realise how terribly I have missed him. I tell myself he did not deserve to die in the way he did. I must make it up to him" (31). When Kehinde awakens after the abortion, she tells her friend Moriammo, "The child I just flushed away was my father's *chi*, visiting me again. But I refused to allow him to stay in my body" (32). Like Manzoni portraying the Unnamed's conversion, Emecheta presents this scene in such a way that it can be read as either an actual meeting of Kehinde and her parents' spirits or "just a dream," in which her sense of guilt is invested with the material of traditional Igbo piety.

Nwoga points out that among "the West Niger Igbo the . . . concept of *chi* as 'the person who has reincarnated in the individual' is . . . prevalent," and cites Francis Okoafor Isichie's description: "The deceased who is believed to be reborn in the new child is generally called the child's *agu* or *chi*. A man's *chi* is the *alter ego* of the person concerned, whose present life must be supervised, ruled and guided by the circumstances of the *agu*'s or *chi*'s life in his or her previous world existence. For example, if one's *chi* was killed or kidnapped at Ibusa, the child would be forbidden to go to Ibusa." Nwoga adds, "Buchi Emecheta . . . uses this same conceptualisation of *chi* in her novels."[26]

In *Head above Water*, Emecheta describes how, born two months premature and devalued as a girl, she was expected to die and so she was fed only drops of water for the first days of her life, until her father recognized in her determination to live "the fighting spirit of [his] mother, Agbodo," which prompted her mother to take the tiny yellow infant to the hospital, declaring, "I know she has not got much chance of living but my husband said that she is his come-back mother. And he will not forgive me if I let his come-back mother die." The nurses immediately ordered the mother to begin breast-feeding, and Emecheta flourished. Her father gave her the name Onyebuchi, meaning "Are you my God?" and called her familiarly Nnenna, meaning "father's mother."[27] Indigenous sexism nearly condemned Emecheta to starve to death as an infant; on the other hand, her father's patriarchal authority, combined with his sense of indebtedness to his own mother, saved her life.

Emecheta does, as Berrian argues, use the Taiwo to specify "a paradigm of transcendence for Kehinde." However, the association of Taiwo with the *chi*, and the *chi* with western Igbo understandings of how the reborn one's guidance is shaped by his or her previous life's experience (how another's life guides one's own, how the past guides the present and future), complicates any treatment of "transcendence" as co-extensive with "conjur[ing] up [one's] own self-definition," which seems to signify only postmodernism's version of negative liberty. Berrian argues that Taiwo, "as both Kehinde's twin and *chi*, is the carrier of wisdom by which Kehinde is to live. . . . As a result, Taiwo's intervention confirms that contact with the ancestors is transformational for Kehinde," but this wisdom apparently consists in exactly what postmodernism has long taught—that freedom comes "through rebellion," through multiple positionalities, through being "not . . . alienated from [the] Ibusa society whose laws she transgresses. Neither defeated by the Igbo world nor totally assimilated into the Western world, Kehinde embraces those values which are the most beneficial for her lifestyle."[28]

Hawley also assimilates the Taiwo and *chi* to a model of freedom comfortable for Western readers, arguing that Emecheta's "*kehinde*-protagonist chooses to step into this brave new world with *no* guide. Kehinde has, so her neighbors tell her, 'eaten' Taiwo in the womb—and she now carries the twin's spirit, her '*chi*,' within her."[29] Such a reading exposes the antisocial implications of modern Western notions of freedom (only by devouring the other can we be free, because any guidance by another must be colonizing). This reading, however, does violence to the text: Kehinde does not *choose* to enter the world alone, and the imputation that she has "eaten" her twin is consistently portrayed as slander.

"The Dream" begins with Kehinde's memory of playing, as a child, "a game of families. Olu is refusing to play mother, because her mother has died, gone away, neglecting Olu and her brother Akintunde. Each time we remember, we are silent with sorrow" (28). The childish conflation of death and abandonment is counterbalanced by the children's intuitive understanding of the tragedy of losing a mother who, among other things, is a "guide" into "brave new worlds." Similarly, the egoism of their enjoyment, evident in their forgetfulness, is counterbalanced by their being "silent with sorrow" each time they remember. Olu's loss of a mother makes Kehinde ask about her father. The need to be loved is inseparable from the need to bestow love. Unable to sleep

because of her unanswered questions, Kehinde gives her Taiwo "the only comfortable part of the mat, . . . so she can lie in comfort and listen to all my
mutterings and questions" (30).

Emecheta's deliberate ambiguity about the ontological status of Kehinde's
"dream" prevents its moral significance from being relativized. Because there
is room for a psychological explanation, what is peculiarly Igbo, even West
Igbo, in Kehinde's dream may suggest that Igbo culture can offer metaphorical
insight into moral significance embedded, nonarbitrarily, in the situation. The
father is willing to come back not because life is sweet or because self-fulfillment and will to power are to be had, but because life gives us opportunities
for ethical activity (he was coming "to look after" Kehinde) and those opportunities are cherished because we know ourselves as guilty before others: "He
feels guilty about not looking after you the last time." Kehinde was raised by
her aunt and then sent to boarding school. She barely knew her father, yet her
response to the possibility of getting him back was to realize how "terribly" she
missed him. Even though her father did not treat her with much consideration, Kehinde thinks that "he did not deserve to die in the way he did."

The ethical relation involves treating people better than they deserve, returning good for ill. Kehinde senses that she must "make it up to him" by
bringing him into life again. Thus, the father's willingness to return and the
daughter's willing to bear him depend upon a recognition that the Other calls
us to ethical obligation. Just as ethical obligation underlies coming into (human) life, so ethical activity ("looking after," "making up") constitutes the substance of a genuinely human life—and not desire, will to power, resistance, or
lifestyle benefits. It is this understanding of the meaning of life that Kehinde
does violence to through agreeing to the abortion. That such a vision should
come to her, reinstating this understanding, at the very moment of the abortion indicates, whatever the ontological status of the vision, that what abortion
violates is not simply Igbo custom but moral intuitions constitutive of our humanity.

Relativism, Chauvinism, and Postcolonial
Deformations of Character

It might seem strange that Emecheta would begin a story about Kehinde's
growing resistance to patriarchal oppression with this account of what is at
stake in her abortion. Emecheta argues that effective self-assertion depends

upon situating the self within contexts where its assertion is more than a matter of desire or will to power, for if self-assertion comes to be seen as bare egotism, one cannot articulate *reasons*, even to oneself, why its claims should matter. Emecheta distinguishes between forms of acculturation that allow us to lay claim to our full humanity and forms of acculturation which *do* underwrite patriarchy and other modes of oppression. The same Igbo culture that gives Kehinde resources to resist Albert's demands also endorses female subordination. Albert longs to return to a world where, on Sundays, "his father and his mates would put on crisp *agbadas* which their wives had spent the greater part of the week bleaching and starching," going "from house to house, drinking palm wine, eating kolanuts and dried fish." He resents a Kehinde who in London "was full of herself, playing the role of a white, middle-class woman, forgetting that she was not only black, but an Igbo woman" (35).

Fishburn argues that Emecheta's portraits of boorish, self-centered Nigerian men do not necessarily indict Igbo culture, because these men are often portrayed as "corrupted" by Western individualism.[30] While selfish and materialistic impulses are certainly reinforced by Western models, Emecheta explores, in *Kehinde* at least, what aspects of Igbo culture make its men ripe for such "corruption." There is an implied link between Albert's nostalgic memory of his father's life, his resentment of Kehinde's "forgetting" herself, and the image he and his friends have of the life he would lead at home: "taking his ease in a large, airy white bungalow, with white verandahs shaded by palm-fronds . . . , with laughter and more friends than you could count" (37). Money has value to Albert as a means to "our new image." The send-off party Albert stages follows the Lagos custom of lavish display: "In the course of the evening, she changed clothes ten times, as rich men's wives did in Nigeria, to advertise their wealth and boost the ego of the man of the house" (37). This custom combines Western materialism with Igbo cultural patterns delineated in *Efuru*: competitiveness, linking wealth and status, viewing wives as markers of male status.

What distinguishes Albert's masculine self-importance from Achebe's Okonkwo's self-importance is the disdain Albert exhibits toward hard work. His idea of being a "big man" is inseparable from imagining himself "taking his ease." This might suggest that Albert has been "colonized" by a Western consumer culture. It certainly implies on Albert's part a fundamentally appropriative orientation toward exteriority. However, notions that one accumulates in order to display, that status and power rest upon claiming the service of others who—whether kin or not—are essentially clients, that leisure is both the sign of and reward for competitive success, are central to noncapitalist, patriarchal, warrior cultures in which accumulation, through plunder, tribute, and territorial expansion, necessarily bears the stamp of triumphant violence. Despite overpopulation in Igboland in the nineteenth century, the Igbo dictim that "people are wealth" implies a context of abundant unclaimed land and scarce human resources; whoever can command human resources has an ever-increasing competitive advantage. Within such a socioeconomic context, a woman acquires security and status through attaining and retaining affiliation with a "big man." A woman's independent accumulation of wealth, through farming and trading, is protected, in the absence of a modern nation-state, in the same way any client's accumulation would be protected, by the "big man's" prestige and human resources.[31]

Kehinde accepts the patriarchal assumptions that follow from such modes of social organization, despite her own career in the capitalistic institution of banking, sufficiently to scorn one of her guests, Mary Elikwu, who has recently left her husband "because, she claimed, he beat her. She had taken her six children with her" (38). By dismissing Mary's "claim" of abuse, Kehinde exhibits a naive confidence that, unless one makes some foolish mistake, life can be easy and uncomplicated. But while Kehinde's notion that losers have only themselves to blame may be consistent with the ideology a consumerist, capitalistic culture promotes, she takes as "natural" that a woman's foremost duty is to maintain the networks of affiliation that offer security and social identity: Kehinde thinks, "For all her qualifications [Mary is a university graduate], she, Kehinde, was worth more than a woman like Mary Elikwu who couldn't even keep her husband" (39).

At the same time, Kehinde feels "she deserve[s] more consideration than Albert [gives] her," she wonders why she finds it difficult "to join in" the enthusiasm about returning to Nigeria, and she resents Albert's selfish lovemaking (41–42). Kehinde willfully refuses, however, to explore the implications of what her body and her common sense intrude upon her consciousness. After Albert returns to Nigeria, leaving her in London to sell their house, she struggles to believe that his infrequent letters do not indicate that his affection and loyalty have waned. As she struggles to convince herself that return to Nigeria is a good thing, and thus to maintain her view of herself as a good Igbo wife, "the intrusive inner voice" (45) of her Taiwo "articulat[es] her vaguely acknowledged fears": "See, our father was coming to protect you from this, but you killed him. . . . Have you forgotten that in Nigeria it's considered manly for men to be unfaithful?" (46). "Her mischievous *chi*, in the voice of Taiwo," hints that Albert has acquired a girlfriend (47).

The utterances of this inner voice may be seen, in accord with Western secular realism, as Kehinde's interpretation of what is "really" her own practical rationality. But if we follow this reading, we are led to see that practical rationality, because it resists and ultimately slips away from colonization by those cultural patterns that would violate our humanity, does indeed act *as though* it were the voice of another that is yet us, a voice which gives us access to a context of identity and value that, as if it were a spiritual or divine context, disputes the totalizing claims of particular colonizing cultural patterns as well as our own propensity to value ideological consistency for the mere pleasure — what Žižek, following Lacan, calls *jouis-sense* — of consistency.[32] To accept this "realistic" account of Kehinde's Taiwo's voice is to dispute postmodern claims that subjectivity can be resolved entirely into networks of cultural, linguistic inscription and to dispute postmodern equations of freedom's possibility with instability, with incessant shifting among multiple positionalities. If practical rationality may indeed act as though it were the voice of another guiding us to a "transcendence" of totalizing, colonizing cultural patterns, then a natural — i.e., materially grounded, species-wide — human capacity for transcending both cultural contexts and libidinal economies comes into view.

The voice Kehinde hears makes reasoned arguments. Freedom lies in acknowledging the claims of reason within us, not in locating ourselves in desire's revolt against reason. Rather than argue with her inner voice, Kehinde dismisses it with a "genealogical" critique: "The voice of Taiwo was simply being mischievous" (47). Kehinde ignores her Taiwo's urging to return to save her marriage (52), but talks herself into wanting to live in Nigeria to gratify two sorts of corrupt desire: first, the desire to conform to what her husband wants; and second, the desire to be admired and powerful among her female Nigerian friends. She thinks, "Which Nigerian girlfriend would be able to stand the presence of a rich, been-to madam?" (47) which shows that desire can easily lead to isolating pride, a pride that, moreover, proves delusory. Kehinde organizes her ego not only around finding pleasure in her own ideological consistency but also in seeking pleasure in a specifically female version of the "ease" and prestige Albert imagines awaits him. When she becomes estranged from her friend, Moriammo, in part because Moriammo is absorbed in her newborn son, in part because her husband resents Kehinde's independence,

Kehinde abruptly resigns her bank position and returns to Nigeria rather than lay "herself open to anyone who cared to ugly her name, simply because she was not under a man's protection" (58).

Emecheta highlights the endemic racism Kehinde faces in London by noting that her "immediate boss" over the last ten years "never called her by her full name, making light of his failure to pronounce it correctly" (62). But the escape she desires proves no less alienating and oppressive. When she tells Albert she is coming, he is furious, and her initial contact with Nigeria, at the airline counter in London and baggage claim in Lagos, reveals a world in which influence and bribery alone allow one to claim public services and "commercial" civility (64–68). When Kehinde arrives at Albert's Lagos home, she discovers a house full of his relations and a "very beautiful, sophisticated, young, pregnant woman, with a baby on her left hip" (68). Her older sister, Ifeyinwa, attempts to acclimate a stunned Kehinde, telling her she must call Albert "Joshua's father" now, and stop referring to him as her husband: "You must learn to say 'our.' He is Rike's husband too" (71). Indirectly, Ifeyinwa consoles her sister, telling her that Rike, with a Ph.D. in literature and a university position, pressed herself upon Albert, a well-off been-to man. That she would do so suggests chilling realities about the status and opportunities of women in postcolonial Nigeria. When Kehinde is greeted by one of Albert's aunts, her own value is clearly defined: "You are the senior wife of a successful Nigerian man, the first wife of the first son of our father, Okolo" (73).

Kehinde's entrance into her husband's house full of strangers parallels her entrance, at age eleven, into her father's house; sent without explanation from her aunt in Lagos, Kehinde encounters a father, a second wife, and relations she has never met, as well as Ifeyinwa, her only sister: "Ifeyinwa and I quickly became very close. . . . Ifeyinwa showed me the kind of love and closeness I had never before experienced" (80). Kehinde has been denied closeness in part because of the circumstances of her birth. Ifeyinwa explains, "They believed you ate your sister in our mother's tummy" (80) She has also been denied closeness because hierarchical and polygamous Igbo culture creates barriers to intimacy. Her father notes, "In our culture, few people are raised by their real parents" (79). The intimacy between Ifeyinwa and Kehinde is soon broken by the older sister's marriage, but she frequently visits Kehinde at her convent school, "trying to make up for the time [they] had lost as children" (84). Kehinde senses that her sister's life "was not easy" (84). Both Kehinde's return and her lost opportunity for intimacy with Ifeyinwa suggest that certain

Igbo cultural practices do violence to that culture's own intuitions of human beings' constitutive need for others, of the interdependence at the core of identity: Ifeyinwa notes that Kehinde bears not only her own *chi* but that of her Taiwo and mother (80–81).

Repeatedly, Emecheta suggests that the cultural beliefs we should value are those that come from intuitions constantly renewed by our experience—in diverse cultural contexts—of the human condition. By contrast, other cultural beliefs, based upon false ideologies, show themselves in the course of lived experience to be ultimately only means of justifying power inequities. Kehinde's and Ifeyinwa's sudden, passionate friendship underscores the human need for nonhierarchical solidarity, which reconfirms what the portrait of Kehinde's prenatal relationship with her Taiwo suggests. We are defined at once as innately sociable and as morally conscious of how the reality of the Other puts in question the appropriativeness internal to our unfolding or becoming; what we are exceeds what sociohistorical conditioning would "construct" or what our willful pursuit of power or pleasure would fashion.

In that excess (which Levinas links to the infinity, the abiding resistance to conceptual colonization manifest in the human face)[33] lies the possibility of transcendence. The diversity of moralities does not suggest that ethics is something culture imposes upon people. When the family goes to visit Kehinde's children at their boarding school, Kehinde seeks to get into the front seat, "as she had done in London, daring Rike to challenge her right to sit next to Albert" (88), but she is stopped by Albert's aunt, who declares, "When we, the relatives of the head of the family, are here, we take the place of honour by our Albert. When you visit your brother's houses, the same honour will be accorded you" (88). Kehinde responds with mortification, having committed a social faux pas that only "young brides with poor training" would make, but more is involved here than mistakenly doing in Lagos what is appropriate in London. As they drive to the school, Kehinde sees Albert catch her eye in the mirror, but then look away, "so the others would not notice." She realizes that "in his heart of hearts he was not enjoying all this" (88). The cultural denial of spatial intimacy between husband and wife denotes the denial of intimacy in marriage to which the Western seating arrangement points. Of course, not all Western marriages are intimate, but the social formalities point to, and help reproduce, a cultural ideal. Kehinde's sense of violation and Albert's signs of regret or conscience indicate that more than a westernized conditioning is involved. Some cultural notions, such as the companionable marriage and the connection of personal identity to one's *chi* and one's relatives' *chis*, have a moral authority independent of being "the way people conventionally think in this or that place" because they do justice to or offer insight into constitutive aspects of our humanity.

Conversely, some cultural notions necessarily do violence to the humanity of those they affect. Emecheta portrays polygamy as precluding marital intimacy and setting women against each other: Kehinde knows she does not "stand a chance" against Rike, even though she recognizes that Rike married not for intimacy but for security: by "bowing down to tradition . . . , she had acquired a home and a big extended family (89). Rike's need to secure herself through marriage is grimly close to that of East African women of the 1880s threatened by the slave trade: "The woman of the period understood that her life chances were defined by the constellation of relationships of dependency. . . . Narwimba was clearly willing to accept the possibility of extreme and relatively brutal subordination in marriage because a marriage, even of this kind, was protection against enslavement."[34]

Finding herself radically devalued and unable to get a job—in part because of Nigerian sexism, in part because she does not have formal certificates—Kehinde writes to Moriammo: "Albert has humiliated me, and the worst is, I have to depend on him financially. He gave me the first housekeeping money in over eighteen years of marriage. . . . When I refused to kneel to take it, his sisters levied a fine of one cock" (94). Of course, the sisters reinforce the patriarchy because they are its victims, too, but the Nigeria Emecheta portrays is one in which self-destructive, antisocial behavior is endemic. When Kehinde posts the letter, she witnesses a fight between an unemployed university graduate and the wealthy man he has just robbed. When a crowd gathers, the graduate claims to be unjustly impoverished. When the crowd wants the two men to share the money, the graduate appeals "to the man whose money it was to let him have it, and God would bless him for it" (96). This cynical appeal to religion sways the crowd. Kehinde knows that he has won, and all this happens "not too far away from the police station" where an officer "yawn[s] and look[s] the other way, provoking laughter" (96). There is an implicit connection between the sterile power games and male bravado of private life and the relentless cynicism and corruption of public life. There is no respect for the rich man's property because, in a world where material reward is disconnected from both effort and public service, no property claims have moral legitimacy. Emecheta's portrait of institutionalized corruption and incompetence accords with Hountondji's,[35] and her portrait of the systemic disjunction between effort and reward echoes Irele's observation that the "idea that there should be a relation . . . has become openly laughable."[36] The effective absence of a nation-state's system of protections for individuals forces postcolonial people to seek refuge in improvised versions of precolonial patron-client networks, where the need to stroke connections, fork out considerations, and flatter superiors is a constant and humiliating necessity.

Kehinde escapes subordination to this system only because Moriammo sends her a plane ticket and has the foresight to have it hand-delivered by a Nigerian flight attendant "brought up in a polygamous family" who "knew the necessity of hiding from the rest of the family, especially from a younger wife" (100). Kehinde is saved by the unselfish goodness of another. The kind of female solidarity Moriammo is able to achieve contrasts with that available to Ifeyinwa. After Kehinde leaves, Ifeyinwa revenges herself and her sister upon Rike by announcing, with ritualist mock unconcern, that Albert is about to marry a third wife: "[Kehinde] wasn't going to lower herself to the level of sharing her husband with a child like that—sixteen or so. Hm! Our men, they poke any hole" (113): "She gave Rike one long animal stare, like a predator assessing its victim" (113–14). Poor Rike goes to her evangelical church, where, in return for her substantial contributions, she is reassured through dubious "prophecies," which underscores her poignant powerlessness.

The Way Home: Narrative Consistency and the Work Ethic

Returning to 1980s London, Kehinde discovers that the opportunities of the 1960s are over. Not only can she not retrieve her bank position; even after she puts herself through the university and earns a sociology degree, she can only find a job as a hotel chambermaid. However, through a plaintive letter from her daughter, we learn that things are worse in Nigeria. Albert has lost his job, Rike's income is not enough, and Kehinde's children need her to send pocket money. Like Albert and like Emecheta's ex-husband, Sylvester, Nigeria reveals itself to be improvident, squandering the money of the oil boom while institutionalizing the kind of eat-or-be-eaten world that erodes the constraints of civil society.[37]

Emecheta portrays the humiliation Kehinde endures in her work, the casual indifference with which she is treated as an easily replaceable employee, and her vulnerability to the sexual curiosity of a jaded wealthy Arab guest, but

the relationship between patriarchy and a wage economy is not seamless. Being able to earn a wage allows Moriammo to extract Kehinde from the postcolonial prisonhouse into which her naiveté and her rash, chauvinistic relativism had plunged her. Being able to earn a wage once she is back in England
provides Kehinde with the material conditions necessary to attain personal,
moral independence: she is able to make mortgage payments on the London
house while financing her own education. Even though she is underem-
ployed, Kehinde has a plurality of options that radically diminish her subjugation to masculine authority. Because her life chances are not defined, as in a
"traditional" noncapitalist patriarchal order, by a "constellation of relationships of dependency," when the Arab, long "accustomed to buying his way"
(128), asks to see her naked, she can simply leave, as opposed to one of his
wives, who "could not have been more than fifteen" and was "obliged to cope
with frequent sexual demands" (130).

While the capitalistic economy has its internal disciplinary mechanisms
(Kehinde works very hard for slender compensation) supporting vested interests (she and other non-Western women do the menial labor that keeps London hotels and their English male managers looking good), there is a fundamental difference between inequitable systems that ultimately allow the least
advantaged to be rewarded for their best efforts and those systems that perpetu-
ate, regardless of what individuals do, the exploitation of the many by the few.
A system that fixes people, permanently, in a disempowered position is unethical not simply because it is inequitable but also because it cuts human beings
off from the narrativity constitutive of human subjectivity itself. The very real
material and power inequities of England's capitalistic economy do not prevent Kehinde from being able to educate herself. Because she is, despite those
inequities, able—unlike in Nigeria, where she is portrayed as isolated and
immobile within enclosed rooms—to enact, narratively, a life plan, Kehinde
eventually is able to get a part-time job as a social worker at the Department of
Health and Social Services.

The novel concludes by linking the financial and social independence possible in the West with fidelity to the voice of the Other within us. Able to act as
an ethical agent (albeit in ways limited by capitalistic power relations, sexism,
and racism), Kehinde is able to build her own life, a life in which respect for
herself is inseparable from making mortgage payments, doggedly going
through night school until she achieves a sociology degree, and sending her
children much needed British currency—in other words, a life composed of

the habitual practice of virtues and humble, middle-class, maternal virtues at that.

In these ways, Kehinde resembles her creator. Emecheta describes how, abandoned by her husband with five small children, she accepted public housing and welfare, but was determined not to sink into a life on the dole: "I knew that I was not going to allow [my children] to grow up there. I had to pull myself out of the ditch for their sake. . . . So for their sake I could not afford to wallow in the mire of our powerlessness for long."[38] Self-assertion here is motivated by being-for-another, by experiencing maternal obligation as undeclinable. Emecheta describes how she wrote, pursued a degree in sociology, and worked as a social worker and teacher, while securing for her children good parochial schooling. This process of self-empowerment culminated in gaining sufficient capital for the down payment on a house and a sufficiently secure career to make the monthly payments.[39]

Upon Kehinde's return to England, "the smell of the London terrace house welcomed her like a lost child" (107–8). The "lost child" who has taken as its abode not a wooden statuette but a London terrace house is her Taiwo: "Before she could suppress it, a voice inside her sang out, 'Home, sweet home!' Taiwo, who had not spoken to her since she had gone to Nigeria, was back. Kehinde rebuked the voice: 'This is not my home. Nigeria is my home.' As she said it, she knew she was deceiving herself, and Taiwo would not let her get away with it" (108). That her Taiwo inhabits the London house and recalls Kehinde from nativist self-deception suggests that Kehinde is being "guided" to the place that should become her own because it is the place where she can compose a life whose narrative structure binds together enduring fidelities (to her children, to Moriammo) and open-ended innovation, the place where a fully realized humanity, interweaving *idem-* and *ipse*-identity, becomes possible. The "unexpected strength" (108) with which Kehinde pulls the For Sale sign out of the ground and declares, "This house is mine," both gives rise to and is reinforced by the practice of virtues through which, in a remarkable, pointed symmetry, she makes mortgage payments and builds a life that gives her, in multiple senses, a "place" of her own.

When Michael Gibson, a longtime boarder at her house, asks her out for Indian or Chinese food, she surprises herself by accepting: "She had stopped protesting that all her thoughts were hers alone, and started accepting Taiwo's voice as a permanent part of her consciousness. . . . Ifeyinwa [would not] understand how she could go out to eat Indian or Chinese with a man who was not her husband or even Nigerian" (135). Emecheta portrays Kehinde's in-creasing self-assertion as nurturing and being reinforced by her increasing re-jection of Nigerian chauvinism. When Mr. Gibson first becomes a boarder, Kehinde wants to have nothing to do with him, because "though black," he is from the Caribbean, and "[s]he and Albert had never had much to do with their fellow black people who were not Nigerians" (47). She is also suspicious of "an attractive black man of over thirty . . . living alone, and a black man with a good job besides" (48). To accept Mr. Gibson's invitation, Kehinde must overcome her nationalistic exclusiveness and her assumption that there is something peculiar about a man who is always considerate and never domi-neering. Similarly, Kehinde revises her opinion of Mary Elikwu and, in the midst of her own problems, has her "on [her] conscience" (95); she also re-tracts her judgment that the woman who approached Albert's car on the way to the abortion must have been a prostitute: "Now she wondered why the woman had been walking down Harley Street if she were a whore as Kehinde had called her. It had never been a red light district. Had she been looking for help?" (132).

In all three cases, moral growth is associated with complicating categorical judgments. While this questioning involves a liberation, it is valuable because it allows us to do better justice to others—for, as Kehinde's relationship with her Taiwo indicates, it is through responsiveness to the Other that our own primordial needs for intimacy are answered. By entering into ethical relations with Mary and Michael, by having the Other on one's conscience, by allowing the concrete humanity of the Other to put aside the hostility to the Other as other with which Kehinde originally approached them both, friendship, com-munity, solidarity can expand in cross-cultural, multiethnic directions. There-fore, Kehinde's movement toward a cosmopolitan rejection of ethnic particu-larism (eating Indian or Chinese with a Caribbean man in London) involves fidelity to the moral intuitions inscribed in the best of Igbo and Yoruba culture (hence, Taiwo urges her to accept Michael Gibson's invitation). However par-adoxical, Kehinde's return to London suggests this responsible life is more likely to be achieved within the (albeit flawed) economic and social conditions of the modern West than in the Nigeria of the 1980s and 1990s.

In the letter enclosing the plane ticket back to London, Moriammo de-clares, "[D]on't let fear of what people will say stop you from doing what your *chi* wants" (100). When she sees Kehinde off at the airport, Ifeyinwa observes, "You must do what your *chi* tells you" (106). Nwoga observes that through having a personal *chi*, "The Igbo person is therefore independent of other deities and forces as far as his existence is concerned. To quote Arinze's version: This idea is even embedded in a proverb. . . . ('If one's *chi* is not party to the arrangement death will not kill that person')."[40] The implication of Moriammo's and Ifeyinwa's usage, and Nwoga's commentary, is that through the *chi* the Igbo open up a way for an individual to stand against the community, and even to stand against the gods, and to be justified in so doing. Emecheta describes her own *chi* repeatedly urging her to resist colonialistic and masculinist oppression, to overcome despondency and lack of self-confidence.[41] The notion of the *chi* articulates an understanding that to be human is to be bound up with an infinity that transcends totality, to be in such intimate, immediate contact with the divine that one cannot be, in justice, contained within any socially constructed totality, nor even within such totality as implied by the Igbo pantheon itself. Resistance to totalization turns out to be a value transmitted by Igbo acculturation, but, unlike postmodern versions of that value, it is combined with an insistence that sociability is equally primordial, equally necessary if the self is not to succumb to its own dehumanization. Just as Kehinde's flight from Nigeria is understood in traditional Igbo terms of listening to one's *chi*, so her dismissal of concern about violating Nigerian norms of respectability by "going out with a Caribbean man over five years her junior" is understood in terms of listening to her Taiwo: "So what if your children notice the relationship when they return? After all, are you hurting anybody?" (136). What gives these particular cultural voices authority, as opposed to the other cultural claims that are being rejected here, is that they speak *through* cultural constructs *about* what is elemental to humanity. When Kehinde takes her leave from Ifeyinwa, she wishes "she could take her sister with her" because she sees that "the body [Ifeyinwa] had used all these years in nurturing and caring still yearned for comfort" (107). Because bodies yearn for comfort, we cannot see others without being called to ethical obligation.

If individuals are called to judgment by the materiality of the Other's humanity, so cultures are also called to judgment. Since the body's yearning for comfort goes unheeded in contemporary Nigeria, it is best to leave. One might think that Kehinde's staying would be a noble self-sacrifice for a sister who, "[g]rowing up among brothers, at the mercy of her step-mother, . . . had woven a fantasy around her missing sister every bit as poignantly felt as Kehinde's for her Taiwo" (109). However, the differences between the ways each sister can assuage the body's yearning for comfort reveal why Kehinde's leaving is not just a selfish rescuing of herself. Ifeyinwa can only assuage her wound by attacking Rike, an act which is a type of triumph, but one that involves becoming "like a predator" and finding one's comforts in "something sweeter than money—the satisfaction of exerting her power in her sister's interests" (114). In a world in which the body's yearning for comfort will remain unattended, one's satisfactions come to rest in exerting power against others. If an "eat-or-be-eaten logic" relentlessly organizes public space, then even good people will come to find what consolation they can in witchlike predation. The following chapter on Rike's desperation and vulnerability (115–19) indicates that such satisfactions as Ifeyinwa (and, vicariously, the reader) can obtain in such a culture depend upon a colonizing inscription of the Other into stereotypical norms that falsify and simplify reality in order to justify aggression and thus savor its pleasures. The ultimate evil of social oppression is not that others deny us our full humanity, but that such a denial makes it humanly impossible to answer adequately the obligations other people's humanity places upon us.[42]

Emecheta's final portrait of Kehinde's self-assertion, against her son's demands that Mr. Gibson be evicted and that the house be placed in the son's name, reveals the connection between listening to her Taiwo, being able to do justice to self and others, and the material conditions regulated by Western property law. When Joshua demands that Mr. Gibson be evicted because it is his house, Kehinde replies, "This is *my* house, though it may be yours one day." She then waits for Joshua to say "that he was his father's first son, and that women don't own houses" (137), for in Nigeria the house always belongs to the man (4). When Joshua reveals that he has seen Kehinde and Mr. Gibson in bed, she replies that it is "not a crime to love," that Albert has two other wives, and then "Taiwo, the spirit of her rebellious sister," asks, "You have girlfriends, don't you?" (138). When Joshua protests that she should "live for [her] children," Kehinde replies that he is a "grown man," that mothers are people, too, that while she needs him, she doesn't have "the energy to be the carrier of everybody's burdens" (139). Joshua consults a lawyer who, after hearing that Kehinde makes the mortgage payments, tells him, "You need to go and sort out your own life" (140). Joshua, who has been "to Africa, where young men were made to feel they owned heaven and earth" (137), is staggered by finding a mother who is "a rebel" (141).

Berrian comments, "At this stage in Kehinde's life, children are neither a binding force nor the only goal. She is not inclined to be exploited by an estranged husband or a son who both see her as a commodity."[43] This is certainly true, but Emecheta has Kehinde stress less the stage of her *own* life than the stage of Joshua's. In response to his insistence that mothers "were supposed to live for [their] children," Kehinde remarks, "I did, when you were young. My whole life was wound around your needs, but now you're a grown man!" (139). Even as a "rebel," Kehinde does not embrace making what is "the most beneficial for [one's own] lifestyle" the ultimate aim of life. Instead, the nature of one's ethical relations with others must depend upon a rational assessment of what is best *for them*. Nothing Kehinde says suggests that she now believes it was wrong, when her son was young, for her whole life to be wound around his needs. While a life wound around the needs of small children did not preclude Kehinde from having a career, it did mean that their needs came first and that such a priority was understood to be not an imposition but an obligation.[44] Now that Joshua is an adult, this should no longer be the case, not because Kehinde now understands that a sense of motherly duty is a patriarchal trap, but because the difference in Joshua alters the way that such duty ought to be rationally articulated.

In treating Joshua's youthful tirade with affectionate firmness, Kehinde is not only doing justice to herself. She is also being a good mother: it is in Joshua's own best interests to unlearn the patriarchal arrogance he picked up. Giddens points out that interests are connected to, but not identical with, wants, and that "a fully elaborated theory . . . requires a philosophical anthropology" if we are not to "*simply identify wants with 'empirical wants'*" (what people actually want in a given time and place), since the latter are conditioned and confined by the nature of the society of which an individual is a member."[45] We might see Kehinde's feminist treatment of Joshua as ethically responsive to his true wants and interests, but only if we surrender the notion that humans are defined entirely by their cultural, historical constructedness.

Implicitly, Emecheta is criticizing what Joshua takes as culturally normative—"Most Igbo women liked taking on the whole family's burden, so that they would be needed" (141)—not only because it victimizes women but also because it juvenilizes men. Such maternal self-sacrifice is ethically irresponsible precisely because it is governed by a (tragically misguided) assessment of what is most beneficial for one's own lifestyle (what will make one "needed"). If it is, paradoxically, in our real interest to achieve the "otherwise than being" of disinterested non-indifference to the Other,[46] then Kehinde is helping Joshua achieve his full humanity by forcing him to deal with the culturally uncomfortable notion, at the core of feminism, that mothers are people, too.

Emecheta makes clear that Kehinde's ability to protect herself, to answer to a degree her body's yearning for comfort, and to do what she thinks right for her son depends upon Western property law. As tainted by racism and egoistic individualism as it is, Western culture provides a legal basis for Kehinde's ability to act upon the voice of her Taiwo: "Claiming my right does not make me less of a mother, not less of a woman. If anything it makes me more human" (141). Hawley argues that "Kehinde's 'seizure' [his scare quotes] of her property is a liberating act of possession, a laying claim to an identity."[47] Identity and liberation are tied, strikingly, to the ability to acquire private property, but Hawley's metaphors of violence and of onetime revolutionary ruptures obscure how significant it is that private property, in this sociolegal context, constitutes what cannot be "seized"—what becomes one's right not through "a liberating act" but through years of monthly payments, years in which one's right emerges from the narrative that one's ethical agency, over time, enacts.

Berrian comments, "The symbolic reference to the London home in connection with Kehinde's self-actualization goes full circle. . . . What Albert does not take into consideration [in his effort to get Joshua to claim the house] . . . is the reformed Kehinde who has more space in which to maneuver (reflecting the duality of bi-cultural identity and the convention of using the rules of one or the other as the situation or need warrants)."[48] Like Hawley, Berrian depicts Kehinde's possession of the house in terms of violence or clever manipulation. Emecheta stresses, however, through Joshua's conversation with the lawyer, that Kehinde can lay claim to the house not because she is the cleverer strategist in an eat-or-be-eaten world but because she is the one who has been paying the mortgage (140). Kehinde keeps the house because she has a moral claim that can be rationally articulated and that is legally recognized. British property law is not depicted as a "rule" to exploit when convenient, nor as simply "more space in which to maneuver," but, in this instance at least, as institutionalized justice. Only within sociopolitical contexts where the aspiration to institute justice displaces an eat-or-be-eaten zero-sum economy of predation can lives that bind together self-esteem and ethical solicitude, that actualize themselves in narrative unities of reiterated, nonviolent practices of virtues, become not only possible but normative. By contrast, Emecheta suggests that Nigerian property law is not just another rule but institutionalized injustice: "In Nigeria, the home belonged to the man, even if the woman spent her entire life keeping it in order" (4). Where injustice is institutionalized, the self cannot achieve narrative consequentiality (how a woman spends "her entire life" becomes irrelevant). Only by taking seriously the thematic centrality of property law in *Kehinde*, its integral relation to Kehinde's ability to become, in multiple senses, "more human," can we appreciate the significance of what Hawley calls the "positioning of Emecheta's spokesperson on *London* ground," the "end[ing of] the tentative emigrant status that would not let Kehinde—or Emecheta—settle."[49]

When Kehinde says to the spirit of her long dead twin, "Now we are one" (141), she indicates that through action, and through living in a sociopolitical world where, despite its very real imperfections, action can and does assume rational, effective form, she has made the dead living, has made spiritual forces participants in material life, and so has achieved an identity, like Rama-toulaye's, in which modern self-assertion and traditional piety are interfused. In describing herself, Emecheta has linked piety—a sense of elemental in-debtedness—to ethical responsibility and to successful self-assertion: "Despite everything I am very religious. . . . I say, 'God, this idea has come to me, help me to treat it responsibly.' I do this because people will quote what you have written in a book, so it is a tremendous responsibility."[50] Authorial responsibil-ity asks to be met, on the reader's side, by what Newton calls "a hermeneutic ethics (the ethico-critical accountability which acts of reading hold their read-ers to)."[51] The ethical use of language, as Emecheta makes clear, is neither a lifestyle choice nor a career move, but an unconditional obligation. That obli-gation imposes itself not only on all who would write feminist literature and all who practice literary criticism, but more broadly on all who use language.

Conclusion

The Challenge of Decolonizing
the West's Reading of African Fiction

From the novels explored above, we may see that at least some African fiction demands a literary theory that challenges notions that heterogeneity and ambiguity are ends in themselves, that treating authors and characters as rational, coherent interlocutors is New Critical folly, that realism is necessarily hegemonic, that acculturation is always totalizing. Fishburn begins one of her chapters by quoting Mary Jacobus to the effect that difference should be understood "as a multiplicity, ambiguity and heterogeneity which is that of textuality itself," so that, Fishburn argues, Jacobus can claim that "language makes it possible for writers to achieve a 'traversal' of sexual boundaries that reveals them to be nothing more than 'the product of phallocentric discourse' — and thus subject to change. . . . Multiplicity. Ambiguity. Heterogeneity. Open-endedness. Surely all of these terms also describe Buchi Emecheta's fiction. Could we not say, then, that the difference in her writing violates sexual, textual, *and cultural* boundaries—that she, too, is engaged in reconstituting the subject?"[1]

While multiplicity, ambiguity, and heterogeneity may be deeply valuable in specific contexts, as abstract ends they are simply vacuous. If multiplicity, etc., are goods simply because they allow us to recognize that all boundaries are discursively constructed, then only negative textual work can be legitimate: we must see ourselves as defined by negative liberty and so able to choose amid a heterogeneity whose value resides in serving an egoistic identity in ways that must be entirely formal (the more multiplicity, ambiguity, heterogeneity the better, for quantity becomes the only nonarbitrary measure of value). This position suggestively parallels that of the consumer in advanced capitalism. A text, like a store, is valued only for how many free choices it allows, and since any concrete discussion of the good might constrain freedom to choose, the valued text will reaffirm "liberalism's [and capitalism's] (illusory) agnostic stance towards the question of the good life."[2]

The demand that texts can be valuable only to the extent that they reaffirm what contemporary Western theory takes as axiomatic precludes appreciation of any text whose difference is tied to arguing for specific conceptions of *phronêsis* that justify determinate forms of *praxis*. Instead, freedom and fulfillment are understood in terms of mixing and matching heterogeneous cultural resources in order to gain an identity that is as capable of delivering power and pleasure to itself as possible. For novels to be able to make genuine and specific claims upon readers, it must be possible for *phronêsis* and *praxis* not to collapse into abstract affirmations of consumerist free choice.

Aptness to discount what a text actually *says* in favor of abstract affirmations of difference may arise from fears of falling into New Critical assumptions about unified, centered subjectivity with universal attributes.[3] While one must be wary of forced "organic unities," there are dangers in too hasty assumptions of disconnection and incoherence. Linda Hutcheon has noted that "challenges to the coherent, autonomous subject" might not be appropriate for "feminist and post-colonial discourses" that "must work first to assert and affirm a denied or alienated subjectivity."[4] More broadly, Ferry and Renault question the ethics of reading encouraged by postmodernism: Communication appears "not as free debate among subjects responsible for what they say but simply as the sublimation of relations of force or, if you wish, as a euphemistic form of war (class struggle, intermittent conflicts, clashes of desires for power, etc.)."[5]

If fear of New Critical universalizing leads to an a priori discounting of the possibility of a rational articulation of cross-cultural ethics, it becomes impossible to read fiction in ways that pursue Said's suggestion that real materialism grounds real humanism. Equating realism with mimesis, postmodernism views realism as an illicit attempt to "naturalize" an interpretation or a value judgment on the basis of description.[6] Behind the assumption that realism illicitly moves from description to prescription, and thus literature is better to the extent that it approaches postmodern self-reflexivity, lies the further assumption that movements from description to prescription can never be rationally justified.

Both Levinas's insistence that ethics is "first philosophy" and Ricoeur's treatment of narration as "between description and prescription" challenge this Humean legacy,[7] while the way that legacy works out in practice is that the realm of *is*, description, is given over to the ubiquitous play of violences (hence

Hawley's and Berrian's characterizations of Kehinde's acquisition of the London house) while the realm of *ought*, prescription, is given over, usually through indirection, to negative liberty, self-aestheticization, and consumerist self-fashionings.

This dualism, however, is not only distinctive to Western modernity. It is also a naturalization of a divorce between facts and values effected in eighteenth-century Britain through early capitalism: "Unable to derive values from facts—which is to say, to ground moral ideology in bourgeois social practice—the moral sense theorists turn instead to the notion of value as autotelic."[8] Independently of Levinas and Ricoeur, Hilary Putnam points out that "the requirement that a description be adequate is implicitly a requirement that the describer have available a certain set of *concepts*. . . . The use of the word 'inconsiderate' seems . . . a very fine example of the way in which the fact/value distinction is hopelessly fuzzy in the real world and in the real language. . . . Just as we criticize a describer who does not employ the concepts of *table* and *chair* when their use is called for, so also, someone who fails to remark that someone is *considerate* or *spontaneous* may open himself to the criticism that he is imperceptive or superficial."[9] For this reason, what is mimetic and what is realistic need not be the same; the former may appeal to a network of facts, a state of affairs, but the latter must speak to the "fuzziness" of fact/value distinctions in "the real world and in the real language," that is, it must answer to the *phronêsis* inseparable from communication, the origin of language itself in responsibility. Novelistic realism's movement from description to prescription need not be coercive; indeed, such a movement underlies the possibility of making a searching, *responsible* depiction of what is at stake in the lives of real women in real circumstances.

Thus, assimilating African feminist fiction to postmodern or Western postcolonial categories occludes as much as, if not more than, it illuminates. McWilliams argues that regardless of whether "Dangarembga herself is aware" of it, her text "resounds with black voices emerging from within the shadow and oppression of colonial rule." *Nervous Conditions* is construed as an object resounding with black voices; moreover, the voices turn out to be those of Western postcolonial theory—JanMohamed, Memmi, Fanon, Bhabha—modified and enhanced by the voices of Western postmodern feminism—Irigaray, Cixous, Trinh Minh-ha. While all of these writers might illuminate Dangarembga's novel, the equation of the voices of postcolonial, postmodern theorists with black voices emerging from colonial rule is troubling. Instead of tracing how Dangarembga engages (implicitly, perhaps) any of these voices in reasoned discourse, McWilliams focuses on her own ability to "hear" these voices within a text perhaps unaware of them. The effect is to suggest that the novel's value rests in its illustration of current Western theory. While McWilliams praises Dangarembga's "specificity," her account of that specificity is entirely vague: "Tambu prepares to use her past and her country's history to carve out new positions of action."[10] Like Fishburn's account of Emecheta's violation of boundaries, this is either vacuous or consistent with the notion of selfhood (free choice, instrumental rationality) encouraged by consumer capitalism.

The forms of misunderstanding that have shaped the Western academic reception of African feminist fiction fit into a broader context of the West's assimilation of African fiction, beginning with the work of the major male writers of the 1950s, into strictly Western categories of value and meaning—first existentialism, Sartrean anticolonial theory, then Western Marxism, liberal individualism, postmodernism, or some combination thereof. Similarly, the novelistic articulations of feminist moral discourse developed in these novels may be situated within patterns established by early male African writers, such as Camara Laye and Ferdinand Oyono in Francophone literature, and Amos Tutuola and Chinua Achebe in Anglophone literature, of making novelistic prose not only a means of contesting colonialistic, chauvinistic Western ideas but also a means of vindicating and modernizing indigenous structures of value in ways that challenge the egocentric philosophical anthropology of *Western* anticolonial theory and politics. Above all, many pioneering male writers, just as the feminist novelists studied here, offer reasoned repudiations of the notion that the master trope for understanding human relations and language should be that of warfare. In Islamic contexts, the realm of warfare is what piety and civility overcome; in non-Islamic contexts, the reduction of social relations to relations of war is the essence of malevolent witchcraft. From African contexts of value and meaning, the propensity of the modern West to totalize the metaphor of war appears as a violent denial of all that makes humans distinct from beasts of the bush.

Both the depth of African ethical unease with the trope of warfare and the intensity of the hold of that trope upon Western academic discourse may be glimpsed by juxtaposing Aidoo's response to suggestions that she writes about "sexual warfare" with the subtitles Uwakweh chooses for her essay on *Changes*. When Adeola James asks whether one "can read sexual warfare" into her writings, Aidoo replies, "I don't believe in sexual warfare and I don't believe that we are here to wage war against one another, at all."[11] Uwakweh divides her essay, "Free but Lost: Variations in the Militant's Song," into the following sections: "Breaking New Grounds," "The Making of a Militant," "Negotiating the Battlefront," and "Counting Gains and Losses."[12] Aidoo's rejection of a metaphorics of warfare makes it unlikely that analyzing her discourse through tropes of war will do it critical justice. We are not here "to wage war against one another" because, as Achebe has argued, the modern Western view "of society and of culture as a prisonhouse from which the individual must escape in order to find space and fulfillment" is fundamentally misguided.[13] This way of conceiving fulfillment cannot sustain rational deliberation about moral goods because it rests upon an understanding of the self that makes the ethical somehow secondary or disposable.

Achebe describes fulfillment as "a presence — a powerful demanding presence limiting the space in which the self can roam uninhibited. . . . Fulfillment is other-centered, a giving or subduing of the self."[14] This is because intersubjectivity is constitutive of subjectivity and there is no self-consciousness anterior to moral consciousness. The feminist fictions here, and earlier anticolonial fictions written by men, do not simply argue that Africans have their own cultural viewpoints that are no less "valid" than those of the modern West; they argue that in specific and crucial respects African moral discourses are better, more responsive to the demands of the ethical relation, than what the West would have African peoples, no less than fictional characters and authors, accept as fulfillment and liberation.

There is a story to be told of how, in the 1940s and 1950s, the West began theorizing anticolonial activity in terms of its own egocentric philosophical anthropology and its own eurocentric monopolizing of conceptuality, of how actual, contemporaneous African resistance, especially peasant resistance, to colonial authority drew fruitfully and innovatively upon indigenous moral discourse, and of how the Western reception of African fiction, from the 1950s on, reiterated the terms of its own conceptuality at the expense of any consideration of how early male African writers, much as the women writers studied here, brought indigenous structures of value to bear upon their novels in ways that simultaneously gave those structures a cross-cultural relevance and challenged the terms of thought and value that the West, even in the guise of championing anticolonialism, incessantly naturalized. That story, however, exceeds the bounds of this study.

What is at stake in freeing a reading of African feminist fiction from hegemonic Western critical assumptions goes beyond the considerable value of these novels. If all acculturation is, of necessity, indirect colonization, then anticolonialism (or feminism) can only be successful if the individual is liberated from cultural forms of identity altogether, which would mean that anticolonialism (or feminism) must end in an affirmation of Western negative liberty, whether in the guise of liberal individualism or antiessentialism. But part of the "difference" that African narrative presents to Western theory is the reasoned rejection of these alternatives, a rejection that implies that if the West is ever to cease patronizing Africa it must begin to grasp the narrowness and nonnecessity of its own conception of modernity. Only if the West grows willing to become strange to itself, to accept the possibility of modernities, and feminisms, rationally critical of its own dominant modes of realizing modernity, and feminism, will African feminist fiction become accessible as more than the echo of Western voices, as speech whose difference matters.

Notes

1. Encountering Africa in Contemporary Western Theory and Representation

1. Chandra Talpade Mohanty, "Under Western Eyes," 196; Obioma Nnaemeka, "Urban Spaces, Women's Places," 164.

2. For the introductory phase, see esp. Eustace Palmer, *Growth of the African Novel*; Charles Larson, *The Emergence of the African Novel*. For the second phase, see esp. Abiola Irele, *The African Experience in Literature and Ideology*; Emmanuel Ngara, *Art and Ideology in the African Novel*. For the third phase, see esp. Kenneth W. Harrow, *Thresholds of Change in African Literature*; Richard Bjornson, *The African Quest for Freedom and Identity*; Simon Gikandi, *Reading Chinua Achebe*; Christopher L. Miller, *Theories of Africans*.

3. For discussions of the political psychology of colonialism, see esp. Ngũgĩ wa Thiong'o, *Decolonising the Mind*; Christopher L. Miller, *Blank Darkness*; Abdul JanMohamed, *Manichean Aesthetics*.

4. See Bjornson, *African Quest*, 197–376; Miller, *Theories of Africans*, 31–67, 246–93.

5. Kwame Anthony Appiah, *In My Father's House*, 155. For the confluence of antihumanism and postmodernism, see esp. Michel Foucault, *Language, Counter-Memory, Practice*, 113–64; Jacques Derrida, *Margins of Philosophy*, esp. 111–36. For critiques of postmodern antihumanism, see John McGowan, *Postmodernism and Its Critics*; Peter Dews, *Logics of Disintegration*; Richard J. Bernstein, *The New Constellation*; Albrecht Wellmer, *The Persistence of Modernity*; Luc Ferry and Alain Renault, *French Philosophy of the Sixties*.

6. See esp. Chinua Achebe, *Anthills of the Savannah*; Ousmane Sembène, *Le Dernier de l'Empire*.

7. See Yambo Ouologuem, *Le devoir de violence*; Wole Soyinka, *Myth, Literature, and the African World*; Paulin J. Hountondji, *African Philosophy*, esp. 33–70. For critiques of "traditional" African sexual politics, see Calixthe Beyala, *Tu t'appelleras Tanga*; Buchi Emecheta, *The Joys of Motherhood*; Mariama Bâ, *Une si longue lettre*. For a critique of traditionalism, see Adewale Maja-Pearce's *A Mask Dancing*.

8. See esp. the discussion of witchcraft in the essays collected in Jean Comaroff and John Comaroff, eds., *Modernity and Its Malcontents*.

9. See esp. Michael McKeon, *The Origins of the English Novel*; J. Paul Hunter, *Before the Novel*.

10. For the distinction between genre and kind, see Alistair Fowler, *Kinds of Literature*, 20–22.

11. See Gikandi, *Reading Chinua Achebe*, 1–3; Fredric Jameson, *The Political Unconscious*, esp. 90–107, 281–99.

12. See Chatterjee, *The Nation and Its Fragments*.

13. Whereas Palmer argues that the novel is a Western, modern form (*Growth of the African Novel*, 1–10), Chinweizu, Jemie, and Madubuike insist that contemporary African fiction draws upon oral narrative traditions (*Towards the Decolonization of African Literature*, 1:1–146). Appiah's judgment of the later work, however, is telling: its "nativism . . . is simply the reflection of [Euro-American inspired romantic racisms] in the domain of academic literary criticism" (*In My Father's House*, 73).

14. See Kalu Ogbala, *Gods, Oracles, and Divination*; Isidore Okpewho, *Myth in Africa*.

15. See Dr. Samuel Johnson, *Rambler*, no. 4; G. W. F. Hegel, *Aesthetics*, 573–611, 1040–1110; Georg Lukács, *The Theory of the Novel*.

16. See M. M. Bakhtin, *Speech Genres and Other Late Essays*, 7, 89; see also Gary Saul Morson and Caryl Emerson, *Mikhail Bakhtin: Creation of a Prosaics*.

17. See esp. Rev. Samuel Johnson, *The History of the Yorubas*; Vincent Mulago, *La Religion traditionnelle des Bantu et leur vision du monde*.

18. See Kwasi Wiredu in "Formulating Modern Thought in African Languages"; V. Y. Mudimbe, *The Invention of Africa*; Alexis Kagame, *La Philosophie bantu comparée*; Kwame Gyekye, *An Essay on African Philosophical Thought*, esp. 24–57; V. Y. Mudimbe, *Parables and Fables*, esp. 124–65.

19. Appiah, *In My Father's House*, 155; Paulin J. Hountondji, "Recapturing," 238–48.

20. See Appiah, *In My Father's House*, 47–72; Kwasi Wiredu, *Philosophy and an African Culture*, 1–36; Hountondji, *African Philosophy*, 33–70.

21. Wiredu, *Philosophy and an African Culture*, 39; see also 37–50.

22. See Appiah, *In My Father's House*, 155; see also 137–57.

23. See Alasdair MacIntyre, *Three Rival Versions of Moral Enquiry*, 105–48.

24. "Aquinas was able to show how the will, conceived in Augustinian fashion, could both serve and yet mislead the mind, as conceived in Aristotelian fashion" (ibid., 124).

25. See E. D. Hirsch Jr., *Cultural Literacy*, 93.

26. See MacIntyre, *Whose Justice? Which Rationality?* 349–403; MacIntyre, *Three Rival Versions of Moral Enquiry*, 105–26.

27. See Bjornson's account of Negritude and political repression in *African Quest*, 108–46, 170–96; Soyinka's critique of "neo-Tarzanism" in *Art, Dialogue, and Outrage*, 86–109, 315–29; Appiah, *In My Father's House*, 56–60.

28. Eugene Goodheart, *The Reign of Ideology*, 27–28; Marianna Torgovnik, *Gone Primitive*, 245.

29. Goodheart, *The Reign of Ideology*, 31.

30. Selwyn R. Cudjoe, *V. S. Naipaul*, 191–92; the quotations from Naipaul refer to an interview in *Vogue*, August 1981, 130.

31. See Maja-Pearce, "The Naipauls on Africa"; T. R. S. Sharma, "Chinua Achebe and V. S. Naipaul"; Peter Nazareth, "Out of Darkness"; Neil ten Kortenaar, "Beyond Authenticity and Creolization"; Juhani Koponen, *People and Production in Late*

Precolonial Tanzania, 54. For critiques of postulates of a "passive" Africa, see Steven Feierman, "African Histories and the Dissolution of World History," 167–212; Frederick Cooper, "Africa and the World Economy."

32. See Christopher L. Miller, *Blank Darkness*; Appiah, *In My Father's House*, 3–27.

33. Patrick Manning, *Slavery and African Life*, esp. 8–37, 86–100; John Ralph Willis, ed., *Slaves and Slavery in Muslim Africa*, 2 vols., esp. vol. 1; and J. O. Hunwick, "Notes on Slavery in the Songhay Empire," 2:16–32; Polly Hill, "Comparative West African Farm-Slavery Systems"; Mordechi Abir, "The Ethiopian Slave Trade and Its Relation to the Islamic World"; A. M. H. Sheriff, "The Slave Mode of Production along the East African Coast, 1810–1873."

34. Rob Nixon, *London Calling*, 76–77.

35. See V. S. Naipaul, *Finding the Center*, 87–89, 119–27.

36. Ibid., 149.

37. Ibid., 156–68.

38. Goodheart, *The Reign of Ideology*, 178n. 12.

39. Wiredu, *Philosophy and an African Culture*, 11.

40. Appiah, *In My Father's House*, 134–35.

41. See Appiah, *In My Father's House*, 135–36; Wiredu, *Philosophy and an African Culture*, 12–15; Hountondji, *African Philosophy*, 71–107; Abiola Irele, "In Praise of Alienation," 217, 216.

42. See esp. Gordon Innes, *Sunjata*; Camara Laye, *Le Maître de la parole*.

43. See Nixon, *Homelands, Harlem, and Hollywood*.

44. Appiah, *In My Father's House*, 134.

45. T. O. Beidelman, *Moral Imagination in Kaguru Modes of Thought*, 107–8.

46. Beidelman addresses such details. Ibid., 111–19.

47. See Koponen, *People and Production in Late Precolonial Tanzania*, 70; Edward A. Alpers, *Ivory and Slaves*, 58–64.

48. See Koponen, *People and Production in Late Precolonial Tanzania*, 53–76; Abdul M. H. Sheriff, *Slaves, Spices, and Ivory in Zanzibar*; Frederick Cooper, *Plantation Slavery on the East Coast of Africa*.

49. Koponen, *People and Production in Late Precolonial Tanzania*, 101–25 (quote on 108), 127–39, 150–78.

50. J. M. Bernstein, *The Fate of Art*, 2.

51. Pearl Cleage, "A Stunning Journey to 'Joy,'" N8; Laura Shapiro, "Possessing the Secret of Joy," 57.

52. Kimberley Joyce Pollock, "A Continuum of Pain," 38–39.

53. Nwikali Kieti, "Homesick and Eurocentric? Alice Walker's Africa," 157, 158, 164.

54. Alice Walker, *Possessing the Secret of Joy*, 23. All further citations are to this edition.

55. For Freud, see esp. *Civilization and Its Discontents*. For the turn away from Freud, see esp. Herbert Marcuse, *Eros and Civilization*; Wilhelm Reich, *Selected Writings*; R. D. Laing, *Self and Others*. For a critique of linking erotic and political revolution, see Richard J. Bernstein, *Philosophical Profiles*, 176–96.

56. Jean Comaroff, *Body of Power, Spirit of Resistance*, 117; see also 114–18.

57. Kieti, "Homesick or Eurocentric?" 164.

58. The excisions were not always only metaphorical. See Robin Morgan and Gloria Steinem, "The International Crime of Genital Mutilation," in Steinem, *Outrageous Acts and Everyday Rebellions*, 292–300.

59. See esp. Jean-Jacques Rousseau, *Émile ou de l'éducation*. For a critique of this legacy in feminism, see Sandra M. Gilbert and Susan Gubar, "The Mirror and the Vamp."

60. See Pollock, "A Continuum of Pain," 50–51, for a discussion of Walker's treatment of gendering as social violence. Walker's notion of acultural selfhood is closely allied with "womanism." As Tuzyline Jita Allan points out in *Womanist and Feminist Aesthetics*, 1–17, the term has been appropriated for essentialist and antiessentialist positions.

61. For feminist utopianism, see Mary Daly, *Gyn/Ecology*; Sara Ruddick, *Maternal Thinking*. For speculative matriarchal prehistory, see Luce Irigaray, *Je, tu, nous*. For idealizations of feminine "life forces" in Negritude, see Lloyd W. Brown, *Women Writers in Black Africa*, 7–8.

62. See Carl Jung, *The Portable Jung*, esp. 59–162, 273–300.

63. Pollock, "A Continuum of Pain," 53.

64. Despite significant differences, these theorists imply that complicity with one's own victimization attends socialization.

65. See Foucault, *The History of Sexuality, Volume One*, 17–49.

66. Dews, *Logics of Disintegration*, 231–32.

67. For the paradox of trying to valorize freedom while denying agency, see Stanley Rosen, *The Ancients and the Moderns*, 189–234, and *Hermeneutics as Politics*, 175–93; see also McGowan, *Postmodernism and Its Critics*, 70–88.

68. Richard J. Bernstein, *The New Constellation*, 164, 191; see also McGowan, *Postmodernism and Its Critics*, 101–16; 134–36.

69. J. M. Bernstein, *The Fate of Art*, 183, 185–86; see also McGowan, *Postmodernism and Its Critics*, 117–21.

70. See Gayatri Chakravorty Spivak, *The Post-Colonial Critic*, 10–12.

71. See, for example, Katherine Fishburn, *Reading Buchi Emecheta*, 146–52.

72. Anthony Giddens, *Central Problems in Social Theory*, 52.

73. Ibid., 50–53, 155–60, 179–81; Giddens, *Social Theory and Modern Sociology*, 213–15.

74. See Homi K. Bhabha, "DissemiNation," 291–97.

75. Edward Said, *Culture and Imperialism*, 79–80; see esp. Nancy Armstrong and Lenard Tennenhouse, eds., *The Violence of Representation*; D. A. Miller, *The Novel and the Police*; Nancy Armstrong, *Desire and Domestic Fiction*; John Bender, *Imagining the Penitentiary*.

76. See Paul Ricoeur's discussion of the entwinement of agency and narrative unity in *Oneself as Another*, esp. 88–168.

77. Heidegger ascribes the essence of man to that which allows man to "stand out" from the ontic realm of beings (Martin Heidegger, *Letter on Humanism*, 204). For a

critique of the essentialism in Heidegger's antiessentialism, see Derrida, *Margins of Philosophy*, 111–36.

78. See Catherine Belsey and Jane Moore, introduction to *The Feminist Reader*, 1–20.

79. Mudimbe, *Parables and Fables*, 11; Irele, introduction to *African Philosophy*, by Paulin J. Hountondji, 14.

80. Friedrich Nietzsche, *On the Genealogy of Morals/Ecce Homo*, 22.

2. Postmodernism, Cultural Otherness, and the Ethical Stake in Close Reading

1. See Appiah, *In My Father's House*, 155.

2. Leela Gandhi, *Postcolonial Theory*, viii-ix. See the indexes of Bill Ashcroft, Gareth Griffiths, and Helen Tiffen, eds., *A Post-Colonial Reader*, and Patrick Williams and Laura Chrisman, eds., *Colonial Discourse and Post-Colonial Theory*. For the importance of parastatals in postcolonial Africa political history, see Bruce J. Berman and Colin Leys, eds., *African Capitalists in African Development*.

3. Rosemary Marangoly George, *The Politics of Home*, 119; see also Rosemary Marangoly George and Helen Scott, "A New Tail to an Old Tale," in *NOVEL: A Forum for Fiction* 26, no. 3 (1993): 305.

4. See Bill Ashcroft, Gareth Griffiths, and Helen Tiffin, *The Empire Writes Back*, 15, 41, 74, 97–104, 149–54, 180.

5. Vijay Mishra and Bob Hodge, "What Is Post(-)Colonialism?" *Textual Practice* 5, no. 3 (1991): 399.

6. Ashcroft, Griffiths, and Tiffin, *The Empire Writes Back*, 41, 153; see also Gandhi's critique of the tendency to treat "indigeneity" as "raw material" (*Postcolonial Theory*, 175–76).

7. Mishra and Hodge, "What Is Post(-)Colonialism?" 401, 402, 403, 405, 411; Ashcroft, Griffiths, and Tiffin, *The Empire Writes Back*, 179, 180.

8. Mishra and Hodges, "What Is Post(-)Colonialism?" 406.

9. Robert J. C. Young, *Colonial Desire*, 4.

10. Homi K. Bhabha, "Signs Taken for Wonders," *Critical Inquiry* 12, no. 1 (1985): 156, 154; quoted in Young, *Colonial Desire*, 23.

11. Kobena Mercer, "Diaspora Culture and the Dialogic Imagination: The Aesthetics of Black Independent Film in Britain," 57; quoted in Young, *Colonial Desire*, 25.

12. See Richard J. Bernstein, *The New Constellation*, esp. 31–56, see also 142–98; Wellmer, *The Persistence of Modernity*, 38–71.

13. Young, *Colonial Desire*, 21.

14. Bakhtin, *Speech Genres and Other Late Essays*, 68–69.

15. Ibid., 10, 111.

16. Emmanuel Levinas, *Totality and Infinity*, 203–4. See also Levinas, "Ethics as First Philosophy"; and Mikhail Bakhtin, *Art and Answerability* and *Toward a Philosophy of the Act*.

17. For an exception, see Satya Mohanty, "Colonial Legacies, Multicultural Futures."

18. Bhabha, "DissemiNation," 291, 293, 295, 297.

19. See ibid., 303; Jacques Derrida, *Dissemination*, 64–173; Paul de Man, *The Resistance to Theory*, 3–20; J. Hillis Miller, *The Ethics of Reading*.

20. Bhabha, "DissemiNation," 306, 312, 314.

21. G. W. F. Hegel, *The Phenomenology of Mind*, 79. For parallels between Schelling and Derrida, see Dews, *Logics of Disintegration*, 19–31. See also Alex Callinicos, "Wonders Taken for Signs"; Asha Varadharajan, *Exotic Parodies*, 16–17, 21–23; Aijaz Ahmad, *In Theory*, 68–69.

22. Harrow, *Thresholds of Change*, 21, 52–60, 69, 70; see also Dennis Duerden, *African Art and Literature*.

23. Harrow, *Thresholds of Change*, 73, 78, 83; see also 60–60, 77–78, 79–85.

24. Seyla Benhabib, "Autonomy, Modernity, and Community," 46; Gayatri Spivak, *Outside in the Teaching Machine*, 63.

25. Geoffrey Galt Harpham, *Getting It Right*, 156.

26. See Derrida's claim in *Aporias*, 19, that ethical injunctions must resemble the propositions of negative theology least.

27. See Derrida, *Limited Inc.*, 7; Harpham, *Getting It Right*, 147–48.

28. Derrida, *Limited Inc.*, 152.

29. See Derrida's stress on "responsibility" in *Limited Inc.*, 152.

30. See Simon Critchley, *The Ethics of Deconstruction*, 13–44, 188–247; J. M. Bernstein, *The Fate of Art*, 175–87; Richard J. Bernstein, *The New Constellation*, 172–98; Rosen, *The Ancients and the Moderns*, 189–234, Rosen, *Hermeneutics as Politics*, 50–86; McGowan, *Postmodernism and Its Critics*, 1–30, 89–210; Dews, *Logics of Disintegration*, 34–44, 128–43, 186–99; Ferry and Renault, *French Philosophy of the Sixties*, 3–32, 122–52.

31. Spivak, *Outside in the Teaching Machine*, 60.

32. Ibid., 64.

33. Spivak, *The Post-Colonial Critic*, 10–12. See also Varadharajan, *Exotic Parodies*, 75–112.

34. For examples of work directly or indirectly inspired by Said, see esp. Young, *Colonial Desire*; Christopher Miller, *Blank Darkness*.

35. James Clifford, *The Predicament of Culture*, 259.

36. See Lyotard, *The Postmodern Condition*, 9–11, 26–27, 66.

37. Clifford, *The Predicament of Culture*, 261.

38. McGowan, *Postmodernism and Its Critics*, 166–67, 175; the citation is from Edward W. Said, "Interpreting Palestine," *Harper's* 274: 19. For related discussions, see Varadharajan, *Exotic Parodies*, 113–36; Ahmad, *In Theory*, 159–219; Young, *White Mythologies*, 126–40.

39. Said, *Culture and Imperialism*, xix,

40. Ibid., 33–34, 312–13.

41. For alternative descriptions of Quranic hermeneutical tradition, see Andrew Rippen, ed., *Approaches to the History of the Interpretation of Qur'ān*; M. E. Combs-Schilling, *Sacred Performances*; Ira M. Lapidus, "Knowledge, Virtue, and Action."

42. Said, *Culture and Imperialism*, 211–15, 279–80.

43. Ibid., 55, 54. See also Edward W. Said, *The World, the Text, and the Critic*, esp. 1–53, 158–77.

44. Said, *Culture and Imperialism*, 269, 270, 271; see also McGowan's discussion in *Postmodernism and Its Critics*, 165–67.

45. Said, *Culture and Imperialism*, 269; Frantz Fanon, *Les damnés de la terre*, 138: "Le nationalisme s'il n'est pas explicité, enrichi et approfondi, s'il ne se transforme très rapidement en conscience politique et sociale, en humanisme, conduit à une impasse." [Nationalism if it is not explicated, enriched and deepened, if it does not transform itself very rapidly into political and social consciousness, into humanism, leads to a impasse.]

46. Said, *Culture and Imperialism*, 274.

47. See George Lukács, *History and Class Consciousness* and *Theory of the Novel*, 29–39, 56–93.

48. Spivak, *Outside in the Teaching Machine*, 56.

49. Said, *Culture and Imperialism*, 270–71. For the link between modernity and Romanticism, see McGowan, *Postmodernism and Its Critics*, 3–12. George provides an analogous reading of Jameson's postcolonial theorizing in *The Politics of Home*, 113–17.

50. Theodor W. Adorno, *Negative Dialectics*, 23. Varadharajan argues in *Exotic Parodies* for Adorno's usefulness in postcolonial studies. See *Exotic Parodies*, 34–74, 113–36.

51. Adorno, *Negative Dialectics*, 12, 6.

52. Eagleton, *The Ideology of the Aesthetic*, 354; see also Said, *The World, the Text, and the Critic*, 224.

53. Adorno, *Negative Dialectics*, 207.

54. Eagleton, *The Ideology of the Aesthetic*, 222, 223, 226.

55. Ibid., 37–38.

56. See Wellmer, *The Persistence of Modernity*, 1–35. J. M. Bernstein argues against Wellmer that Adorno does not associate conceptual reason, but its deformation, with violence (see *The Fate of Art*, 244–47, 255–57); his overall argument is that Adorno valorizes modern art because it points to a desirable connection of *phronêsis* and *praxis* foreclosed everywhere *outside* art (188–274).

57. Levinas, *Totality and Infinity*, 303.

58. Harpham, *Getting It Right*, 23, 182.

59. J. M. Bernstein, *The Fate of Art*, 216; see Adorno, *Negative Dialectics*, 127.

60. Harpham, *Getting It Right*, 181–82.

61. Brian Schroeder, *Altared Ground*, 101–2; see also Harpham, *Getting It Right*, 24. Jean Cohen and Andrew Arato critique Gramsci's theorizing of postrevolutionary society in similar terms in *Civil Society and Political Theory*, 149–74.

62. Chinua Achebe, *Hopes and Impediments*, 53. Some African writers do follow these Western narratives, most prominently Ngũgĩ wa Thiong'o in *Writers in Politics*, 3–33.

63. Harrow, *Thresholds of Change in African Literature*, 129.

64. Dews, *Logics of Disintegration*, 237–38.

65. Derrida argues that Levinas makes sexual difference secondary (54–55). Levinas contends that differences of gender, class, and race do not displace the primacy of the ethical relation but acquire significance through that primacy. See Emmanuel Levinas,

Otherwise than Being, 153–62, 165–71; Critchley, *The Ethics of Deconstruction*, 107–44, 219–36.

66. Hans-Georg Gadamer, *Truth and Method*, 304–5; Hans-Georg Gadamer, *Wahrheit und Methode*, 308–9.

67. See Martha C. Nussbaum, *Love's Knowledge*; Charles Taylor, *Sources of the Self*, *The Ethics of Authenticity*; Bernard Williams, *Ethics and the Limits of Philosophy*; Stanley Cavell, *Must We Mean What We Say?* and *The Claim of Reason*; Ricoeur, *Oneself as Another*; Hans-Georg Gadamer, *The Relevance of the Beautiful and Other Essays*.

68. See esp. Goodheart, *The Reign of Ideology*; Adam Zachary Newton, *Narrative Ethics*; Christopher Norris, *Truth and the Ethics of Criticism*; Harpham, *Getting It Right*.

69. Although Levinas's career began in the 1930s, his work did not acquire prominence in the academy until the 1980s.

70. Zygmunt Bauman, *Postmodern Ethics*, 62, 72, 73. See Levinas, *Totality and Infinity*, 194–219; "Ethics as First Philosophy."

71. Bauman, *Postmodern Ethics*, 76, 77, 112, 132.

72. I am drawing upon the title of Levinas's collection of essays on Judaism, *Difficult Freedom*.

73. Harpham, *Getting It Right*, 55; Emmanuel Levinas and Richard Kearney, "Dialogue with Emmanuel Levinas," in *Face to Face with Levinas*, ed. Richard Cohen, 29.

74. Harpham, *Getting It Right*, 57–58.

75. Bauman, *Postmodernity and Its Discontents*, 47, 53.

76. Levinas, *Totality and Infinity*, 200–201, 203–4, 207, 219.

77. Levinas, *Otherwise than Being*, 5–6.

78. Ibid., 165.

79. Norris, *Truth and the Ethics of Criticism*, 48.

80. See Ricoeur's discussion of Levinas in *Oneself as Another*, 188–89, 335–41, 354–55.

81. Ibid., 168; Levinas, *Otherwise than Being*, 138.

82. Ricoeur, *Oneself as Another*, 337.

83. Levinas, *Otherwise than Being*, 158–59.

84. See Levinas, "The Other in Proust"; Schroeder, *Altared Ground*, 102; Eaglestone, *Ethical Criticism*, 98–128, 156–66.

85. See Simone de Beauvoir, *The Second Sex*, xix; Luce Irigaray, *An Ethics of Sexual Difference*, 185–217.

86. See Derrida, "En ce moment même dans cet ouvrage me voici."

87. Tina Chanter, "Feminism and the Other," 34, 36.

88. Ibid., 42.

89. Harpham, *Getting It Right*, 180–81.

90. See esp. Armstrong, *Desire and Domestic Fiction*; Miller, *The Novel and the Police*.

91. Newton, *Narrative Ethics*, 17–19.

92. Ibid., 28–29; see also 37–69. This is a problem that afflicts other recent efforts to delineate Levinas's signficance for literary studies. See Eaglestone's *Ethical Criticism* and Jill Robbins's *Altered Reading*, esp. xxiv.

93. See David P. Haney, "Aesthetics and Ethics in Gadamer, Levinas, and Romanticism," *PLMA* 114, no. 1 (1999): 32–45; Luc Ferry, *Homo Aestheticus*, 71–76.

94. Giddens, *Beyond Left and Right*, 5.

95. See Haney, "Aesthetics and Ethics," 40.

3. Culture's Relation to Identity and Value in *Efuru* and *The Stillborn*

1. Lloyd W. Brown, *Women Writers in Black Africa*, 144.

2. Countering monolithic theories of culture, Derrida in *The Other Heading* postulates, "What is proper to a culture is to not be identical with itself" (9). See also Michel de Certeau, *The Practice of Everyday Life*; Giddens, *Central Problems in Social Theory*, 96–164; Trinh T. Minh-ha, *Woman, Native, Other*; Jameson, *The Political Unconscious*, 74–102.

3. Brown, *Women Writers in Black Africa*, 141–42, 145, 147, 151.

4. Naana Banyiwa-Horne, "African Womanhood: The Contrasting Perspectives of Flora Nwapa's *Efuru* and Elechi Amadi's *The Concubine*," 125, 126, 128; Theodora Akachi Ezeigbo, "Myth, History, Culture, and Igbo Womanhood in Flora Nwapa's Novels," 70.

5. Elleke Boehmer, "Stories of Women and Mothers: Gender and Nationalism in the Early Fiction of Flora Nwapa," 15, 17; Ada Uzoamaka Azodo, "*Efuru* and *Idu*: Rejecting Women's Subjugation," 176.

6. Carole Boyce Davies, "Motherhood in the Works of Male and Female Igbo Writers," 251.

7. Obioma Nnaemeka, introduction to *The Politics of (M)Othering*, 3–4.

8. Ibid., 18–19.

9. Ibid., 21.

10. Heidegger separates himself from Sartre in *Letter on Humanism*, 204–11. However, Sartre's theorizing of the "for-itself" draws upon Heidegger's account of the "ecstatic" condition of Dasein's "being-in-the-world." See Sartre, *Being and Nothingness*, 133, 145, 367; Heidegger, *Being and Time*, 377–80, 387–89, 414–15. Both thinkers argue that the antiessential essence of human being can be found in how humans "stand out" in ways that make objectification violent.

11. See Thomas Hobbes's account of worth, natural law, and legitimacy in *Leviathan*, 78–79, 109–19, 139–43, 170–80, 251–61; see also C. B. Macpherson, *The Rise and Fall of Economic Justice and Other Papers*, 1–20, 86–91, 133–46.

12. For an exception, see Emelia C. Oko, "Woman, the Self-Celebrating Heroine: The Novels of Flora Nwapa."

13. See Maryse Condé, "Three Female Writers in Modern Africa: Flora Nwapa, Ama Ata Aidoo, and Grace Ogot," *Présence Africaine* 82, no. 2 (1972): 134–36; Davies, "Motherhood in the Works of Male and Female Igbo Writers," 241–56; Susheila Nasta, introduction to *Motherlands*, xxi; Boehmer, "Stories of Women and Mothers," 11–12.

14. Bakhtin, *Speech Genres and Other Late Essays*, 7; for the value of outside understanding, see 132–72; Bakhtin, *Art and Answerability*, 61–93.

15. Harrow, *Thresholds of Change in African Literature*, 28, 27.

16. On such dangers, see Spivak, *Outside in the Teaching Machine*, 53–76, 277–78.

17. See Banyiwa-Horne, "African Womanhood," 125; Davies, "Womanhood in the Works of Male and Female Igbo Writers," 250; Boehmer, "Stories of Women and Mothers," 15; Susan Z. Andrande, "Rewriting History, Motherhood, and Rebellion: Naming an African Women's Literary Tradition," *Research in African Literature* 21, no. 2 (1990): 91–110.

18. "Marriage Is a Private Affair" is reprinted in Achebe, *Girls at War and Other Stories,* 22–30. For arguments that Efuru's "bath" creates a permanent psychic wound, see Linda Strong-Leek, "The Quest for Spiritual/Sexual Fulfillment in Flora Nwapa's *Efuru* and *The Lake Goddess,*" and Shivaji Sengupta, "Desire, the Private, and the Public in Flora Nwapa's *Efuru* and *One Is Enough.*"

19. See Brown, *Women Writers in Black Africa,* 137–41; Banyiwa-Horne, "African Womanhood," 121–22; Davies, "Womanhood in the Works of Male and Female Igbo Writers," 249–50; Boehmer, "Stories of Women and Mothers," 15–17.

20. Ricoeur, *Oneself as Another,* 2–3.

21. Ibid., 330–31.

22. See Pierre Bourdieu, *The Logic of Practice,* 69–72; see also 52–97.

23. Adeola James, ed., *In Their Own Voices,* 114.

24. See Ifi Amadiume, *Male Daughters, Female Husbands,* 30–40.

25. Maja-Pearce, *A Mask Dancing,* 28. On linguistic inscriptions of inequality, see Felix K. Ekechi, "Pawnship in Igbo Society," 92–94.

26. See J. M. Bernstein's commentary in *The Fate of Art,* 216–24; Walter Benjamin, *Illuminations,* 258.

27. Levinas, *Totality and Infinity,* 215.

28. Levinas, *Otherwise than Being,* 138–39.

29. Ibid., 48.

30. See Chinua Achebe, *Things Fall Apart,* 123–25; Ousseynou B. Traoré, "Why the Snake-Lizard Killed His Mother: Inscribing and Decentering 'Nneka' in *Things Fall Apart.*"

31. Ricoeur, *Oneself as Another,* 193.

32. Ibid., 218–55.

33. See Toyin Falola and Paul E. Lovejoy, "Pawnship in Historical Perspective," and Ekechi, "Pawnship in Igbo Society," in *Pawnship in Africa.*

34. See Newton, *Narrative Ethics,* 17–23.

35. Susan Arndt, "Applauding a 'Dangerous Luxury,'" 211.

36. Ibid., 212.

37. For historical contexts, see esp. David Northrup, "The Ideological Context of Slavery in Southeastern Nigeria in the Nineteenth Century"; Herbert S. Klein, "African Women in the Atlantic Slave Trade"; John Thornton, "Sexual Demography: The Impact of the Slave Trade on Family Structure"; Claude Meillassoux, "Female Slavery"; Martin A. Klein, "Women in Slavery in the Western Sudan"; and Claude Meillassoux, *The Anthropology of Slavery.* For the gradual cessation of slavery, see Don Ohadike, "The Decline of Slavery among the Igbo People." For a similar folktale, see "The Disobedient Sisters," in *African Folktales,* ed. Roger D. Abrahams, 143–45. Simon Ottenberg notes the

fear about leaving children unattended outdoors in *Boyhood Rituals in an African Society*, 47.

38. Arndt, "Applauding a 'Dangerous Luxury,'" 218, 221.

39. Levinas, *Otherwise than Being*, 124.

40. Giddens, *Beyond Left and Right*, 5.

41. Roberto Mangabiera Unger, *Social Theory*, 23–24.

42. See Richard L. Roberts, *Warriors, Merchants, and Slaves*, 89. Stuart Brown notes that Alkali, a native Hausa speaker, spent the first ten years of her life in the mostly Christian village of Garkida. See Brown's introduction to *The Stillborn*, viii.

43. See Catherine Coles and Beverly Mack, "Women in Twentieth-Century Hausa Society"; Barbara J. Callaway, *Muslim Hausa Women in Nigeria*, 1–20.

44. See Callaway, *Muslim Hausa Women*, 28–35.

45. Unger, *Social Theory*, 32–33.

46. Faku's views are conventional. See Callaway, *Muslim Hausa Women*, 35–47.

47. See Adeola James's remarks in *In Their Own Voices*, 30.

48. See Combs-Schilling, *Sacred Performances*, 95; Mernissi, *Beyond the Veil*, 31, 39, 41–42, 53–54.

49. Mernissi, *Beyond the Veil*, 31. Callaway notes that the Hausa word *karuwa* (single or unmarried woman, with implications of sexual and economic independence) has the connotation of "prostitute." See Callaway, *Muslim Hausa Women*, 42–44, 84.

50. For discussions of the rejection of the West among educated women, see Callaway, *Muslim Hausa Women*, 109–30, 168–80, 187–212; Bilkisu Yusuf, "Hausa-Fulani Women: The State of the Struggle"; Ayesha M. Iman, "Ideology, the Mass Media, and Women: A Study from Radio Kaduna, Nigeria."

51. See Callaway's discussion of repudiation in *Muslim Hausa Women*, 47–51.

52. Maja-Pearce, *A Mask Dancing*, 152–53.

53. For the centrality of Hegel's master-slave dialectic to anticolonialist theory, see Sartre, *Being and Nothingness*, 301–400; Fanon, *Peau noire, masques blanches*; Memmi, *The Colonizer and the Colonized*; Said, *Culture and Imperialism*, 270–71.

54. For Hegel, realized freedom, as opposed to an abstract potential for freedom, is achieved through determinate identity (*Philosophy of Right*, 107, sec. 149). Sartre argues that freedom is the opposite of being, of determinateness (*Being and Nothingness*, 567). For Levinas, freedom transcends the bond between essence and self-interest (*Totality and Infinity*, 303; *Otherwise than Being*, 3–4, 135–40).

55. Sartre, *Being and Nothingness*, 384; see also Hegel, *The Phenomenology of Mind*, 229–40; Sartre, *Being and Nothingness*, 340–400.

56. On the status of prostitution, see Callaway, *Muslim Hausa Women*, 44; Coles and Mack, "Women in Twentieth-Century Hausa Society," 18–19; Roberta Ann Dunbar, "Islamic Values, the State, and 'the Development of Women': The Case of Niger," 76; Catherine Coles, "Hausa Women's Work in a Declining Urban Economy: Kaduna, Nigeria, 1980–1985," 175; Alan Frishman, "Hausa Women in the Urban Economy of Kano," 193, 200.

57. Trinh T. Minh-ha, "Mother's Talk," 29.

58. See Mohamed Ahmed Sherif, *Ghazali's Theory of Virtue*, 30–35; Callaway, *Muslim Hausa Women*, 23–27; Mernissi, *Women's Rebellion and Islamic Memory*.

59. Minh-ha, "Mother's Talk," 31; Connie Stephens, "Marriage in the Hausa *Tatsuniya* Tradition: A Cultural and Cosmic Balance," 223.

60. Stephens, "Marriage," 224–25, 231.

61. Levinas, *Otherwise than Being*, 48, 55, 56.

62. Mernissi, *Islam and Democracy*, 95.

63. Ibid., 85, 86. In "Reality and Its Shadow," Levinas also links the image with idolatry (137–38, 141–42).

64. Mernissi, *Women's Rebellion and Islamic Memory*, 111, 110, 118.

65. Clifford Geertz, *Local Knowledge*, 110.

66. See Haney, "Aesthetics and Ethics."

67. Alkali, interview in James, *In Their Own Words*, 29.

68. Newton, *Narrative Ethics*, 13.

69. Fielding, *Tom Jones*, 80.

70. Battestin's note in Fielding, *Tom Jones*, 79–80.

71. Levinas, *Otherwise than Being*, 148.

72. Callaway, *Muslim Hausa Women*, 191.

73. Mernissi, *Islam and Democracy*, 84.

74. Alkali, interview in James, *In Their Own Words*, 31.

75. Nicole Echard, "Gender Relationships and Religion: Women in the Hausa *Bori* of Ader, Nigeria," 212; see also 207–20; Callaway, *Muslim Women in Nigeria*, 82–84, 196–97.

76. Yusuf, "Hausa-Fulani Women," 102–3, see also 90–106; Barbara J. Callaway, "The Role of Women in Kano City Politics" and *Muslim Hausa Women*, 85–130.

77. See Mernissi, *Women's Rebellion and Islamic Memory*, esp. 95–106.

78. Mernissi, *Islam and Democracy*, 99–100.

4. Tenderness, Piety, and Cosmopolitan Humanism in *Une si longue lettre*

1. See esp. Keith L. Walker, "Postscripts: Mariama Bâ, Epistolarity, Menopause, and Postcoloniality"; Dorothy Davis Willis, "Economic Violence in Postcolonial Senegal: Noisy Silence in Novels by Mariama Bâ and Aminata Sow Fall"; Glenn W. Fetzer, "Women's Search for Voice and the Problem of Knowing in the Novels of Marima Bâ," *CLA Journal* 35, no. 1 (1991): 31–41; Mildred Mortimer, *Journeys through the French African Novel*, 133–47. Florence Stratton, in "The Shallow Grave: Archetypes of Female Experience in African Fiction," *Research in African Literatures* 19, 1(1988): 143–69, argues that Ramatoulaye's rebellion is unsuccessful. Irene Assiba d'Almeida, in "The Concept of Choice in Mariama Bâ's Fiction," views "choice" being validated, but also implies that Aïssatou's actions are better (171). For discussions of Bâ's views on polygamy, see esp. Susan Stringer, *The Senegalese Novel by Women*, 68–69; Edris Makward, "Marriage, Tradition, and Woman's Pursuit of Happiness in the Novels of Mariama Bâ."

2. Walker, "Postscripts," 257, 259.

3. Fetzer, "Women's Search for Voice," 39, 40. See also C. L. Innes, "Mothers or

Sisters? Identity, Discourse, and Audience in the Writing of Ama Ata Aidoo and Mariama Bâ," 146.

4. Mariama Bâ, *Une si longue lettre*, 7; Bâ, *So Long a Letter*, 1. Henceforth parenthetical citations in the text will be to these editions. At times I will modify the translation, as indicated by brackets, and indicate the French edition as *USLL*.

5. Annemarie Schimmel, *My Soul Is a Woman*, 93–94.

6. Levinas, *Totality and Infinity*, 204.

7. Levinas, *Otherwise than Being*, 106, 108.

8. Ibid., 109, 110.

9. Levinas, "God and Philosophy," 179, 185, 184.

10. Muhammad Abdul Quasem, *The Recitation and Interpretation of the Qur'an*, 18–19

11. Walker, "Postscripts," 252. Shaun Irlam emphasizes Ramatoulaye's empowering relation to the Quran in "Mariama Bâ *Une si longue lettre:* The Vocation of Memory and the Space of Writing," *Research in African Literatures* 29, no. 2 (1998): 81.

12. Mernissi, *Islam and Democracy*, 85. The connections that Bâ's French discourse builds with Islamic thought are weakened in translation.

13. Levinas, "Revelation in the Jewish Tradition," 208, 209. In *Death and Responsibility*, Dennis King Keenan argues, "For Levinas, God is only the interruption of order" (19). However, Keenan largely neglects how Levinas binds ethical interruption to the redemption of reason.

14. Barbara Freyer Stowasser, *Women in the Qur'an, Tradition, and Interpretation*, 134.

15. Quasem, *The Recitation and Interpretation of the Qur'an*, 88, 104.

16. See Charles Taylor, *Sources of the Self.* By "inwardness," Taylor refers to the deepening of subjectivity; "the affirmation of ordinary life" refers to the claim that everyday, prosaic life is invested with significance; "the voice of nature" refers to Rousseauian-Romantic notions that "nature" can speak to us, act as a moral guide; "subtler languages" refers to efforts to find ways of expressing what supersedes ordinary, conventional language.

17. Julia Kristeva, *Time and Sense*, 108, 109; see also Irlam, "Mariama Bâ *Une si longue lettre*," 77.

18. See esp. Proust's account of the relation of body position and memory in the "Ouverture," the genesis of young Marcel's love of Gilberte in "Combray," the structuring of Marcel's desire for cities and Balbec in "Place-names: The Name."

19. Taylor, *Sources of the Self*, 479.

20. Kristeva, *Time and Sense*, 171; *Le temps sensible*, 211.

21. On public ritual praise, see Graham Furniss and Liz Gunner, eds., *Power, Marginality, and African Oral Literature.*

22. Mortimer, *Journeys through the French African Novel*, 135, 137, 146–47. See also Nnaemeka, "Mariama Bâ," *Feminist Issues* 10, no. 1 (1990): 13–35.

23. Mortimer, *Journeys*, 143.

24. Kristeva, *Time and Sense*, 331.

25. Stringer, *The Senegalese Novel by Women*, 54.

26. Mbye B. Cham, "Contemporary Society and the Female Imagination: A Study of the Novels of Mariama Bâ," 91–92.

27. Nnaemeka, "Mariama Bâ," 13–16; in "Urban Spaces, Women's Places," Nnaemeka argues that polygamy in an urban, middle-class space victimizes women more than in earlier times.

28. Uzo Esonwanne, "Enlightenment Epistemology and 'Aesthetic Cognition': Mariama Bâ's *So Long a Letter,*" 85, 86–87.

29. Stringer, *The Senegalese Novel by Women,* 54.

30. Mortimer, *The Journey through French African Fiction,* 138–39.

31. Esonwanne, "Enlightenment Epistemology and 'Aesthetic Cognition,'" 86–87.

32. Stowasser notes that the Quran portrays Adam and Eve are equal partners in sin, while later traditions recast Eve in a misogynistic light. See *Women in the Qur'an, Traditions, and Interpretation,* 25–38.

33. Irène Assiba d'Almeida, "The Concept of Choice in Mariama Bâ's Fiction," 161, 170.

34. Mortimer, *The Journey through the French African Novel,* 139.

35. Ibid.

36. Esonwanne, "Enlightenment Epistemology and 'Aesthetic Cognition,'" 89.

37. Mortimer, *The Journey through the French African Novel,* 140.

38. For the relationship between Aristotelian ethics and educational theory, see esp. T. H. Irwin, *Aristotle's First Principles,* 416–23; see also Plutarch, *Moralia,* vol. 1.

39. See Lapidus, "Knowledge, Virtue, and Action"; Peter Brown, "Late Antiquity and Islam: Parallels and Contrasts."

40. Cheryl Wall Staunton, "Marima Bâ: Pioneer Senegalese Woman Novelist," *CLA Journal* 37, no. 3 (1994): 330, 332, 329; see also János Riesz, "Mariama Bâ *Une si longue lettre*: An *Erziehungsroman,*" *Research in African Literatures* 22, no. 1 (1991): 27–42.

41. For Renaissance humanist education, see esp. Erasmus, *A Declamation on the Subject of Early Liberal Education for Children*; Charles Trinkaus, *In Our Image and Likeness.*

42. Leonardo A. Villalón, *Islamic Society and State Power in Senegal,* 51.

43. See David C. Conrad and Barbara E. Frank, eds., *Status and Identity in West Africa,* and Patrick R. McNaughton, *The Mande Blacksmiths.*

44. Villalón, *Islamic Society,* 56–57.

45. Ibid., 61–62; see also Sheldon Gellar, *Senegal,* 1–8; Donal B. Cruise O'Brien, *Saints and Politicians,* 1–56.

46. On the silence of Francophone women before Bâ, see Miller, *Theories of Africans,* 246–93.

47. See Levinas, *Difficult Freedom,* 59–96, 226–27; *Totality and Infinity,* 281–85.

48. Esonwanne, "Enlightenment Epistemology and 'Aesthetic Cognition,'" 88–91; Lapidus, "Knowledge, Virtue, and Action," 39.

49. Gérard Genette, *Narrative Discourse,* 116; see also 117.

50. Kristeva, *Time and Sense,* 331.

51. Levinas, *Totality and Infinity,* 147.

52. Charles Ponnuthurai Sarvan, "Feminism and African Fiction: The Novels of Mariama Bâ," *Modern Fiction Studies* 34, 3 (1988): 457–58.

53. See Christopher L. Delgado and Sidi Jammeh, eds., *The Political Economy of Senegal under Structural Adjustment.*

54. Catherine Boone, *Merchant Capital and the Roots of State Power in Senegal, 1930–1985,* 11.

55. See Levinas, "Reality and Its Shadow." However, Levinas's position here may be contrasted with his claim that "across all literature the human face speaks" in *Ethics and Infinity,* 117.

56. Esonwanne, "Enlightenment Epistemology and 'Aesthetic Cognition,'" 87.

57. Muhammad Adbul Haq Ansari, *Sufism and Sharî'ah,* 35, 51, 131.

58. See David Haney, "Wordsworth and Levinas: Making a Habit of the Sublime."

59. See Ansari's discussion in *Sufism and Sharî'ah,* 101–17.

60. Levinas, *Totality and Infinity,* 148.

61. Villalón, *Islamic Society,* 62–63

62. Miller, *Theories of Africans,* 282, 283.

63. Sarvan, "Feminism and African Fiction," 458.

64. Miller, *Theories of Africans,* 281.

65. Mernissi, *Islam and Democracy,* 89.

66. Taylor uses "moral space" to describe how the self locates itself in relation to goods toward which it moves or from which it strays. See *Sources of the Self,* 25–52.

67. Villalón, *Islamic Society,* 35.

68. See Donal B. Cruise O'Brien, *The Mourides of Senegal, Saints, and Politicans;* see also Villalón, *Islamic Society,* esp. 115–99.

69. Villalón, *Islamic Society,* 229–30.

70. Mernissi, *Islam and Democracy,* 101, 99.

71. Sherif, *Ghazali's Theory of Virtue,* 30, 34–35.

72. Seyyed Hossein Nasr, *Sufi Essays,* 35.

73. Miller, *Theories of Africans,* 275. See Riesz's defense of Ramatoulaye's affirmation of acculturation in "Mariama Bâ *Une si longue lettre,*" 28–29.

74. See, for example, Cicero, *De Officiis,* 1:iv–viii, 12–29.

75. Miller, *Theories of Africans,* 275.

76. Mernissi, *Islam and Democracy,* 105.

77. Walker, "Postscripts," 259.

78. Mernissi, *Islam and Democracy,* 117, 118–19.

79. Julia Kristeva, *Interviews,* 10.

80. Julia Kristeva, *Tales of Love,* 34.

81. Kristeva, *Interviews,* 62.

82. Esonwanne, "Enlightenment Epistemology and 'Aesthetic Cognition,'" 94.

83. Sarvan, "Feminism and African Fiction," 459; see also Irlam, "Mariama Bâ *Une si longue lettre,*" 80.

84. Stowasser, *Women in the Qur'an, Traditions, and Interpretation,* 86.

85. Ibid., 114.

86. Sarvan, "Feminism and African Fiction," 459; d'Almeida, "The Concept of Choice in Mariama Bâ's Fiction," 167.

87. Levinas, *Otherwise than Being*, 108–9.

88. Combs-Schilling, *Sacred Performances*, 92; see also Abdelwahab Bouhdiba, *Sexuality in Isalm*, esp. 19–57.

89. Combs-Schilling, *Sacred Performances*, 239, 240–41.

90. Levinas, *Difficult Freedom*, 9.

91. Stowasser, *Women in the Qur'an, Traditions, and Interpretation*, 5, 6–7.

92. See Mernissi, *The Veil and the Male Elite*, 115–40.

93. Sarvan, "Feminism and African Fiction," 460.

94. Esonwanne, "Enlightenment Epistemology and 'Aesthetic Cognition,'" 94; see also Innes, "Mothers or Sisters?" 148.

95. See Irwin's account of Aristotelian rational and ethical agency in *Aristotle's First Principles*, 329–46; on "choiceworthy" (*hairetos*), see Aristotle, *Nicomachean Ethics*, 390.

96. Levinas, *Totality and Infinity*, 279.

97. Ibid., 279–80.

5. Acculturation and Decolonization in Tsitsi Dangarembga's *Nervous Conditions*

1. Tsitsi Dangarembga, *Nervous Conditions*, 1. All further citations are to this edition.

2. For such readings, see Charles Sugnet, "*Nervous Conditions*: Dangarembga's Feminist Reinvention of Fanon"; Lindsay Pentolfe Aegerter, "A Dialectic of Autonomy and Community: Tsitsi Dangarembga's *Nervous Conditions*," *Tulsa Studies in Women's Literature* 15, no. 2 (1996): 231–40; Pauline Ada Uwakweh, "Debunking Patriarchy: The Liberational Quality of Voicing in Tsitsi Dangarembga's *Nervous Conditions*," *Research in African Literature* 26, 1 (1995): 75–84; Supriya Nair, "Melancholic Women: The Intellectual Hysteric(s) in *Nervous Conditions*," *Research in African Literature* 26, 2 (1995): 130–39; Sue Thomas, "Killing the Hysteric in the Colonized House: Tsitsi Dangarembga's *Nervous Conditions*," *Journal of Commonwealth Literature* 24, 1 (1992): 26–36; Michelle Vizzard, "'Of Mimicry and Woman': Hysteria and Anticolonial Feminism in Tsitsi Dangarembga's *Nervous Conditions*," *Span: Journal of the South Pacific Association for Commonwealth Literature and Language Studies* 36 (1993): 202–10; Miki Flockemann, "'Not-Quite Insiders and Not-Quite Outsiders': The 'Process of Womanhood' in *Beka Lamb, Nervous Conditions*, and *Daughters of the Twilight*," *Journal of Commonwealth Literature* 24, 1 (1992): 37–47; Sally McWilliams, Tsitsi Dangarembga's *Nervous Conditions*: At the Crossroads of Feminism and Post-Colonialism," *World Literature Written in English* 31, 1 (1991): 103–12.

3. Sugnet, "*Nervous Conditions*," 40.

4. Ibid., 36.

5. Elizabeth Schmidt, *Peasants, Traders, and Wives*, 1–2.

6. Ibid., 14–21.

7. On the colonial efforts to displace Shona trade and agriculture, see Schmidt, *Peasants, Traders, and Wives*, 43–97; on the colonialist gender ideology and efforts to control women, see 98–121; on the mission schools, see 122–54.

8. Juliana Makuchi Nfah-Abbenyi, *Gender in African Women's Writing*, 62.

9. See, for example, Immanuel Kant, "What Is Enlightenment? Idea for a Universal History from a Cosmopolitan Point of View," in Kant, *On History*, 3–26.

10. Nussbaum, *Love's Knowledge*, 308–9.

11. Rosemary Marangoly George and Helen Scott, "An Interview with Tsitsi Dangarembga," *NOVEL: A Forum for Fiction* 26, 3 (1993): 313.

12. Martin Jay, *Fin de Siècle Socialism and Other Essays*, 143, 146; see also Richard J. Bernstein, *The New Constellation*, 142–71, 199–229; Jürgen Habermas, *The Philosophical Discourse of Modernity*, 106–30, 238–93.

13. Schmidt, *Peasants, Traders, and Wives*, 140; see also 140–45. Riesz, "Mariama Bâ *Une si longue lettre*," 30–35.

14. Schmidt, *Peasants, Traders, and Wives*, 154.

15. See Schmidt's account of the suppressing of African trade (ibid., 74–76, 78).

16. Jean-Paul Sartre, preface to Frantz Fanon, *The Wretched of the Earth*, 16–17; quoted in Thomas, "Killing the Hysteric in the Colonized's House," 27.

17. Thomas, "Killing the Hysteric in the Colonized's House," 27.

18. Sugnet, "*Nervous Conditions*," 35.

19. Thomas, "Killing the Hysteric in the Colonized's House," 28, 33, 32.

20. Uwakweh, "Debunking Patriarchy," 77.

21. Sugnet, "*Nervous Conditions*," 34.

22. Nfah-Abbenyi, *Gender in African Women's Writing*, 65, 66, 71.

23. Some uses of the trickster figure assimilate it to a purely "disruptive" narrative function. See Fishburn's discussion, in *Reading Buchi Emecheta*, 71–72. Robert D. Pelton notes in *The Trickster in West Africa* that the Yoruba and other West African trickster figures help *establish* as well as violate cosmic and social orders.

24. Ricoeur, *Oneself as Another*, 113.

25. Ibid., 140, 166.

26. See Schmidt, *Peasants, Traders, and Wives*, 17–18, 23–28.

27. David Beach, *The Shona and Their Neighbours*, 154.

28. Sugnet, "*Nervous Conditions*," 40.

29. See the distinctions between good and bad sorcery elaborated in Jean Comaroff and John Comaroff, eds., *Modernity and Its Malcontents*.

30. Ricoeur, *Oneself as Another*, 177.

31. Ibid., 179–80.

32. Ibid., 180.

33. See Unger's account of the "paradox" of the inevitability of contexts and their constant revision in *Social Theory*, 18–25; see also Gadamer's account of "horizons" in *Truth and Method*, 302–7.

34. Beach, *The Shona and Their Neighbours*, 154–55.

35. Ibid., 82–108.

36. Thomas, "Killing the Hysteric in the Colonized's House," 35.

37. Flockemann, "Not-Quite Insiders and Not-Quite Outsiders," 41. Sugnet does ac-

knowledge that some aspects of Western acculturation play a positive role in Tambu's ability to "reinvent herself" ("*Nervous Conditions*," 42), but does not explore how.

38. Nfah-Abbenyi, *Gender in African Women's Writing*, 66

39. Thomas, "Killing the Hysteric in the Colonized's House," 35.

40. Gadamer, *Truth and Method*, 299, 305, 306.

41. Abiola Irele, "In Praise of Alienation," 214–15.

42. Ibid., 202.

43. Thomas, "Killing the Hysteric in the Colonized's House," 34, 33.

44. Ricoeur, *Oneself as Another*, 180.

45. Ibid., 181.

46. Ibid., 186.

47. George Eliot, *Middlemarch*, 613.

48. See Wolfgang Iser, *The Fictive and the Imaginary*, esp. 1–86.

49. Sugnet, "*Nervous Conditions*," 45, 47.

50. See Schmidt, *Peasants, Traders, and Wives*, 19, 21.

51. McWilliams, "Tsitsi Dangarembga's *Nervous Conditions*," 109.

52. Sugnet, "*Nervous Conditions*," 44.

53. Beach, *The Shona and the Neighbours*, 156–57.

54. See McWilliams, "Tsitsi Dangarembga's *Nervous Conditions*," 105.

55. See Irele's account of "cultural nationalism" in "In Praise of Alienation."

56. Lucia's and Maiguru's manipulation of Shona and Western patriarchal self-images exemplifies the "ruse" of the disempowered as analyzed by Michel de Certeau in *The Practice of Everyday Life*, esp. 15–42.

57. Sugnet, "*Nervous Conditions*," 45.

58. Jean-Paul Sartre, "'*Les damnés de la terre*,'" 181. The translations are mine.

59. Sartre, "'*Les damnés de la terre*,'" 183.

60. See Beach, *The Shona and Their Neighbours*, 180–83.

61. For treatments of Nyasha as Dangaremgba's mouthpiece, see Thomas, "Killing the Hysteric in the Colonized's House," 31–32, 34; McWilliams, "Tsitsi Dangarembga's *Nervous Conditions*," pp.105, 111; Sugnet, "*Nervous Conditions*," 37; Aegerter, "A Dialectic of Autonomy and Community," 236–37, 238.

62. Schmidt notes that in precolonial Shona culture a wife was often viewed with suspicion because she was seen as loyal to a different set of ancestral spirits. See Schmidt, *Peasants, Traders, and Wives*, 16–19, 24–26.

63. See Camara Laye, *L'Enfant noir*, 215–19.

64. See Sugnet, "*Nervous Conditions*," 36–38.

65. Nfah-Abbenyi, *Gender in African Women's Writing*, 68.

66. Sugnet, "*Nervous Conditions*," 43.

67. Nfah-Abbenyi, *Gender in African Women's Writing*, 69, 71; Nfah-Abbenyi quotes on 71 Ellen Willis, in "Discussion" with Gayatri Spivak and Catharine MacKinnon, 118.

68. George and Scott, "An Interview with Tsitsi Dangarembga," 311.

69. Sugnet, "*Nervous Conditions*," 47.

70. Levinas, *Otherwise than Being*, 64.

71. For intimate connections between the moral discourse of good and bad wizardry, on the one hand, and the mobilization of political and military resistance to white colonial rule, on the other hand, see David Lan, *Guns and Rain* and T. O. Ranger, *Peasant Consciousness and Guerrilla War in Zimbabwe*.

72. Newton, *Narrative Ethics*, 18, 14.

73. Sartre argues that Negritude poetry reverses the values of the terms of the Western schema through which the West "sees" the black colonized. See Jean-Paul Sartre, *Black Orpheus*, esp. 16–21, 57–65; *Orphée noir*, 229–86. The pattern of equating the position of colonizer and colonized to Sartre's analysis of "the look" (*Being and Nothingness*, 340–400), where the observer objectifies and dehumanizes the observed, is elaborated in the binary structure of Memmi's *The Colonizer and the Colonized*. For the view that realistic fiction "naturalizes" interpretations, see Harrow, *Thresholds of Change in African Literature*, 60–68, 78–85 and Fishburn, *Reading Buchi Emecheta*, 46–48, 128.

74. Bakhtin, *Art and Answerability*, 82.

75. Ibid., 50.

6. Ambiguous Freedom in Ama Ata Aidoo's *Changes*

1. Ama Ata Aidoo, *Changes: A Love Story*, no page number, henceforth cited parenthetically in the text.

2. See James, *In Their Own Voices*, 14.

3. See Miller, *The Ethics of Reading*, and Derrida's discussion of "making the *archê* tremble" in *Writing and Difference*, 141.

4. See James, *In Their Own Voices*, 12.

5. James Joyce, *Portrait of the Artist as a Young Man*, 215.

6. Kwesi Yankah *Speaking for the Chief*, 51.

7. Ibid., 52,

8. See Levinas's discussion of communication in *Otherwise than Being*, 118–21.

9. Kwasi Wiredu, *Cultural Universals and Particulars*, 65, 159; see also Kwame Gyekye, *An Essay on African Philosophical Thought*, 85–103.

10. Yankah, *Speaking for the Chief*, 79; for a discussion of women and public discourse, see 68–79.

11. See Juliana Makuchi Nfah-Abbenyi, "Flabberwhelmed or Turning History on Its Head? The Postcolonial Woman-as-Subject in Aidoo's *Changes: A Love Story*," 284.

12. This is how Slavoj Zˇizˇek might describe it. See Sjavoj Zˇizˇek, "'I Hear You with My Eyes'; or, The Invisible Master," in *Gaze and Voice as Love Object*, ed. Renata Saleci and Slavoj Zˇizˇek (Durham: Duke University Press, 1996); see also Miriam C. Gyimah, "Sexual Politics and Phallocentric Gaze in Ama Ata Aidoo's *Changes: A Love Story*," 385–96.

13. Charles Taylor, *The Ethics of Authenticity*, 27.

14. Gay Wilentz, "African Woman's Domain: Demarcating Political Space in Nwapa, Sutherland, and Aidoo," 276; Nfah-Abbenyi, "Flabberwhelmed or Turning History on Its Head," 296; Nfah-Abbenyi, *Gender in African Women's Writing*, 57.

15. Elizabeth Willey, "National Identities, Tradition, and Feminism: The Novels of Ama Ata Aidoo Read in the Context of the Works of Kwame Nkrumah," 19.

16. Ibid., 21.

17. Nfah-Abbenyi, *Gender in African Women's Writing*, 60–61; "Flabberwhelmed or Turning History on Its Head," 297.

18. Sally McWilliams, "'Strange as It May Seem': African Feminism in Two Novels by Ama Ata Aidoo," 351.

19. Pauline Onwubiko Uwakweh, "Free but Lost: Variations in the Militant's Song," 363, 369; Miriam C. Gyimah, "Sexual Politics and Phallocentric Gaze in Ama Ata Aidoo's *Changes: A Love Story*," 395.

20. Vincent O. Odamtten, *The Art of Ama Ata Aidoo*, 163, 172–73.

21. James, *In Their Own Voices*, 19.

22. Wiredu, *Cultural Universals and Particulars*, 170.

23. James, *In Their Own Voices*, 13.

24. Ibid., 16, 17, 19.

25. Odamtten, *The Art of Ama Ata Aidoo*, 112–20; for the dialogic structure of oral storytelling sequences, see esp. Michael Jackson, *Allegories of the Wilderness*.

26. Odamtten, *The Art of Ama Ata Aidoo*, 172, 5.

27. See Roman Ingarden, *The Cognition of the Literary Work of Art*, esp. 94–145; Wolfgang Iser, *The Act of Reading*, esp. 107–59.

28. See esp. Levinas, *Totality and Infinity*. 42–48, 109–10.

29. Levinas, *Otherwise than Being*, 80.

30. Wiredu, *Cultural Universals and Particulars*, 158.

31. Ama Ata Aidoo, "Unwelcome Pals and Decorative Slaves or Glimpses of Women as Writers and Their Characters in Contemporary African Literature," 12.

32. On Akan understandings of marriage, see Wiredu, *Cultural Universals and Particulars*, 72–73; Christine Oppong, *Middle Class African Marriage*, 28–51.

33. Aidoo, "Unwelcome Pals and Decorative Slaves," 12.

34. Wiredu, *Cultural Universals and Particulars*, 158–59.

35. Robert B. Edgerton, *The Fall of the Asante Empire*, 24.

36. Edgerton, *The Fall of the Asante Empire*, 24.

37. Ibid., 14. On the sources of Asante military and political power, see Ivor Wilks, *Forests of Gold*, 1–167; T. C. McCaskie, *State and Society in Pre-Colonial Asante*, 25–65; see also R. A. Kea, *Settlements, Trade, and Politics in the Seventeenth-Century Gold Coast*.

38. McCaskie, *State and Society in Pre-Colonial Asante*, 35–36; see also Wilks, *Forests of Gold*, 293–328.

39. Gyimah, "Sexual Politics and Phallocentric Gaze," 390.

40. See Yankah, *Speaking for the Chief*, 68; Minh-ha, "Mother's Talk," 26–32.

41. Jane Austen, *Pride and Prejudice*, 142.

42. Levinas, *Otherwise than Being*, 67.

43. Ibid., 80.

44. Gyimah, "Sexual Politics and Phallocentric Gaze," 391.

45. See esp. Jean Comaroff and John Comaroff, eds., *Modernity and Its Malcontents*, 89–220; see also Edwin M. Lemert, *The Trouble with Evil: Social Control at the Edge of Morality*, esp. 33–92.

46. Gyimah, "Sexual Politics and Phallocentric Gaze," 388.

47. Yankah, *Speaking for the Chief*, 100.

48. See esp. Ralph A. Austen, "The Moral Economy of Witchcraft: An Essay in Comparative History."

49. Gyekye, *An Essay on African Philosophical Thought*, 95.

50. R. S. Rattray, *Religion and Art in Ashanti*, 29–30. Readers may compare this account to Misty L. Bastian, "'Bloodhounds Who Have No Friends': Witchcraft and Locality in the Nigerian Popular Press"; Pamela G. Schmoll, "Black Stomachs, Beautiful Stones: Soul-Eating among Hausa in Niger"; Peter Geschiere, *Village Communities and the State*.

51. Jean Comaroff and John Comaroff, *Modernity and Its Malcontents*, xxv, xxix.

52. Gyekye, *An Essay on African Philosophical Thought*, 132.

53. Ibid., 147–48.

54. Wiredu, *Cultural Universals and Particulars*, 160.

55. Rattray, *Religion and Art in Ashanti*, 28.

56. See Erik Erikson, *Childhood and Society*, 219–33, esp. 219–22.

57. Kristeva, *Tales of Love*, 41. 42.

58. Ibid., 42.

59. McWilliams, "'Strange as It May Seem,'" 348.

60. McWilliams, "Strange as It May Seem," 354, and Gyimah, "Sexual Politics and Phallocentric Gaze," 392.

61. See esp. Isaacman, "Peasants and Rural Social Protest in Africa," and Frederick Cooper, "Africa and the World Economy."

62. See Wilks's discussion in *Forests of Gold*, 41–63.

63. Ibid., 96; Peter Shinnie argues that archaeological evidence pushes the process back from the 1500s to the 1200s in "Early Asante: Is Wilks Right?"

64. See Wilks, *Forests of Gold*, 127–67; McCaskie, *State and Society in Pre-Colonial Asante*, 37–49.

65. See Paul Nugent, *Big Men, Small Boys, and the Politics of Ghana*, 15–39.

66. McCaskie, *State and Society in Pre-Colonial Asante*, 78.

67. Nugent, *Big Men, Small Boys, and the Politics of Ghana*, 27.

68. Ibid., 78–79; see also 40–105.

69. McWilliams, "'Strange As It May Seem,'" 354.

70. Tuzyline Jita Allan, afterword to Aidoo, *Changes*, 184.

71. McWilliams, "'Strange as It May Seem,'" 353.

72. Gyimah, "Sexual Politics and Phallocentric Gaze," 381, 382; see also 383–85.

73. See Nugent, *Big Men, Small Boys and Politics in Ghana*, 15–59; see also Youry Petchenkine, *Ghana*, 3–116.

74. The distinction is axiomatic in contemporary Africa studies. See esp. Jackson, *Allegories of the Wilderness*; McNaughton, *The Mande Blacksmith*; Beidelman, *Moral*

Imagination in Kaguru Modes of Thought; Jean Comaroff, *Body of Power, Spirit of Resistance.*

75. See McCaskie's extended account in *State and Society in Pre-Colonial Asante*, 144–242; on human sacrifices, see Wilks, *Forests of Gold*, 215–40.

76. Rattray, *Religion and Art in Ashanti*, 28.

77. Alasdair MacIntrye, *After Virtue*, 1.

78. Allan, afterword to Aidoo, *Changes*, 180.

79. On the collusion of being and self-interest, see Levinas, *Otherwise than Being*, 3–5, 15–19.

80. See Uwakweh, "Free but Lost," 373; Willey, "National Identities, Tradition, and Feminism," 23.

81. Hillary Rodham Clinton, *It Takes a Village*, 96.

82. See Nugent, *Big Men, Small Boys, and Politics in Ghana*, 19–35; Petchenkine, *Ghana*, 33–94.

83. See Nugent, *Big Men, Small Boys, and Politics in Ghana*, 105–62.

84. Ibid., 126–27.

85. Ibid., 130–31.

86. On the stifling of legitimate private accumulation, see Iliffe, *The Emergence of African Capitalism*; Paul Kennedy, *African Capitalism*; Berman and Leys, *African Capitalists in African Development.*

87. Nugent, *Big Men, Small Boys, and Politics in Ghana*, 204.

88. Ibid., 146.

89. Ibid., 28.

90. McWilliams, "'Strange as It Seems,'" 355.

91. Uwakweh, "Free but Lost," 373.

92. Gyimah, "Sexual Politics and Phallocentric Gaze," 395, 396.

93. Ada Uzoamaka Azodo, "Facing the Millennium: An Interview with Ama Ata Aidoo," 440.

7. Self-Assertion, Piety, and Ethical Responsibility in Buchi Emecheta's *Kehinde*

1. Buchi Emecheta, *Kehinde*, 3, 1, 15–16. All further citation are to this edition.

2. John C. Hawley, "Coming to Terms: Buchi Emecheta's *Kehinde* and the Birth of a 'Nation,'" 341.

3. Buchi Emecheta, *Head above Water*, 70.

4. Ibid., 33.

5. Bakhtin, *Art and Answerability*, 40.

6. Ricoeur, *Oneself as Another*, 3.

7. See Levinas, *Otherwise than Being*, 4–5, 11–19, 135–40; *Difficult Freedom*, 6–10, 16–17.

8. Hobbesian egotistic materialism presupposes a centered, unified subject, whereas the egotistic materialism of Nietzsche and Foucault posits a decentered subjectivity. However, the various competing, disunified elements function as though they were the

possessive individuals. See Friedrich Nietzsche, *The Will to Power*, 267; Foucault, *Language, Counter-Memory, Practice*, 151–52.

9. Levinas, *Otherwise than Being*, 6; see also 5–15, 45–59, 65–72; Critchley, *The Ethics of Deconstruction*, 4–9, 145–82, 219–36.

10. Levinas, *Totality and Infinity*, 148.

11. Levinas, *Difficult Freedom*, 16, 17; "Ethics as First Philosophy," 85.

12. On postmodernism's tendency to treat violence or totalizing as normative, see Richard Bernstein, *The New Constellation*, 172–91; Critchley, *The Ethics of Deconstruction*, 9–20, 31–44; McGowan, *Postmodernism and Its Critics*, 89–145; Dews, *Logics of Disintegration*, 34–44, 150–99; Ferry and Renault, *French Philosophy of the Sixties*, 3–32.

13. Fishburn, *Reading Buchi Emecheta*, 26, xii. It should be noted that Fishburn's study was completed before the publication of *Kehinde*.

14. Levinas, "Ethics as First Philosophy," 82.

15. Fishburn, *Reading Buchi Emecheta*, 8

16. Ibid., 4, 18, 8.

17. Gadamer, *Truth and Method*, 320, 324.

18. Fishburn, *Reading Buchi Emecheta*, 28.

19. See Donatus Ibe Nwoga, *The Supreme God as Stranger in Igbo Religious Thought*, 64–65.

20. Kofi Asara Opoku, *West African Traditional Religion*, 106–7; quoted in Brenda F. Berrian, "Her Ancestor's Voice: The *Ibéji* Transcendence of Duality in Buchi Emecheta's *Kehinde*," 170.

21. Berrian, "Her Ancestor's Voice," 171.

22. Spivak, *Outside in the Teaching Machine*, 58.

23. Gabriel García Márquez, *Cien años de soledad*, 190, 279–80.

24. Alessandro Manzoni, *I promessi sposi*, 281, 308; *The Betrothed*, 378, 415.

25. Feroza Jussawalla and Reed Way Dasenbrock, *Interviews with Writers of the Post-Colonial World*, 85; quoted in Hawley, "Coming to Terms," 336.

26. Nwoga, *The Supreme God as Stranger in Igbo Religious Thought*, 64–65; Nwoga cites Elizabeth Isichei, *Igbo Worlds*, 178.

27. Emecheta, *Head above Water*, 10, 11.

28. Berrian, "Her Ancestor's Voice," 173, 181.

29. Hawley, "Coming to Terms," 340.

30. See Fishburn, *Reading Buchi Emecheta*, 59–63, 111–16.

31. For discussions of precapitalist accumulation and domination, see Catherine Coquery-Vidrovitch, *Africa*, 50–111; Mahmood Mamdani, *Citizen and Subject*, 43–48. See also Anthony Giddens, *The Nation-State and Violence*, esp. 48–67, and *A Contemporary Critique of Historical Materialism*, esp. 49–68, 90–108.

32. See Žižek, *The Sublime Object of Ideology*, 47–132.

33. See Levinas, *Totality and Infinity*, 194–97.

34. Steven Feierman, "African Histories and the Dissolution of World History," in *Africa and the Disciplines*, 189, 194–95.

35. See Paulin J. Hountondji, "Daily Life in Black Africa: Elements for a Critique"; see also Emecheta's comments in James, *In Their Own Words*, 35, 40.

36. Irele, "In Praise of Alienation," 212.

37. See Joseph, *Democracy and Prebendal Politics*; David E. Sahn, ed., *Adjusting to Policy Failure in African Economies*; Iliffe, *The Emergence of African Capitalism*, 82.; Julius Edo Nyang'oro, *The State and Capitalist Development in Africa*, 132–39; Mamdani, *Citizen and Subject*, 170–79.

38. Emecheta, *Head above Water*, 39.

39. Ibid., esp. 204–8

40. Nwoga, *The Supreme God as Stranger in Igbo Religious Thought*, 65.

41. See Emecheta, *Head above Water*, 21–22.

42. For Emecheta's views, see James, *In Their Own Words*, 35–36, 38–39, 40–41.

43. Berrian, "Her Ancestor's Voice," 179.

44. This seems to have been the case in Emecheta's life as well. See James, *In Their Own Words*, 37.

45. Giddens, *Central Problems in Social Theory*, 189–90.

46. See Levinas, *Otherwise than Being*, 45–59, 77–78.

47. Hawley, "Coming to Terms," 344.

48. Berrian, "Her Ancestor's Voice," 178.

49. Hawley, "Coming to Terms," 344.

50. James, *In Their Own Words*, 45.

51. Newton, *Narrative Ethics*, 17–18.

Conclusion: The Challenge of Decolonizing the West's Reading of African Fiction

1. Fishburn, *Reading Buchi Emecheta*, 127–28.

2. J. M. Bernstein, *The Fate of Art*, 183.

3. See Fishburn, *Reading Buchi Emecheta*, 22–25.

4. Linda Hutcheon, "Circling the Downspout of Empire: Post-colonialism and Post-modernism," *Ariel* 20, 4 (1989): 151.

5. Ferry and Renault, *French Philosophy in the Sixties*, 18.

6. See Harrow, *Thresholds of Change in African Literature*, 63, 76.

7. See Levinas, "Ethics as First Philosophy," 76–87; Ricoeur, *Oneself as Another*, 152–68.

8. Eagleton, *The Ideology of the Aesthetic*, 40; see also 45–52.

9. Hilary Putnam, *Reason, Truth, and History*, 138–39.

10. McWilliams, "Tsitsi Dangarembga's *Nervous Conditions*," 106–11.

11. James, *In Their Own Words*, 18.

12. See Uwakweh, "Free but Lost," 363–75.

13. Achebe, *Hopes and Impediments*, 53.

14. Ibid.

Bibliography

Abir, Mordechi. "The Ethiopian Slave Trade and Its Relation to the Islamic World." In *Slaves and Slavery in Muslim Africa*, 2 vols., ed. John Ralph Willis, 2:123–36. London: Frank Cass, 1985.

Achebe, Chinua. *Anthills of the Savannah*. New York: Doubleday, 1987.

———. *Girls at War and Other Stories*. New York: Fawcett, 1972.

———. *Hopes and Impediments: Selected Essays*. New York: Doubleday, 1989.

———. *No Longer at Ease*. New York: Fawcett, 1970.

———. *Things Fall Apart*. New York: Fawcett, 1959.

Adorno, Theodor W. *Negative Dialectics*. Translated by E. B. Ashton. New York: Continuum, 1973.

Aegerter, Lindsay Pentolfe. "A Dialectic of Autonomy and Community: Tsitsi Dangarembga's *Nervous Conditions*." *Tulsa Studies in Women's Literature* 15, no. 2 (1996): 231–40.

Ahmad, Aijaz. *In Theory: Classes, Nations, Literatures*. London: Verso, 1992.

Aidoo, Ama Ata. *Changes: A Love Story*. New York: Feminist Press, City University of New York, 1993.

———. "Unwelcome Pals and Decorative Slaves or Glimpses of Women as Writers and Their Characters in Contemporary African Literature." In *Emerging Perspectives on Ama Ata Aidoo*, ed. Ada Uzoamaka Azodo and Gay Wilentz, 11–24. Trenton, N.J.: Africa World Press, 1999.

Alkali, Zaynab. *The Stillborn*. London: Longman, 1988.

Allan, Tuzyline Jita. Afterword to *Changes: A Love Story*, by Ama Ata Aidoo, 171–96. New York: Feminist Press, City University of New York, 1993.

———. *Womanist and Feminist Aesthetics: A Comparative Review*. Athens: Ohio University Press, 1995.

Alpers, Edward A. *Ivory and Slaves: Changing Patterns of International Trade in East Central Africa to the Later Nineteenth Century*. Berkeley: University of California Press, 1975.

Amadiume, Ifi. *Male Daughters, Female Husbands: Gender and Sex in an African Society*. London: Zed, 1987.

Andrande, Susan Z. "Rewriting History, Motherhood, and Rebellion: Naming an African Women's Literary Tradition. *Research in African Literatures* 21, no. 2 (1990): 91–110.

Ansari, Muhammad Abdul Haq. *Sufism and Sharī'ah: A Study of Shaykh Ahmad Sirhindi's Efforts to Reform Sufism*. Leicester, U.K.: Islamic Foundation, 1986.

Appiah, Kwame Anthony. *In My Father's House: Africa in the Philosophy of Culture.* New York: Oxford University Press, 1992.

Aristotle. *Nicomachean Ethics.* Translated by Terence Irwin. Indianapolis: Hackett, 1985.

Armstrong, Nancy. *Desire and Domestic Fiction: A Political History of the Novel.* Oxford: Oxford University Press, 1987.

Armstrong, Nancy, and Lenard Tennenhouse, eds. *The Violence of Representation.* New York: Routledge, 1989.

Arndt, Susan. "Applauding a 'Dangerous Luxury': Flora Nwapa's Womanist Re-Interpretation of the *Ifo* about the 'Handsome Stranger.'" In *Emerging Perspectives on Flora Nwapa: Critical and Theoretical Essays,* ed. Marie Umeh, 205–22. Trenton, N.J.: Africa World Press, 1998.

Ashcroft, Bill, Gareth Griffiths, and Helen Tiffen, eds. *A Post-Colonial Reader.* New York: Routledge, 1996.

———. *The Empire Writes Back: Theory and Practice in Post-Colonial Literatures.* New York: Routledge, 1989.

Austen, Jane. *Pride and Prejudice.* New York: Norton, 1966.

Austen, Ralph A. "The Moral Economy of Witchcraft: An Essay in Comparative History." In *Modernity and Its Malcontents,* ed. Jean Comaroff and John Comaroff, 89–110. Chicago: University of Chicago Press, 1993.

Azodo, Ada Uzoamaka. "*Efuru* and *Idu*: Rejecting Women's Subjugation." In *Emerging Perspectives on Flora Nwapa: Critical and Theoretical Essays,* ed. Marie Umeh, 161–87. Trenton, N.J.: Africa World Press, 1998.

———. "Facing the Millennium: An Interview with Ama Ata Aidoo." In *Emerging Perspectives on Ama Ata Aidoo,* ed. Ada Uzoamaka Azodo and Gay Wilentz, 429–41. Trenton, N.J.: Africa World Press, 1999.

Bâ, Mariama. *Une si longue lettre.* Dakar: Nouvelles Éditions Africaines, 1980.

———. *So Long a Letter.* Translated by Modupé Bodé-Thomas. Portsmouth, N. H.: Heinemann, 1981.

Bakhtin, Mikhail. *Art and Answerability: Early Philosophical Essays.* Edited by Michael Holquist and Vladimir Liapunov. Austin: University of Texas Press, 1990.

———. *Speech Genres and Other Late Essays.* Translated by Vern W. McGee. Austin: University of Texas Press, 1986.

———. *Toward a Philosophy of the Act.* Translated by Vadim Liapunov. Austin: University of Texas Press, 1993.

Banyiwa-Horne, Naana. "African Womanhood: The Contrasting Perspectives of Flora Nwapa's *Efuru* and Elechi Amadi's *The Concubine.*" In *Ngambika: Studies of Women in African Literature,* ed. Carole Boyce Davies and Anne Adams Graves, 119–29. Trenton, N.J.: African World Press, 1986.

Bastian, Misty L. "'Bloodhounds Who Have No Friends': Witchcraft and Locality in the Nigerian Popular Press." In *Modernity and Its Malcontents,* ed. Jean Comaroff and John Comaroff, 129–66. Chicago: University of Chicago Press, 1993.

Bauman, Zygmunt. *Postmodern Ethics.* Cambridge: Blackwell, 1993.

———. *Postmodernity and Its Discontents*. Cambridge: Polity Press, 1997.

Beach, David. *The Shona and Their Neighbours*. Oxford: Blackwell, 1994.

Beauvoir, Simone de. *The Second Sex*. Translated by H. M. Parshley. New York: Vintage, 1974.

Beidelman, T. O. *Moral Imagination in Kaguru Modes of Thought*. Bloomington: Indiana University Press, 1986.

Belsey, Catherine, and Jane Moore. "Introduction: The Story So Far." In *The Feminist Reader: Essays in Gender and the Politics of Literary Criticism*, ed. Catherine Belsey and Jane Moore, 1–20. New York: Basil Blackwell, 1989.

Bender, John. *Imagining the Penitentiary: Fiction and the Architecture of Mind in Eighteenth-Century England*. Chicago: University of Chicago Press, 1987.

Benhabib, Seyla. "Autonomy, Modernity, and Community: Communitarianism and Critical Social Theory in Dialogue." In *Cultural-Political Interventions in the Unfinished Project of Enlightenment*, ed. Axel Hommeth, Thomas McCarthy, Clauss Offee, and Albrecht Wellmer, 39–59. Cambridge: MIT Press, 1992.

Benjamin, Walter. *Illuminations*. Translated by Harry Zohn. London: Fontana, 1970.

Berman, Bruce J., and Colin Leys, eds. *African Capitalists in African Development*. Boulder, Colo.: Lynne Reimer, 1994.

Bernstein, J. M. *The Fate of Art: Aesthetic Alienation from Kant to Derrida and Adorno*. University Park: Pennsylvania State University Press, 1992.

Bernstein, Richard J. *The New Constellation: The Ethico-Political Horizons of Modernity/Postmodernity*. Cambridge: MIT Press, 1992.

———. *Philosophical Profiles: Essays in a Pragmatic Mode*. Cambridge: Polity Press, 1986.

Berrian, Brenda F. "Her Ancestor's Voice: The *Ibéji* Transcendence of Duality in Buchi Emecheta's *Kehinde*." In *Emerging Perspectives on Buchi Emecheta*, ed. Marie Umeh, 169–84. Trenton, N.J.: Africa World Press, 1996.

Beyala, Calixthe. *Tu t'appelleras Tanga* (You shall be called Tanga). Paris: Stock, 1988.

Bhabha, Homi K. "DissemiNation: Time, Narrative, and the Margins of the Modern Nation." In *Nation and Narration*, ed. Homi K. Bhabha, 291–322. London: Routledge, 1990.

———. "Signs Taken for Wonders: Questions of Ambivalence and Authority under a Tree Outside Dehli, May 1817." *Critical Inquiry* 12, no. 1 (1985): 144–65.

Bjornson, Richard. *The African Quest for Freedom and Identity: Cameroonian Writing and the National Experience*. Bloomington: Indiana University Press, 1991.

Boehmer, Elleke. "Stories of Women and Mothers: Gender and Nationalism in the Early Fiction of Flora Nwapa." In *Motherlands: Black Women's Writing from Africa, the Caribbean, and South Asia*, ed. Susheila Nasta, 3–23. New Brunswick, N.J.: Rutgers University Press, 1992.

Boone, Catherine. *Merchant Capital and the Roots of State Power in Senegal, 1930–1985*. Cambridge: Cambridge University Press, 1992.

Bouhdiba, Abdelwahab. *Sexuality in Islam*. Translated by Alan Sheridan. London: Routledge and Kegan Paul, 1985.

Bourdieu, Pierre. *The Logic of Practice*. Translated by Richard Nice. Stanford, Calif.: Stanford University Press, 1990.

Brown, Lloyd W. *Women Writers in Black Africa*. Westport, Conn.: Greenwood Press, 1981.

Brown, Peter. "Late Antiquity and Islam: Parallels and Contrasts." In *Moral Conduct and Authority: The Place of "Adab" in South Asia Islam*, ed. Barbara Daly Metcalf, 23–37. Berkeley: University of California Press, 1984.

Brown, Stuart. Introduction to *The Stillborn*, by Zaynab Alkali, vii–xxi. London: Longman, 1988.

Callaway, Barbara J. *Muslim Hausa Women in Nigeria: Tradition and Change*. Syracuse: Syracuse University Press, 1987.

Callinicos, Alex. "Wonders Taken for Signs: Homi Bhabha's Postcolonialism." *Transformation* 1 (1995): 98–112.

Cavell, Stanley. *The Claim of Reason: Wittgenstein, Skepticism, Morality, and Tragedy*. New York: Oxford University Press, 1979.

———. *Must We Mean What We Say? A Book of Essays*. Cambridge: Cambridge University Press, 1976.

Certeau, Michel de. *The Practice of Everyday Life*. Translated by Steven F. Rendall. Berkeley: University of California Press, 1984.

Cham, Mbye B. "Contemporary Society and the Female Imagination: A Study of the Novels of Mariama Bâ." In *Women in African Literature Today: A Review*, ed. Eldred Durosimi Jones, 89–101. London: James Currey, 1987.

Chanter, Tina. "Feminism and the Other." In *The Provocation of Levinas: Rethinking the Other*, ed. Robert Bernasconi and David Wood, 32–56. New York: Routledge, 1988.

Chatterjee, Partha. *The Nation and Its Fragments: Colonial and Postcolonial Histories*. Princeton: Princeton University Press, 1993.

Chinweizu, Onwuchekwa Jemie, and Ikechukwa Madubuike. *Towards the Decolonization of African Literature*. 2 vols. Washington, D.C.: Howard University Press, 1983.

Cicero. *De Officiis*. Translated by Walter Miller. London: William Heinemann, 1913.

Cleage, Pearl. "A Stunning Journey to 'Joy.'" *Atlanta Journal/Atlanta Constitution*, July 14, 1992, N8.

Clifford, James. *The Predicament of Culture: Twentieth-Century Ethnography, Literature, and Art*. Cambridge: Harvard University Press, 1988.

Clifford, James, and George E. Marcus, eds. *Writing Culture: The Poetics and Politics of Ethnography*. Berkeley: University of California Press, 1986.

Clinton, Hillary Rodham. *It Takes a Village, and Other Lessons Children Teach Us*. New York: Simon and Schuster, 1996.

Cohen, Jean, and Andrew Arato. *Civil Society and Political Theory*. Cambridge: MIT Press, 1992.

Cohen, Richard A. *Face to Face with Levinas*. Albany: State University of New York Press, 1986.

Coles, Catherine. "Hausa Women's Work in a Declining Urban Economy: Kaduna,

Nigeria 1980–1985." In *Hausa Women in the Twentieth Century*, ed. Catherine Coles and Beverly Mack, 163–91. Madison: University of Wisconsin Press, 1991.

Coles, Catherine, and Beverly Mack. "Women in Twentieth-Century Hausa Society." In *Hausa Women in the Twentieth Century*, ed. Catherine Coles and Beverly Mack, 3–26. Madison: University of Wisconsin Press, 1991.

Comaroff, Jean. *Body of Power, Spirit of Resistance: The Culture and History of a South African People.* Chicago: University of Chicago Press, 1985.

Comaroff, Jean, and John Comaroff, eds. *Modernity and Its Malcontents.* Chicago: University of Chicago Press, 1993.

Combs-Schilling, M. E. *Sacred Performances: Islam, Sexuality, and Sacrifice.* New York: Columbia University Press, 1989.

Condé, Maryse. "Three Female Writers in Modern Africa: Flora Nwapa, Ama Ata Aidoo, and Grace Ogot." *Présence Africaine* 82, no. 2 (1972): 134–36.

Conrad, David C., and Barbara E. Frank, eds. *Status and Identity in West Africa: Nyamakalaw of Mande.* Bloomington: Indiana University Press, 1995.

Cooper, Frederick. "Africa and the World Economy." In Frederick Cooper et al., *Confronting Historical Paradigms: Peasants, Labor, and the Capitalist World System in Africa and Latin America*, 84–201. Madison: University of Wisconsin Press, 1993.

———. *Plantation Slavery on the East Coast of Africa.* New Haven: Yale University Press, 1977.

Coquery-Vidrovitch, Catherine. *Africa: Endurance and Change South of the Sahara.* Translated by David Maisell. Berkeley: University of California Press, 1988.

Critchley, Simon. *The Ethics of Deconstruction: Derrida and Levinas.* Oxford: Blackwell, 1992.

Cudjoe, Selwyn R. *V. S. Naipaul: A Materialist Reading.* Amherst: University of Massachusetts Press, 1988.

d'Almeida, Irene Assiba. "The Concept of Choice in Mariama Bâ's Fiction." In *Ngambika: Studies of Women in African Literature*, ed. Carole Boyce Davies and Anne Adams Graves, 161–71. Trenton, N.J.: Africa World Press, 1986.

Daly, Mary. *Gyn/Ecology: The Metaethics of Radical Feminism.* Boston: Beacon Press, 1978.

Dangarembga, Tsitsi. *Nervous Conditions.* Seattle: Seal Press, 1988.

Davies, Carole Boyce. "Motherhood in the Works of Male and Female Igbo Writers: Achebe, Emecheta, Nwapa, and Nzekwu." In *Ngambika: Studies of Women in African Literature*, ed. Carole Boyce Davies and Anne Adams Graves, 241–56. Trenton, N.J.: Africa World Press, 1986.

Delgado, Christopher L., and Sidi Jemmeh, eds. *The Political Economy of Senegal under Structural Adjustment.* New York: Praeger, 1991.

de Man, Paul. *The Resistance to Theory.* Minneapolis: University of Minnesota Press, 1986.

Derrida, Jacques. "Afterword: Toward an Ethic of Discussion." In Jacques Derrida, *Limited Inc.*, 111–54. Translated by Samuel Weber. Evanston: Northwestern University Press, 1988.

———. *Aporias: Dying—awaiting (one another at) the "limits of truth."* Translated by Thomas Dutoit. Stanford, Calif.: Stanford University Press, 1993.

———. *Dissemination.* Translated by Barbara Johnson. Chicago: University of Chicago Press, 1981.

———. "En ce moment même dans cet ouvrage me voici" (In this very moment in this work here I am). In *Textes pour Emmanuel Levinas*, ed. F. Laruelle, 21–60. Paris: Jean-Michel Place, 1980.

———. *Margins of Philosophy.* Translated by Alan Bass. Chicago: University of Chicago Press, 1982.

———. *The Other Heading: Reflections on Today's Europe.* Translated by Pascalle-Anne Brault and Michael B. Naas. Bloomington: Indiana University Press, 1992.

———. *Writing and Difference.* Translated by Alan Bass. Chicago: University of Chicago Press, 1978.

Dews, Peter. *Logics of Disintegration.* London: Verso, 1987.

"The Disobedient Sisters." In *African Folktales*, ed. Roger D. Abrahams, 145–47. New York: Pantheon, 1983.

Duerden, Dennis. *African Art and Literature: The Invisible Present.* New York: Harper and Row, 1975.

Dunbar, Roberta Ann. "Islamic Values, the State, and 'the Development of Women': The Case of Niger." In *Hausa Women in the Twentieth Century*, ed. Catherine Coles and Beverly Mack, 69–84. Madison: University of Wisconsin Press, 1991.

Eaglestone, Robert. *Ethical Criticism: Reading after Levinas.* Edinburgh: Edinburgh University Press, 1997.

Eagleton, Terry. *The Ideology of the Aesthetic.* Oxford: Basil Blackwell, 1990.

Echard, Nicole. "Gender Relationships and Religion: Women in the Hausa *Bori* of Ader, Nigeria." In *Hausa Women in the Twentieth Century*, ed. Catherine Coles and Beverly Mack, 207–20. Madison: University of Wisconsin Press, 1991.

Edgerton, Robert B. *The Fall of the Asante Empire: The Hundred-Year War for Africa's Gold Coast.* New York: Free Press, 1995.

Ekechi, Felix K. "Pawnship in Igbo Society." In *Pawnship in Africa: Debt Bondage in Historical Perspective*, ed. Toyin Falola and Paul E. Lovejoy, 83–104. Boulder, Colo.: Westview Press, 1994.

Eliot, George. *Middlemarch.* Edited by Gordon S. Haight. Boston: Houghton Mifflin, 1956.

Emecheta, Buchi. *Head above Water: An Autobiography.* Portsmouth, N. H.: Heinemann, 1986.

———. *The Joys of Motherhood.* New York: George Braziller, 1979.

———. *Kehinde.* Portsmouth, N. H.: Heinemann, 1994.

Erasmus. *A Declamation on the Subject of Early Liberal Education for Children.* Translated by Beert C. Verstraete. In *Collected Works of Erasmus*, ed. J. K. Sowards, 26:297–346. Toronto: University of Toronto Press, 1985.

Erikson, Erik. *Childhood and Society.* New York: Norton, 1950.

Esonwanne, Uzo. "Enlightenment Epistemology and 'Aesthetic Cognition': Mariama

Bâ's *So Long a Letter.*" In *The Politics of (M)othering: Womanhood, Identity, and Resistance in African Literature,* ed. Obioma Nnaemeka. London: Routledge, 1997. 82–100.

Ezeigbo, Theodora Akachi. "Myth, History, Culture and Igbo Womanhood in Flora Nwapa's Novels." In *Emerging Perspectives on Flora Nwapa: Critical and Theoretical Essays,* ed. Marie Umeh, 51–75. Trenton, N.J.: Africa World Press, 1998.

Falola, Toyin, and Paul E. Lovejoy. "Pawnship in Historical Perspective." In *Pawnship in Africa: Debt Bondage in Historical Perspective,* ed. Falola Toyin and Paul E. Lovejoy, 1–26. Boulder, Colo.: Westview Press, 1994.

Fanon, Frantz. *Les Damnés de la terre* (The wretched of the earth). Paris: Maspero, 1975.

———. *Peau noire, masques blanches* (Black skin, white masks). Paris: Éditions du Seuil, 1975.

Feierman, Steven. "African Histories and the Dissolution of World History." In *Africa and the Disciplines: The Contributions of Research in Africa to the Social Sciences and Humanities,* ed. Robert H. Bates, V. Y. Mudimbe, and Jean O'Barr, 167–212. Chicago: University of Chicago Press, 1993.

Ferry, Luc. *Homo Aestheticus: The Invention of Taste in the Democratic Age.* Translated by Robert de Loaiza. Chicago: University of Chicago Press, 1993.

Ferry, Luc, and Alain Renault. *French Philosophy of the Sixties: An Essay on Antihumanism.* Translated by Mary H. S. Cattani. Amherst: University of Massachusetts Press, 1990.

Fetzer, Glenn W. "Women's Search for Voice and the Problem of Knowing in the Novels of Mariama Bâ." *CLA Journal* 35, no. 1 (1991): 31–41.

Fielding, Henry. *The History of Tom Jones, a Foundling.* Edited by Martin Battestin. Middletown, Conn.: Welseyan University Press, 1975.

Fishburn, Katherine. *Reading Buchi Emecheta: Cross-Cultural Conversations.* Westport, Conn.: Greenwood Press, 1995.

Flockemann, Miki. "Not-Quite Insiders and Not-Quite Outsiders': The 'Process of Womanhood' in *Beka Lamb, Nervous Conditions,* and *Daughters of the Twilight.*" *Journal of Comparative Literature* 24, no. 1 (1992): 37–47.

Foucault, Michel. *The History of Sexuality, Volume One: An Introduction.* Translated by Robert Hurley. New York: Vintage, 1978.

———. *Language, Counter-Memory, Practice: Selected Essays and Interviews.* Edited by Donald F. Bouchard. Translated by Donald F. Bouchard and Sherry Simon. Ithaca: Cornell University Press, 1977.

Fowler, Alistair. *Kinds of Literature: An Introduction to the Theory of Genres and Modes.* Cambridge: Harvard University Press, 1982.

Freud, Sigmund. *Civilization and Its Discontents.* Translated by James Strachey. New York: Norton, 1961.

Frishman, Alan. "Hausa Women in the Urban Economy of Kano." In *Hausa Women in the Twentieth Century,* ed. Catherine Coles and Beverly Mack, 192–203. Madison: University of Wisconsin Press, 1991.

Furniss, Graham, and Liz Gunner, eds. *Power, Marginality, and African Oral Literature.* Cambridge: Cambridge University Press, 1995.

Gadamer, Hans-Georg. *The Relevance of the Beautiful and Other Essays.* Edited by Robert Bernasconi. Translated by Nicholas Walker. Cambridge: Cambridge University Press, 1986.

———. *Truth and Method.* Translated by Joel Weinsheimer and Donald G. Marshall. Rev. ed. New York: Crossroads, 1989.

———. *Wahrheit und Methode: Grundzüge einer philosophischen Hermeneutik* (Truth and Method: fundamentals of a philosophical hermeneutic). Tübingen: J.C.B. Mohr (Paul Siebeck), 1986.

Gandhi, Leela. *Postcolonial Theory: A Critical Introduction.* New York: Columbia University Press, 1998.

García Márquez, Gabriel. *Cien años de soledad* (One hundred years of solitude). Madrid: Espasa Calpe, 1982.

Geertz, Clifford. *Local Knowledge: Further Essays in Interpretative Anthropology.* New York: Basic Books, 1983.

Gellar, Sheldon. *Senegal: An African Nation between Islam and the West.* 2d ed. Boulder, Colo.: Westview Press, 1995.

Gennette, Gérard. *Narrative Discourse: An Essay in Method.* Translated by Jane E. Lewin. Ithaca: Cornell University Press, 1980.

George, Rosemary Marangoly. *The Politics of Home: Postcolonial Relocations and Twentieth-Century Fiction.* Cambridge: Cambridge University Press, 1996.

George, Rosemary Marangoly, and Helen Scott. "A New Tail to an Old Tale: An Interview with Ama Ata Aidoo." *NOVEL: A Forum for Fiction* 26, no. 3 (1993): 297–308.

———. "An Interview with Tsitsi Dangarembga." *NOVEL: A Forum for Fiction* 26, no. 3 (1993): 309–19.

Geschiere, Peter. *Village Communities and the State: Changing Relations among the Maka of South-eastern Cameroon since the Colonial Conquest.* London: Kegan Paul, 1982.

Giddens, Anthony. *A Contemporary Critique of Historical Materialism.* Vol. 1: *Power, Property, and the State.* Berkeley: University of California Press, 1981.

———. *Beyond Left and Right: The Future of Radical Politics.* Stanford, Calif.: Stanford University Press, 1994.

———. *Central Problems in Social Theory: Action, Structure, and Contradiction in Social Analysis.* Berkeley: University of California Press, 1979.

———. *The Nation-State and Violence.* Vol. 2 of *A Contemporary Critique of Historical Materialism.* Berkeley: University of California Press, 1987.

———. *Social Theory and Modern Sociology.* Stanford: Stanford University Press, 1987.

Gikandi, Simon. *Reading Chinua Achebe.* London: James Currey, 1991.

Gilbert, Sandra M., and Susan Gubar. "The Mirror and the Vamp: Reflections on Feminist Criticism." In *The Future of Literary Theory,* ed. Ralph Cohen, 144–66. New York: Routledge, 1989.

Goodheart, Eugene. *The Reign of Ideology.* New York: Columbia University Press, 1997.

Gyekye, Kwame. *An Essay on African Philosophical Thought: The Akan Conceptual Scheme.* Cambridge: Cambridge University Press, 1987.

Gyimah, Miriam C. "Sexual Politics and Phallocentric Gaze in Ama Ata Aidoo's *Changes: A Love Story.*" In *Emerging Perspectives on Ama Ata Aidoo*, ed. Ada Uzoamaka Azodo and Gay Wilentz, 377–97. Trenton, N.J.: Africa World Press, 1999.

Habermas, Jürgen. *The Philosophical Discourse of Modernity: Twelve Lectures.* Translated by Frederick G. Lawrence. Cambridge: MIT Press, 1987.

Haney, David P. "Aesthetics and Ethics in Gadamer, Levinas, and Romanticism: Problems in *Phronêsis* and *Techne.*" *PLMA* 114, no. 1 (1999): 32–45.

———. "Wordsworth and Levinas: Making a Habit of the Sublime." In *In Proximity: Levinas and the Eighteenth Century*, ed. Melvyn New, Richard Cohen, and Robert Bernasuoni. Lubbock: Texas Tech University Press, forthcoming.

Harpham, Geoffrey Galt. *Getting It Right: Language, Literature, and Ethics.* Chicago: University of Chicago Press, 1992.

Harrow, Kenneth W. *Thresholds of Change in African Literature: The Emergence of a Tradition.* Portsmouth, N.H.: Heinemann, 1994.

Hawley, John C. "Coming to Terms: Buchi Emecheta's *Kehinde* and the Birth of a 'Nation.'" In *Emerging Perspectives on Buchi Emecheta*, ed. Marie Umeh, 333–48. Trenton, N.J.: Africa World Press, 1996.

Hegel, G. W. F. *Aesthetics: Lectures on Fine Art.* Translated by T. M. Knox. Oxford: Oxford University Press, 1975.

———. *The Phenomenology of Mind.* Translated by J. B. Baillie. New York: Harper and Row, 1967.

———. *Philosophy of Right.* Translated by T. M. Knox. Oxford: Oxford University Press, 1967.

Heidegger, Martin. *Being and Time.* Translated by John Macquarrie and Edward Robinson. Oxford: Blackwell, 1962.

———. *Letter on Humanism.* Translated by Frank A. Capuzzi. In Heidegger, *Basic Writings*, ed. David Farrell Krell, 193–242. New York: Harper and Row, 1977.

Hill, Polly. "Comparative West African Farm-Slavery Systems." In *Slaves and Slavery in Muslim Africa*, ed. John Ralph Willis, 2:33–50. London: Frank Cass, 1985.

Hirsch, E. D., Jr. *Cultural Literacy: What Every American Needs to Know.* Boston: Houghton Mifflin, 1987.

Hobbes, Thomas. *Leviathan, Parts One and Two.* Indianapolis: Bobbs-Merrill, 1958.

Holy Qur'an. Translated by Maulana Muhammad Ali. Chicago: Speciality Promotions, 1985.

Hountondji, Paulin J. *African Philosophy: Myth and Reality.* Translated by Henri Evans with the collaboration of Jonathan Rée. Bloomington: Indiana University Press, 1983.

———. "Daily Life in Black Africa: Elements for a Critique." In *The Surreptitious Speech: Présence Africaine and the Politics of Otherness, 1947–1987*, ed. V. Y. Mudimbe, 244–64. Chicago: University of Chicago Press, 1993.

———. "Recapturing." In *The Surreptitious Speech: Présence Africaine and the Politics of*

Otherness, 1947–1987, ed. V. Y. Mudimbe, 238–48. Chicago: University of Chicago Press, 1993.

Hunter, J. Paul. *Before the Novel.* New York: Barnes and Noble, 1990.

Hunwick, J. O. "Notes on Slavery in the Sonphay Empire." In *Slaves and Slavery in Muslim Africa*, ed. John Ralph Willis, 2:16–32. London: Frank Cass, 1985.

Hutchinson, Linda. "Circling the downspout of empire: post-colonialism and postmodernism." *Ariel* 20, no. 4 (1989): 149–75.

Iliffe, John. *The Emergence of African Capitalism.* Minneapolis: University of Minnesota Press, 1983.

Iman, Ayesha M. "Ideology, the Mass Media, and Women: A Study of Radio Kaduna, Nigeria." In *Hausa Women in the Twentieth Century*, ed. Catherine Coles and Beverly Mack, 244–52. Madison: University of Wisconsin Press, 1991.

Ingarden, Roman. *The Cognition of the Literary Work of Art.* Translated by Ruth Ann Crowley and Kenneth R. Olson. Evanston: Northwestern University Press, 1973.

Innes, C. L. "Mothers or Sisters? Identity, Discourse, and Audience in the Writing of Ama Ata Aidoo and Mariama Bâ." In *Motherlands: Black Women's Writing from Africa, the Caribbean, and South Asia*, ed. Susheila Nasta, 129–51. New Brunswick, N.J.: Rutgers University Press, 1992.

Innes, Gordon. *Sunjata: Three Mandinka Versions.* London: School of Oriental and African Studies, 1974.

Irele, Abiola. *The African Experience in Literature and Ideology.* London: Heinemann, 1981.

———. "In Praise of Alienation." In *The Surreptitious Speech: Prèsence Africaine and the Politics of Otherness, 1947–1987*, ed. V. Y. Mudimbe, 201–24. Chicago: University of Chicago Press, 1993.

———. Introduction to *African Philosophy: Myth and Reality*, by Paulin J. Hountondji, 7–30. Translated by Herni Evans with the collaboration of Jonathan Rée. Bloomington: Indiana University Press, 1983.

Irigaray, Luce. *An Ethics of Sexual Difference.* Translated by Carolyn Burke and Gillian C. Gill. Ithaca: Cornell University Press, 1993.

———. *Je, tu, nous: Toward a Culture of Difference.* Translated by Alison Martin. New York: Routledge, 1993.

Irlam. Shaun. "Mariama Bâ *Une si longue lettre:* The Vocation of Memory and the Space of Writing." *Research in African Literatures* 29, no. 2 (1998): 76–93.

Irwin, T. H. *Aristotle's First Principles.* Oxford: Clarendon Press, 1988.

Isaacman, Alan. "Peasants and Rural Social Protest in Africa." In Frederick Cooper et al., *Confronting Historical Paradigms: Peasants, Labor, and the Capitalist World System in Africa and Latin America*, 205–317. Madison: University of Wisconsin Press, 1993.

Iser, Wolfgang. *The Act of Reading: A Theory of Aesthetic Response.* Baltimore: Johns Hopkins University Press, 1978.

———. *The Fictive and the Imaginary: Charting Literary Anthropology.* Baltimore: Johns Hopkins University Press, 1993.

Isichei, Elizabeth. *Igbo Worlds.* London: Macmillan, 1977.

Jackson, Micheal. *Allegories of the Wilderness: Ethics and Ambiguity in Kuranko Narratives* Bloomington: Indiana University Press, 1982.

James, Adeola. *In Their Own Voices: African Women Writers Talk.* London: James Currey, 1990.

Jameson, Fredric. *The Political Unconscious: Narrative as a Socially Symbolic Act.* Ithaca: Cornell University Press, 1981.

JanMohamed, Abdul. *Manichean Aesthetics: The Politics of Literature in Colonial Africa.* Amherst: University of Massachusetts Press, 1983.

Jay, Martin. *Fin de Siècle Socialism and Other Essays.* New York: Routledge, 1988.

Johnson, Rev. Samuel (d. 1901). *The History of the Yorubas: From the Earliest Times to the Beginning of the British Protectorate.* Edited by Obadiah Johnson. 1921; reprint, Westport, Conn.: Negro University Press, 1970.

Johnson, Dr. Samuel. *Rambler,* no. 4. In *Selected Writings,* ed. Patrick Cruttwell, 149–53. Harmondsworth: Penguin, 1968.

Joseph, Richard A. *Democracy and Prebendal Politics: The Rise and Fall of the Second Republic.* Cambridge: Cambridge University Press, 1988.

Joyce, James. *A Portrait of the Artist as a Young Man.* Harmondsworth: Penguin, 1976.

Jung, Carl. *The Portable Jung.* Edited by Joseph Campbell. Translated by R. F. C. Hull. New York: Vintage, 1971.

Jussawalla, Feroza, and Reed Way Dasenbrock. *Interviews with Writers of the Post-Colonial World.* Jackson: University Press of Mississippi, 1992.

Kagame, Alexis. *La Philosophie bantu comparée* (Bantu philosophy compared). Paris: Présence Africaine, 1976.

Kant, Immanuel. *On History.* Translated and edited by Lewis Beck White. Indianapolis: Bobbs-Merrill, 1963.

Kea, R. A. *Settlements, Trade, and Politics in the Seventeenth-Century Gold Coast.* Baltimore: Johns Hopkins University Press, 1982.

Keenan, Dennis King. *Death and Responsibility: The 'Work' of Levinas.* Albany: State University of New York Press, 1999.

Kennedy, Paul. *African Capitalism: The Struggle for Ascendency.* Cambridge: Cambridge University Press, 1988.

Kieti, Nwikali. "Homesick and Eurocentric? Alice Walker's Africa." In *Of Dreams Deferred, Dead or Alive: African Perspectives on African-American Writers,* ed. Femi Ojo-Ade, 157–69. Westport, Conn.: Greenwood Press, 1996.

Klein, Herbert S. "African Women in the Atlantic Slave Trade." In *Women and Slavery in Africa,* ed. Claire C. Robertson and Martin A. Klein, 29–38. Madison: University of Wisconsin Press, 1983.

Klein, Martin A. "Women in Slavery in the Western Sudan." In *Women and Slavery in Africa,* ed. Claire C. Robertson and Martin A. Klein, 67–92. Madison: University of Wisconsin Press, 1983.

Koponen, Juhani. *People and Production in Late Precolonial Tanzania: History and Structures.* Jyväskylä: Monographs of the Finnish Society for Development Studies no. 2, 1988.

Kortenaar, Neil ten. "Beyond Authenticity and Creolization: Reading Achebe Writing Culture." *PLMA* 110, no. 1 (1995): 30–42.

Kristeva, Julia. *Interviews*. Edited by Ross Mitchell Guberman. New York: Columbia University Press, 1996.

———. *Tales of Love*. Translated by Ross Guberman. New York: Columbia University Press, 1987.

———. *Le temps sensible: Proust et l'expérience littérature* (Time and sense: Proust and the experience of literature). Paris: Gallimard, 1994.

———. *Time and Sense: Proust and the Experience of Literature*. Translated by Ross Guberman. New York: Columbia University Press, 1996.

Laing, R. D. *Self and Others*. London: Tavistock, 1969.

Lan, David. *Guns and Rain: Guerrillas and Spirit Mediums in Zimbabwe*. Berkeley: University of California Press, 1985.

Lapidus, Ira M. "Knowledge, Virtue, and Action: The Classical Muslim Conception of *Adab* and the Nature of Religious Fulfillment in Islam." In *Moral Conduct and Authority: The Place of "Adab" in South Asian Islam*, ed. Barbara Daly Metcalf, 38–61. Berkeley: University of California Press, 1984.

Larson, Charles. *The Emergence of the African Novel*. Bloomington: Indiana University Press, 1971.

Laye, Camara. *L'Enfant noir* (The dark child). Paris: Plon, 1953.

———. *Le Maître de la parole: Kouma Lafôlô Kouma* (The master of the word). Paris: Plon, 1978.

Lemert, Edwin M. *The Trouble with Evil: Social Control at the Edge of Morality*. Albany: State University of New York Press, 1997.

Levinas, Emmanuel. *Difficult Freedom: Essays on Judaism*. Translated by Seán Hand. Baltimore: Johns Hopkins University Press, 1990.

———. *"Ethics and Infinity: Conversations with Philippe Nemo*. Pittsburgh: Duquesne University Press, 1985.

———. "Ethics as First Philosophy." In *The Levinas Reader*, ed. Seán Hand, 76–87. Oxford: Blackwell, 1989.

———. "God and Philosophy." In *The Levinas Reader*, ed. Seán Hand, 166–89. Oxford: Blackwell, 1989.

———. "The Other in Proust." In *The Levinas Reader*, ed. Seán Hand, 161–65. Oxford: Blackwell, 1989.

———. *Otherwise than Being, or Beyond Essence*. Translated by Alphonso Lingis. Pittsburgh: Duquesne University Press, 1981.

———. "Reality and Its Shadow." In *The Levinas Reader*, ed. by Seán Hand, 130–43. Oxford: Blackwell, 1989.

———. "Revelation in the Jewish Tradition." In *The Levinas Reader*, ed. Seán Hand, 190–210. Oxford: Blackwell, 1989.

———. *Totality and Infinity: An Essay on Exteriority*. Translated by Alphonso Lingis. Pittsburgh: Duquesne University Press, 1969.

Lukács, Georg. *History and Class Consciousness*. Translated by Rodney Livingstone. Cambridge: MIT Press, 1968.

———. *The Theory of the Novel*. Translated by Anna Bostock. Cambridge: MIT Press, 1971.

Lyotard, François. *The Postmodern Condition: A Report on Knowledge*. Translated by Geoff Bennington and Brian Massumi. Minneapolis: University of Minnesota Press, 1984.

MacIntyre, Alasdair. *After Virtue*. 2d ed. Notre Dame: Notre Dame University Press, 1984.

———. *Three Rival Versions of Moral Enquiry: Encyclopaedia, Genealogy, and Tradition*. Notre Dame: University of Notre Dame Press, 1990.

———. *Whose Justice? Which Rationality?* Notre Dame: University of Notre Dame Press, 1988.

Macpherson, C. B. *The Rise and Fall of Economic Justice and Other Papers*. Oxford: Oxford University Press, 1985.

Maja-Pearce, Adewale. *A Mask Dancing: Nigerian Novelists in the Eighties*. London: Hans Zell, 1992.

———. "The Naipauls on Africa: An African View." *Journal of Commonwealth Literature* 20, no. 1 (1985): 111–17.

Makward, Edris. "Marriage, Tradition and Woman's Pursuit of Happiness in the Novels of Mariama Bâ." In *Ngambika: Studies of Women in African Literature*, ed. Carole Boyce Davies and Anne Adams Graves, 271–81. Trenton, N.J.: African World Press, 1986.

Mamdani, Mahmood. *Citizen and Subject: Contemporary Africa and the Legacy of Late Colonialism*. Princeton: Princeton University Press, 1996.

Manning, Patrick. *Slavery and African Life: Occidental, Oriental, and African Slave Trades*. Cambridge: Cambridge University Press, 1990.

Manzoni, Alessandro. *The Betrothed*. Harmondsworth: Penguin, 1972.

———. *I promessi sposi* (The betrothed). Milano: Garzanti, 1966.

Marcuse, Herbert. *Eros and Civilization: A Philosophical Inquiry into Freud*. Boston: Beacon Press, 1955.

McCaskie, T. C. *State and Society in Pre-Colonial Asante*. Cambridge: Cambridge University Press, 1995.

McGowan, John. *Postmodernism and Its Critics*. Ithaca: Cornell University Press, 1991.

McKeon, Michael. *The Origins of the English Novel, 1600–1740*. Baltimore: Johns Hopkins University Press, 1987.

McNaughton, Patrick R. *The Mande Blacksmiths: Knowledge, Power, and Art in West Africa*. Bloomington: Indiana University Press, 1988.

McWilliams, Sally. "'Strange as It May Seem': African Feminism in Two Novels by Ama Ata Aidoo." In *Emerging Perspectives on Ama Ata Aidoo*, ed. Ada Uzoamaka Azodo and Gay Wilentz, 333–61. Trenton, N.J.: Africa World Press, 1999.

———. "Tsitsi Dangarembga's *Nervous Conditions*: At the Crossroads of Feminism and Post-Colonialism." *World Literature Written in English* 31, no. 1 (1991): 103–12.

Meillassoux, Claude. *The Anthropology of Slavery: The Womb of Iron and Gold.* Translated by Alide Dasnois. London: Athlone Press, 1991.

———. "Female Slavery." In *Women and Slavery in Africa,* ed. Clarie C. Robertson and Martin A. Klein, 49–66. Madison: University of Wisconsin Press, 1983.

Memmi, Albert. *The Colonizer and the Colonized.* New York: Orion, 1965.

Mercer, Kobena. "Diaspora Culture and the Dialogic Imagination: The Aesthetics of Black Independent Film in Britain." In *Blackframes: Critical Perspectives on Black Independent Cinema,* ed. Mbye B. Cham and Claire Andrade-Watkins, 50–61. Cambridge: MIT Press, 1988.

Mernissi, Fatima. *Beyond the Veil: Male-Female Dynamics in Modern Muslim Society.* Rev. ed. Bloomington: Indiana University Press, 1987.

———. *Islam and Democracy: Fear of the Modern World.* Translated by Mary Jo Lakeland. Reading, Mass.: Addison-Wesley, 1992.

———. *Women's Rebellion and Islamic Memory.* London: Zed, 1996.

———. *The Veil and the Male Elite: A Feminist Interpretation of Women's Rights in Islam.* Translated by Mary Jo Lakeland. Reading, Mass.: Addison-Wesley, 1991.

Miller, Christopher L. *Blank Darkness: Africanist Discourse in French.* Chicago: University of Chicago Press, 1985.

———. *Theories of Africans: Francophone Literature and Anthropology in Africa.* Chicago: University of Chicago Press, 1990.

Miller, D. A. *The Novel and the Police.* Berkeley: University of California Press, 1988.

Miller, J. Hillis. *The Ethics of Reading.* New York: Columbia University Press, 1987.

Minh-ha, Trinh T. "Mother's Talk." In *The Politics of (M)Othering: Womanhood, Identity, and Resistance in African Literature,* ed. Obioma Nnaemeka, 26–32. London: Routledge, 1997.

———. *Woman, Native, Other.* Bloomington: Indiana University Press, 1989.

Mishra, Vijay, and Bob Hodge. "What Is Post(-)Colonialism?" *Textual Practice* 5, no. 3 (1991): 399–414.

Mohanty, Chandra Talpade. "Under Western Eyes: Feminist Scholarship and Colonialist Discourse." In *Colonial Discourse and Post-Colonial Theory: A Reader,* ed. Patrick Williams and Laura Chrisman, 196–220. New York: Columbia University Press, 1994.

Mohanty, Satya P. "Colonial Legacies, Multicultural Futures." *PMLA* 110, no. 1 (1995): 109–13.

Morson, Gary Saul, and Caryl Emerson. *Mikhail Bakhtin: Creation of a Prosaics.* Stanford, Calif.: Stanford University Press, 1990.

Mortimer, Mildred. *Journeys through the French African Novel.* Portsmouth, N. H.: Heinemann, 1990.

Mudimbe, V. Y. *The Invention of Africa: Gnosis, Philosophy, and the Order of Knowledge.* Bloomington: Indiana University Press, 1988.

———. *Parables and Fables: Exegesis, Textuality, and Politics in Central Africa.* Madison: University of Wisconsin Press, 1991.

Mulago, Vincent. *La Religion traditionnelle des Bantu et leur vision du monde* (The traditional religion of the Bantu and their vision of the world). 2d ed. Kinshana: Bibliothèque du Centre d'Etudes des Religiones Africaines, no. 5, 1980.

Naipaul, V. S. *Finding the Center: Two Narratives.* New York: Vintage, 1984.

Nair, Supriya. "Melancholic Women: The Intellectual Hysteric(s) in *Nervous Conditions.*" *Research in African Literatures* 26, no. 2 (1995): 130–39.

Nasr, Seyyed Hossein. *Sufi Essays.* 2d ed. Albany: State University of New York Press, 1991.

Nasta, Susheila. Introduction to *Motherlands: Black Women's Writing from Africa, the Caribbean and South Asia,* ed. Susheila Nasta, xiii–xxx. New Brunswick, N.J.: Rutgers University Press, 1992.

Nazareth, Peter. "Out of Darkness: Conrad and Other Third World Writers." *Conradiana* 14, no. 3 (1982): 173–87.

Newton, Adam Zachary. *Narrative Ethics.* Cambridge: Harvard University Press, 1995.

Nfah-Abbenyi, Juliana Makuchi. "Flabberwhelmed or Turning History on Its Head? The Postcolonial Woman-as-Subject in Aidoo's *Changes: A Love Story.*" In *Emerging Perspectives on Ama Ata Aidoo,* ed. Ada Uzoamaka Azodo and Gay Wilentz, 281–302. Trenton, N.J.: Africa World Press, 1999.

———. *Gender in African Women's Writing: Identity, Sexuality, and Difference.* Bloomington: Indiana University Press, 1997.

Ngara, Emmanuel. *Art and Ideology in the African Novel: A Study of the Influence of Marxism on African Writing.* London: Heinemann, 1985.

Ngũgĩ wa Thiong'o. *Decolonising the Mind: The Politics of Language in African Literature.* London: James Currey, 1986.

———. *The River Between.* London: Heinemann, 1965.

———. *Writers in Politics.* London: Heinemann, 1981.

Nietzsche, Friedrich. *On the Genealogy of Morals/Ecce Homo.* Translated by Walter Kaufmann. New York: Vintage, 1967.

———. *The Will to Power.* Translated by Walter Kaufmann and R. J. Hollingsdale. New York: Vintage, 1967.

Nixon, Rob. *Homelands, Harlem and Hollywood: South African Culture and the World Beyond.* New York: Routledge, 1994.

———. *London Calling: V. S. Naipaul, Postcolonial Mandarian.* Oxford: Oxford University Press, 1992.

Nnaemeka, Obioma. "Mariama Bâ." *Feminist Issues* 10, no. 1 (1990): 13–35.

———, ed. *The Politics of (M)Othering: Womanhood, Identity, and Resistance in African Literature.* London: Routledge, 1997.

———. "Urban spaces, women's places; polygamy as sign in Mariama Bâ's novels." In *The Politics of (M)Othering: Womanhood, Identity, and Resistance in African Literature,* ed. Obioma Nnaemeka, 162–91. London: Routledge, 1997.

Northrup, David. "The Ideological Context of Slavery in Southeastern Nigeria in the Nineteenth Century." In *The Ideology of Slavery in Africa,* ed. Paul E. Lovejoy, 101–22. Beverly Hills: Sage, 1981.

Norris, Christopher. *Truth and the Ethics of Criticism*. Manchester: University of Manchester Press, 1994.

Nugent, Paul. *Big Men, Small Boys and the Politics of Ghana: Power, Ideology and the Burden of History, 1982–1994*. London: Pinter, 1995.

Nussbaum, Martha C. *The Fragility of Goodness: Luck and Ethics in Greek Tragedy and Philosophy*. Cambridge: Cambridge University Press, 1986.

———. *Love's Knowledge: Essays on Philosophy and Literature*. Oxford: Oxford University Press, 1990.

Nwapa, Flora. *Efuru*. London: Heinemann, 1966.

Nwoga, Donatus Ibe. *The Supreme God as Stranger in Igbo Religious Thought*. Ahiazu Mbaise, Nigeria: Hawk Press, 1984.

Nyang'oro, Julius Edo. *The State and Capitalist Development in Africa: Declining Political Economics*. New York: Praeger, 1989.

O'Brien, Donal B. Cruise. *The Mourides of Senegal: The Political and Economic Organization of an Islamic Brotherhood*. Oxford: Clarendon Press, 1971.

———. *Saints and Politicians: Essays in the Organization of a Senegalese Peanut Society*. Cambridge: Cambridge University Press, 1975.

Odamtten, Vincent O. *The Art of Ama Ata Aidoo*. Gainesville: University Press of Florida, 1994.

Ogbala, Kalu. *Gods, Oracles, and Divination: Folkways in Chinua Achebe's Novels*. Trenton, N.J.: Africa World Press, 1992.

Ohadike, Don. "The Decline of Slavery among the Igbo People." In *The End of Slavery in Africa*, ed. Suzanne Miles and Robert Roberts, 437–61. Madison: University of Wisconsin Press, 1988.

Oko, Emelia C. "Woman, the Self-Celebrating Heroine: The Novels of Flora Nwapa." In *Emerging Perspective on Flora Nwapa: Critical and Theoretical Essays*, ed. Marie Umeh, 261–75. Trenton, N.J.: Africa World Press, 1998.

Okpewho, Isidore. *Myth in Africa: A Study of Its Asethetic and Cultural Relevance*. Cambridge: Cambridge University Press, 1983.

Opoku, Kofi Asara. *West African Traditional Religion*. Accra: FEP International, 1978.

Oppong, Christine. *Middle Class African Marriage: A Family Study of Ghanaian Senior Civil Servants*. London: George Allen and Unwin, 1981, rpt. 1974.

Ottenberg, Simon. *Boyhood Rituals in an African Society*. Seattle: University of Washington Press, 1989.

Ouologuem, Yambo. *Le devoir de violence* (The duty of violence). Paris: Éditions du Seuil, 1968.

Palmer, Eustace. *The Growth of the African Novel*. London: Heinemann, 1979.

Pelton, Robert D. *The Trickster in West Africa: A Study of Mythic Irony and Sacred Delight*. Berkeley: University of California Press, 1980.

Petchenkine, Youry. *Ghana: In Search of Stability, 1957–1992*. Westport, Conn.: Praeger, 1993.

Plutarch. *Moralia*, vol. 1. Translated by Frank Cole Babbitt. London: William Heinemann, 1927.

Pollock, Kimberley Joyce. "A Continuum of Pain: A Woman's Legacy in Alice Walker's *Possessing the Secret of Joy.*" In *Women of Color: Mother-Daughter Relationships in Twentieth-Century Literature,* ed. Elizabeth Brown-Guillory, 38–55. Austin: University of Texas Press, 1996.

Putnam, Hilary. *Reason, Truth and History.* Cambridge: Cambridge University Press, 1981.

Quasem, Muhammad Abdul. *The Recitation and Interpretation of the Qur'an: Al-Ghazali's Theory.* London: Kegal Paul, 1982.

Ranger, T. O. *Peasant Consciousness and Guerilla War in Zimbabwe.* Berkeley: University of California Press, 1985.

Rattray, R. S. *Religion and Art in Ashanti.* Oxford: Clarendon Press, 1969, rpt. 1927.

Reich, Wilhelm. *Selected Writings: An Introduction to Orgonomy.* New York: Noonday Press, 1960.

Ricoeur, Paul. *Oneself as Another.* Translated by Kathleen Blamey. Chicago: University of Chicago Press, 1992.

Riesz, János. "Mariama Bâ *Une si longue lettre*: An *Erziehungsroman.*" *Research in African Literatures* 22, no. 1 (1991): 27–42.

Rippen, Andrew, ed. *Approaches to the History of the Interpretation of the Qur'ân.* Oxford: Clarendon Press, 1988.

Roberts, Richard L. *Warriors, Merchants, and Slaves: The State and the Economy in the Middle Niger Valley, 1700–1914.* Stanford, Calif.: Stanford University Press, 1987.

Robbins, Jill. *Altered Reading: Levinas and Literature.* Chicago: University of Chicago Press, 1999.

Rosen, Stanley. *The Ancients and the Moderns: Rethinking Modernity.* New Haven: Yale University Press, 1989.

———. *Hermeneutics as Politics.* New York: Oxford University Press, 1987.

Rousseau, Jean-Jacques. *Émile ou de l'éducation* (Emile; or, of education). Paris: Garnier-Flammarion, 1966.

Ruddick, Sara. *Maternal Thinking: Toward a Politics of Peace.* Boston: Beacon Press, 1989.

Sahn, David E., ed. *Adjusting to Policy Failure in African Economies.* Ithaca: Cornell University Press, 1994.

Said, Edward W. *Culture and Imperialism.* New York: Alfred A. Knopf, 1993.

———. "Interpreting Palestine." *Harper's,* March 1987, 19–20.

———. *Orientalism.* New York: Pantheon, 1978.

———. *The World, the Text, and the Critic.* Cambridge: Harvard University Press, 1983.

Sartre, Jean-Paul. *Being and Nothingness.* Translated by Hazel E. Barnes. New York: Washington Square, 1956.

———. *Black Orpheus.* Translated by S. W. Allen. Paris: Présence Africaine, 1976.

———. "'Les damnés de la terre'" (The wretched of the earth). In Jean-Paul Sartre, *Situations, V: colonialisme et néo-colonialisme* (Situations, V: colonialism and neocolonialism). Paris: Gallimard, 1964.

————. *Orphée noir* (Black Orpheus). In Jean-Paul Sartre, *Situations, III* (Situations, III), 229–86. Paris: Gallimard, 1949.

————. Preface to *The Wretched of the Earth*, by Frantz Fanon. Translated by Constance Farrington. Harmondsworth: Penguin, 1967.

Sarvan, Charles Ponnuthurai. "Feminism and African Fiction: The Novels of Mariama Bâ." *Modern Fiction Studies* 34, no. 3 (1988): 453–64.

Schimmel, Annemarie. *My Soul Is a Woman: The Feminine in Islam.* Translated by Susan H. Ray. New York: Continuum, 1997.

Schmidt, Elizabeth. *Peasants, Traders, and Wives: Shona Women in the History of Zimbabwe, 1870–1939.* Portsmouth, N. H.: Heinemann, 1992.

Schmoll, Pamela G. "Black Stomachs, Beautiful Stones: Soul-Eating among Hausa in Niger." In *Modernity and Its Malcontents*, ed. Jean Comaroff and John Comaroff, 193–220. Chicago: University of Chicago Press, 1993.

Schroeder, Brian. *Altared Ground: Levinas, History, and Violence.* New York: Routledge, 1996.

Sembène, Ousmane. *Le Dernier de l'Empire* (The remains of empire). Paris: L'Harmattan, 1981.

Sengupta, Shivaji. "Desire, the Private, and the Public in Flora Nwapa's *Efuru* and *One Is Enough.*" In *Emerging Perspectives on Flora Nwapa: Critical and Theoretical Essays*, ed. Marie Umeh, 549–65. Trenton, N.J.: Africa World Press, 1998.

Shapiro, Laura. "Possessing the Secret of Joy." *Newsweek*, June 8, 1992: 57.

Sharma, T. R. S. "Chinua Achebe and V. S. Naipaul: One Version and Two Postures on Post-Colonial Societies." In *The Colonial and the Neo-Colonial Encounters in Commonwealth Literature*, ed. M. H. Anniah Gowda, 83–93. Mysore: Prasaragana University Press, 1983.

Sherif, Mohamed Ahmed. *Ghazali's Theory of Virtue.* Albany: State University of New York Press, 1975.

Sheriff, Abdul M. H. "The Slave Mode of Production along the East African Coast, 1810–1873." In *Slaves and Slavery in Muslim Africa*, ed. John Ralph Willis, 2:161–81. London: Frank Cass, 1985.

————. *Slaves, Spices, and Ivory in Zanzibar.* Athens: Ohio University Press, 1987.

Shinnie, Peter. "Early Asante: Is Wilks Right?" In *The Cloth of Many Colored Silks: Papers on History and Society Ghanaian and Islamic in Honor of Ivor Wilks*, ed. John Hunwick and Nancy Lawler, 195–203. Evanston: Northwestern University Press, 1996.

Soyinka, Wole. *Art, Dialogue, and Outrage: Essays on Literature and Culture.* Ibadan: New Horn Press, 1988.

————. *Myth, Literature, and the African World.* Cambridge: Cambridge University Press, 1976.

Spivak, Gayatri Chakravorty. *Outside in the Teaching Machine.* New York: Routledge, 1993.

————. *The Post-Colonial Critic: Interviews, Strategies, Dialogues.* Edited by Sarah Harasym. New York: Routledge, 1990.

Staunton, Cheryl Wall. "Mariama Bâ: Pioneer Senegalese Woman Novelist." *CLA Journal* 37, no. 3 (1994): 328–35.

Steinem, Gloria. *Outrageous Acts and Everyday Rebellions.* New York: Holt, Rinehart, and Winston, 1983.

Stephens, Connie. "Marriage in the Hausa *Tatsuniya* Tradition: A Cultural and Cosmic Balance." In *Hausa Women in the Twentieth Century,* ed. Catherine Coles and Beverly Mack, 221–31. Madison: University of Wisconsin Press, 1991.

Stowasser, Barbara Freyer. *Women in the Qur'an, Tradition, and Interpretation.* New York: Oxford University Press, 1994.

Stratton, Florence. "The Shallow Grave: Archetypes of Female Experience in African Fiction." *Research in African Literatures* 19, no. 1 (1988): 143–69.

Stringer, Susan. *The Senegalese Novel by Women: Through Their Own Eyes.* New York: Peter Lang, 1996.

Strong-Leek, Linda. "The Quest for Spiritual/Sexual Fulfillment in Flora Nwapa's *Efuru* and *The Lake Goddess.*" In *Emerging Perspectives on Flora Nwapa: Critical and Theoretical Essays,* ed. Marie Umeh, 531–48. Trenton, N.J.: Africa World Press, 1998.

Sugnet, Charles. "*Nervous Conditions:* Dangarembga's Feminist Reinvention of Fanon." In *The Politics of (M)Othering: Womanhood, Identity, and Resistance in African Literature,* ed. Obioma Nnaemeka, 33–49. London: Routledge, 1997.

Taylor, Charles. *The Ethics of Authenticity.* Cambridge: Harvard University Press, 1992.

———. *Sources of the Self: The Making of Modern Identity.* Cambridge: Harvard University Press, 1989.

Thomas, Sue. "Killing the Hysteric in the Colonized House: Tsitsi Dangarembga's *Nervous Conditions.*" *Journal of Commonwealth Literature* 24, no. 1 (1992): 6–36.

Thornton, John. "Sexual Demography: The Impact of the Slave Trade on Family Structure." In *Women and Slavery in Africa,* ed. Claire C. Robertson and Martin A. Klein, 39–48. Madison: University of Wisconsin Press, 1983.

Torgovnik, Marianna. *Gone Primitive: Savage Intellectuals, Modern Lives.* Chicago: University of Chicago Press, 1990.

Traoré, Ousseynou B. "Why the Snake-Lizard Killed His Mother: Inscribing and Decentering 'Nneka' in *Things Fall Apart.*" In *The Politics of (M)Othering: Womanhood, Identity, and Resistance in African Literature,* ed. Obioma Nnaemeka, 50–68. London: Routledge, 1997.

Trinkaus, Charles. *In Our Image and Likeness: Humanity and Divinity in Italian Humanist Thought.* 2 vols. Chicago: University of Chicago Press, 1970.

Unger, Roberto Mangabiera. *Social Theory: Its Situation and Its Task.* Cambridge: Cambridge University Press, 1987.

Uwakweh, Pauline Ada. "Debunking Patriarchy: The Liberational Quality of Voicing in Tsitsi Dangarembga's *Nervous Conditions.*" *Research in African Literatures* 26, no. 1 (1995): 75–84.

Uwakweh, Pauline Onwubiko. "Free but Lost: Variations in the Militant's Song." In *Emerging Perspectives on Ama Ata Aidoo,* ed. Ada Uzoamaka Azodo and Gay Wilentz, 363–75. Trenton, N.J.: Africa World Press, 1999.

Varadharajan, Asha. *Exotic Parodies: Subjectivity in Adorno, Said, and Spivak.* Minneapolis: University of Minnesota Press, 1995.

Villalón, Leonardo A. *Islamic Society and State Power in Senegal: Disciples and Citizens in Fatick.* Cambridge: Cambridge University Press, 1995.

Vizzard, Michelle. "'Of Mimicry and Woman:' Hysteria and Anticolonial Feminism in Tsitsi Dangarembga's *Nervous Conditions.*" *Span: Journal of the South Pacific Association for Commonwealth Literature and Language Studies* 36 (1993): 202–10.

Walker, Alice. *Possessing the Secret of Joy.* New York: Harcourt Brace Jovanovich, 1992.

Walker, Keith L. "Postscripts: Mariama Bâ, Epistolarity, Menopause, and Postcoloniality." In *Postcolonial Subjects: Francophone Women Writers,* ed. Mary Jean Green et al., 246–64. Minneapolis: University of Minnesota Press, 1996.

Wellmer, Albrecht. *The Persistance of Modernity: Essays on Aesthetics, Ethics, and Postmodernism.* Translated by David Midgley. Cambridge: MIT Press, 1991.

Wilentz, Gay. "African Woman's Domain: Demarcating Political Space in Nwapa, Sutherland, and Aidoo." In *Emerging Perspectives on Ama Ata Aidoo,* ed. Ada Uzoamaka Azodo and Gay Wilentz, 265–79. Trenton, N.J.: Africa World Press, 1999.

Wilks, Ivor. *Forests of Gold: Essays on the Akan and the Kingdom of Asante.* Athens: Ohio University Press, 1993.

Willey, Elizabeth. "National Identities, Tradition, and Feminism: The Novels of Ama Ata Aidoo Read in the Context of the Works of Kwame Nkrumah." In *Interventions: Feminist Dialogues on Third World Women's Literature and Film,* ed. Bishnupriya Ghosh and Brinda Bose, 3–30. New York: Garland, 1997.

Williams, Bernard. *Ethics and the Limits of Philosophy.* Cambridge: Harvard University Press, 1985.

Williams, Patrick, and Laura Chrisman, eds. *Colonial Discourse and Post-Colonial Theory: A Reader.* New York: Columbia University Press, 1994.

Willis, Dorothy Davis. "Economic Violence in Postcolonial Senegal: Noisy Silence in Novels by Mariama Bâ and Aminata Sow Fall." In *Violence, Silence, and Anger: Women's Writing as Transgression,* ed. Deindre Lashgari, 158–71. Charlottesville: University of Virginia Press, 1995.

Willis, Ellen. In "Discussion" with Gayatri Spivak and Catharine MacKinnon on McKinnon's paper, "Desire and Power: A Feminist Perspective." In *Marxism and the Interpretation of Culture,* ed. Cary Nelson and Lawrence Grossberg, 117–21. Urbana: University of Illinois Press, 1988.

Willis, John Ralph, ed. *Slaves and Slavery in Muslim Africa.* 2 vols. London: Frank Cass, 1985.

Wiredu, Kwasi. *Cultural Universals and Particulars: An African Perspective.* Bloomington: Indiana University Press, 1996.

———. "Formulating Modern Thought in African Languages: Some Theoretical Considerations." In *The Surreptitious Speech: Présence Africaine and the Politics of Otherness, 1947–1987,* ed. V. Y. Mudimbe, 306–31. Chicago: University of Chicago Press, 1993.

————. *Philosophy and an African Culture*. Cambridge: Cambridge University Press, 1980.

Yankah, Kwesi. *Speaking for the Chief: Okyeame and the Politics of Akan Royal Oratory.* Bloomington: Indiana University Press, 1995.

Young, Robert J. C. *Colonial Desire: Hybridity in Theory, Culture and Race.* London: Routledge, 1995.

————. *White Mythologies: Writing History in the West.* London: Routledge, 1990.

Yusef, Bilkisu. "Hausa-Fulani Women: The State of the Struggle." In *Hausa Women in the Twentieth Century,* ed. Catherine Coles and Beverly Mack, 90–106. Madison: University of Wisconsin Press, 1991.

Žižek, Slavoj. "'I Hear You with My Eyes'; or, The Invisible Master." In *Gaze and Voice as Love Object,* ed. Renata Saleci and Slavoj Žižek, 90–126. Durham: Duke University Press, 1996.

————. *The Sublime Object of Ideology.* London: Verso, 1989.

Index

Donald R. Wehrs is associate professor of English at Auburn University, where he teaches postcolonial studies, comparative literature, and eighteenth-century British literature. He has published on African fiction in *Modern Language Notes* and on British and European eighteenth-century literature in *The Eighteenth Century*, *Studies in English Literature*, *Comparative Literature Studies*, and *English Literary History*.